Mellville's BILLY BUDD and the Critics

Wadsworth Guides to Literary Study

Maurice Beebe, General Editor

MELVILLE'S *BILLY BUDD* AND THE CRITICS
  edited by William T. Stafford, Purdue University

LITERARY SYMBOLISM
An Introduction to the Interpretation of Literature
  edited by Maurice Beebe, Purdue University

A *SCARLET LETTER* HANDBOOK
  edited by Seymour L. Gross, University of Notre Dame

THE *KING LEAR* PERPLEX
  edited by Helmut Bonheim, University of California, Santa Barbara

DARWIN AND HIS CRITICS
The Darwinian Revolution
  edited by Bernard R. Kogan, University of Illinois, Chicago

CONRAD'S *HEART OF DARKNESS* AND THE CRITICS
  edited by Bruce Harkness, University of Illinois

APPROACHES TO *WALDEN*
  edited by Lauriat Lane, Jr., University of New Brunswick

THE RIME OF THE ANCIENT MARINER: A HANDBOOK
  edited by Royal A. Gettmann, University of Illinois

CRIME AND PUNISHMENT AND THE CRITICS
  edited by Edward Wasiolek, University of Chicago

LITERARY CENSORSHIP: PRINCIPLES, CASES, PROBLEMS
  *edited by Kingsley Widmer, San Diego State College, and Eleanor
  Widmer*

Melville's

BILLY BUDD

and the Critics

Edited by William T. Stafford
Purdue University

Wadsworth Publishing Company, Inc.
Belmont, California

for Fran, Lindy, Jocy, and Katy

First printing, April 1961
Second printing, December 1962

L.C. Cat. Card No.: 61–9018

Printed in the United States of
America

Manufactured by American Book—
Stratford Press, Inc.

PREFACE

Melville's *Billy Budd* is an instructive example of American fiction. First, it is more *novella* than novel, more the long tale than the novel as we traditionally think of it—as are so many of our most celebrated works of fiction: James's *The Turn of the Screw,* Crane's *The Red Badge of Courage,* Fitzgerald's *The Great Gatsby,* Katherine Anne Porter's *Pale Horse, Pale Rider,* Faulkner's *The Bear,* to name only a few. Like many of them, also, *Billy Budd* joins simplicity of action with complexity of meaning, its surface directness oddly at ease with the moral obliqueness within. It is instructive, finally, in that uniqueness with which major works of any important writer reflect his abiding interests and major themes. No serious student of Melville can ignore *Billy Budd* and pretend to any thorough knowledge of his literary achievement. By similar token, *Billy Budd* is literally a comment on all of Melville's preceding works, just as they are in a sense meaningful preparation for *Billy Budd.* This tale, then, is an ideal introduction to fiction generally, to American fiction specifically, and to the other works of Melville. And when we remember that the tale has been adapted into a highly praised play, a celebrated opera, and a television drama, it may also be, through the study of those works, an ideal introduction to some of the other arts.

The criticism written about *Billy Budd* is equally instructive. No important school of modern critical thought is without representation in this criticism. A study of it therefore becomes a study of modern literary criticism since the early 1920's, when the tale was first published. As a consequence, I have attempted to arrange this criticism in a way that would reflect both the development and the variety of that widespread attention. The first section, for example, contains brief, early notices, all written during the 1920's. The second section joins the first extensive analysis that was made of the tale (in 1933) with a diametrically opposed point of view made by a critic in 1959. The question of whether or not *Billy Budd* is a testament—and, if so, what kind of testament—dominated criticism of the tale until recently. The third section is composed of five different readings—a biographical reading, a social reading, a mythic-psychoanalytical reading, and two esthetic readings—each embodying and operating from a different critical premise and yet each also representing in one sense a total interpretation of the tale. The fourth section is composed of studies of sources and parallels. And the fifth section is an examination of some of the special critical problems posed by the tale. The book concludes with an extensive list of questions and topics for discussion and papers and a checklist of additional studies of *Billy Budd*.

Such an arrangement, I believe, will make this volume useful for a wide variety of purposes. It can be used as a source book in composition courses for both brief and long documented papers. For schools with large library holdings in literary criticism, the checklist provides directions to ample additional studies of the tale. For schools with limited holdings, the collection of criticism within the volume is extensive enough to indicate the various approaches that have been made and that can be made to the story. The book, it is therefore hoped, will also be useful for introductory classes in literature and criticism, for classes in American literature generally, and in the American novel and short story.

For the convenience of the student, page references to the original sources of the critical articles are given in raised numbers between brackets. Whenever a page of the text in its original form ended with a divided word, I have ignored the division and placed the page reference at the end of the completed word. In those articles that contain page references to other editions of *Billy Budd*, I have added, in square brackets, page references to the present volume. The articles have been as accurately reproduced as possible, with the exception of occasional footnotes that have been dropped and the remaining ones renumbered, and with the exception of an occasional creation or substitution of a title. In the case of the latter, a footnote states the original title. Spaced ellipses (. . .) are mine; unspaced ones (...) are the author's.

Finally, I would like to express my appreciation to the various authors and publishers whose works are collected here; to Harrison Hayford of Northwestern University for advice about the text and checklist; to my colleague Maurice Beebe, who, as general editor of this series, has helped me with a variety of problems too numerous to list; and to two other Purdue colleagues, William Braswell and Allen Hayman, who have allowed me to borrow from their excellent collections of studies about Melville more times than I like to remember.

W. T. S.

CONTENTS

CHRONOLOGY*

1819—Herman Melville born as the third of eight children to Allan and Maria Gansevoort Melville on August 1 at No. 6 Pearl Street, New York City.

1830—Moved with family to Albany. Entered the Albany Academy.

1832—Allan Melville died.

1835-37—Clerked in Albany. Taught school near Pittsfield, Massachusetts.

1838—Moved with family to Lansingburgh. Took a course in the Lansingburgh Academy.

1839—Shipped in June as a sailor on the *St. Lawrence* for Liverpool; returned to New York in October. Taught school at Greenbush.

1840—Visited uncle in Galena, Illinois.

1841-44—Shipped as sailor in January on the whaler *Acushnet* from Fairhaven (New Bedford); stopped at Rio de Janeiro in March; rounded the Cape in June; cruised through the Galapagos Islands in fall and winter. Arrived at the Marquesas Islands in June (1842); deserted with Toby Greene to the interior of Nukahiva in July; signed on the Australian whaler *Lucy Ann* in August; left ship at Tahiti, escaped to neighboring island of Eimeo; signed on the whaler *Charles and Henry* in November. Arrived at Hawaiian Islands in April (1843); went to Honolulu in May; signed in August on the frigate *United States*, which sailed to the Marquesas, Tahiti, Valparaiso, Callao, Lima, and Mazatlan. Arrived at Rio in August (1844) and at Boston in October. Rejoined family at Lansingburgh.

1846—*Typee* published in London and New York. *Omoo* completed.

1847—*Omoo* published in London and New York. Married Elizabeth Shaw in Boston on August 4; moved to New York.

1849—*Mardi* published in London and New York. *Redburn* published in London and New York. Completed *White-Jacket*. Visited

---

* With the aid of Jay Leyda's excellent *The Melville Log: A Documentary Life of Herman Melville: 1819–1891*, 2 Vols. (New York: Harcourt, Brace and Co., 1951).

London, Paris, Brussels, Cologne, and the Rhineland. Son, Malcolm, born.

1850—Returned to New York, began book on whaling. *White-Jacket* published in London and New York. Moved to "Arrowhead," near Pittsfield, Massachusetts; there met Hawthorne, who was his neighbor until November, 1851.

1851—*Moby-Dick* published in London (as *The Whale*) and in New York. Began *Pierre*. Second son, Stanwix, born.

1852—*Pierre* published in London and New York.

1853—Began to contribute stories and essays to *Putnam's* and *Harper's* monthlies. Daughter, Elizabeth, born.

1854—*Israel Potter* serialized in *Putnam's*.

1855—*Israel Potter* published in book form. Second daughter, Frances, born.

1856—*The Piazza Tales* published in U.S. and England. Completed *The Confidence-Man*. Sailed to England and the Mediterranean, visiting Malta, Syria, Salonica, Constantinople, Alexandria, Cairo.

1857—*The Confidence-Man* published in U.S. and England. Traveled through Palestine, Italy, Switzerland, Germany, the Netherlands, and (again) England. Returned to America.

1858–60—Lectured in South and Middle West. Worked on poems. Sailed to California and returned to New York (1860).

1863—Moved family to 104 East 26th Street, New York City.

1866—Volume of poems, *Battle-Pieces and Aspects of War*, published. Appointed Inspector of Customs at the Port of New York.

1867—Son Malcolm died of a self-inflicted pistol shot.

1869—Surviving son, Stanwix, went to sea on the *Yokohama*, sailing for China.

1870—Began work on *Clarel*.

1876—Published *Clarel* with a subsidy from uncle, Peter Gansevoort.

1886—Son Stanwix died in San Francisco.

1888—Voyaged to Bermuda, returning by way of Florida. Printed *John Marr and Other Sailors* privately. Began *Billy Budd*.

1891—Completed *Billy Budd*. Printed *Timoleon* privately. Died September 28.

1924—*Billy Budd* published.

A Note about the Text

Because Melville died before having prepared the manuscript of *Billy Budd* for the printers, a good many verbal and mechanical uncertainties about the text still remain. The work was first published in 1924 as a supplement to Raymond Weaver's edition of *The Works of Herman Melville* (1922–1924), but that printing, entitled *Billy Budd, Foretopman,* made no attempt to render literally all parts of the manuscript. In 1948 F. Barron Freeman's edition (*Melville's Billy Budd,* Harvard University Press) attempted to provide a literal transcription of the manuscript, including most of the revisions. And it is this text, as later corrected by Elizabeth Treeman and the *Corrigenda* issued by the Harvard Press, that is followed here. To be sure, some textual problems still exist, and scholars are working on them. But some of the problems are probably ultimately insolvable, for speculation about a text not finally prepared by the author himself must in the end remain as speculation, however persuasive and reasonable. Consequently, I have sometimes inserted additional punctuation and an occasional word (always within brackets) *only* when clarity demanded it. I have, however, made uniform most of the spellings in the text proper and provided a few explanatory notes for those rare other instances that seemed to me to need them.

Melville's original title, *Billy Budd/Foretopman,* on the first page of the manuscript, was later crossed out; but the subtitle, "What befell him . . . ," he left standing. I have therefore substituted *Billy Budd/Sailor* (An inside narrative.), which Melville boxed on the upper left corner of page one of Chapter One of the manuscript, leaving the remainder of his title page exactly as he had it. I have also not corrected the misspelling nor provided any punctuation for the dedication.

Billy Budd
Sailor*
(An inside narrative.)

What befell him
in the year of the
Great Mutiny
etc.

Dedicated to
Jack Chace
Englishman

Wherever that great heart may now be
Here on earth or harboured in Paradise
Captain of the main-top in the year 1843
in the U.S. Frigate "United States"

---

* Reprinted by permission of the publishers from *Melville's Billy Budd*, ed. by Frederick Barron Freeman and corrected by Elizabeth Treeman (Cambridge, Mass.: Harvard University Press, Copyright 1948, 1956, by the President and Fellows of Harvard College).

Preface

The year 1797, the year of this narrative, belongs to a period which[,] as every thinker now feels, involved a crisis for Christendom not exceeded in its undetermined momentousness at the time by any other era whereof there is record. The opening proposition made by the Spirit of that Age involved rectification of the Old World's hereditary wrongs. In France, to some extent, this was bloodily effected. But what then? Straightway the Revolution itself became a wrong-doer, one more oppressive than the kings. Under Napoleon it enthroned upstart kings, and initiated that prolonged agony of continual war whose final throe was Waterloo. During those years not the wisest could have foreseen that the outcome of all would be what to some thinkers apparently it has since turned out to be—a political advance along nearly the whole line for Europeans.

Now, as elsewhere hinted, it was something caught from the Revolutionary Spirit that at Spithead emboldened the man-of-war's men to rise against real abuses, long-standing ones, and afterwards at the Nore to make inordinate and aggressive demands—successful resistance to which was confirmed only when the ringleaders were hung for an admonitory spectacle to the anchored fleet. Yet in a way analogous to the operation of the Revolution at large—the Great Mutiny, though by Englishmen naturally deemed monstrous at the time, doubtless gave the first latent prompting to most important reforms in the British navy.

1

In the time before steamships, or then more frequently than now, a stroller along the docks of any considerable sea-port would occasionally have his attention arrested by a group of bronzed mariners, man-of-war's men or merchant-sailors in holiday attire ashore on liberty. In certain instances they would flank, or, like a body-guard quite surround some superior figure of their own class, moving along with them like Aldebaran among the lesser lights of his constellation. That signal object was the "Handsome Sailor" of the less prosaic time alike of the military and merchant navies. With no perceptible trace of the vainglorious about him, rather with the off-hand unaffectedness of natural regality, he seemed to accept the spontaneous homage of his shipmates. A somewhat remarkable instance recurs to me. In Liverpool, now half a century ago I saw under the shadow of the great dingy street-wall of Prince's Dock (an obstruction long since removed) a common sailor, so intensely black that he must needs have been a native African of the unadulterate blood of Ham. A symmetric figure much above the average height. The two ends of a gay silk handkerchief thrown loose about the neck danced upon the displayed ebony of his chest; in his ears were big hoops of gold, and a Scotch Highland bonnet with a tartan band set off his shapely head.

It was a hot noon in July; and his face, lustrous with perspiration, beamed with barbaric good humor. In jovial sallies right and left[,] his white teeth flashing into view, he rollicked along, the centre of a company of his shipmates. These were made up of such an assortment of tribes and complexions as would have well fitted them to be marched up by Anacharsis Cloots before the bar of the first French Assembly as Representatives of the Human Race. At each spontaneous tribute rendered by the wayfarers to this black pagod of a fellow—the tribute of a pause and stare, and less frequent an exclamation,—the motley retinue showed that they took that sort of pride in the evoker of it which the Assyrian priests doubtless showed for their grand sculptured Bull when the faithful prostrated themselves.

To return.

If in some cases a bit of a nautical Murat in setting forth his person ashore, the handsome sailor of the period in question evinced nothing of the dandified Billy-be-Damn, an amusing character all but extinct now, but occasionally to be encountered, and in a form yet more amusing than the original, at the tiller of the boats on the tempestuous Erie Canal or, more likely, vaporing in the groggeries along the tow-path. Invariably a proficient in his perilous calling, he was also more or less of a mighty boxer or wrestler. It was strength and beauty. Tales of his prowess were recited. Ashore he was the champion; afloat the spokesman; on every suitable occasion always foremost. Close-reefing topsails in a gale, there he was, astride the weather yard-arm-end, foot in the Flemish horse as "stirrup," both hands tugging at the "earring" as at a bridle, in very much the attitude of young Alexander curbing the fiery Bucephalus. A superb figure, tossed up as by the horns of Taurus against the thunderous sky, cheerily hallooing to the strenuous file along the spar.

The moral nature was seldom out of keeping with the physical make. Indeed, except as toned by the former, the comeliness and power, always attractive in masculine conjunction, hardly could have drawn the sort of honest homage the Handsome Sailor in some examples received from his less gifted associates.

Such a cynosure, at least in aspect, and something such too in nature, though with important variations made apparent as the story proceeds, was welkin-eyed Billy Budd, or Baby Budd as more familiarly under circumstances hereafter to be given he at last came to be called[,] aged twenty-one, a foretopman of the British fleet toward the close of the last decade of the eighteenth century. It was not very long prior to the time of the narration that follows that he had entered the King's Service, having been impressed on the Narrow Seas from a homeward-bound English merchantman into a seventy-four outward-bound, H.M.S. *Indomitable;* which ship, as was not unusual in those hurried days[,] having been obliged to put to sea short of her proper complement of men. Plump upon Billy at first sight in the gangway the boarding officer Lieutenant Ratcliffe pounced, even before the merchantman's crew was formally mustered on the quarter-deck for his deliberate inspection. And him only he elected. For whether it was because the other men when ranged before him showed to ill advantage after Billy, or whether he had some scruples in view of the merchantman being rather short-handed, however it might be, the officer contented himself with his first spontaneous choice. To the surprise of the ship's company, though much to the Lieutenant's satisfaction Billy made no demur. But, indeed, any demur would have been as idle as the protest of a goldfinch popped into a cage.

Noting this uncomplaining acquiescence, all but cheerful one might say, the shipmates turned a surprised glance of silent reproach at the sailor. The shipmaster was one of those worthy mortals found in every vocation even the humbler ones—the sort of person whom everybody agrees in calling "a respectable man." And—nor so strange to report as it may appear to be—though a ploughman of the troubled waters, life-long contending with the intractable elements, there was nothing this honest soul at heart loved better than simple peace and quiet. For the rest, he was fifty or thereabouts, a little inclined to corpulence, a prepossessing face, unwhiskered, and of an agreeable color—a rather full face, humanely intelligent in expression. On a fair day with a fair wind and all going well, a certain musical chime in his voice seemed to be the veritable unobstructed outcome of the innermost man. He had much prudence, much conscientiousness, and there were occasions when these virtues were the cause of overmuch disquietude in him. On a passage, so long as his craft was in any proximity to land, no sleep for Captain Graveling. He took to heart those serious responsibilities not so heavily borne by some shipmasters.

Now while Billy Budd was down in the forecastle getting his kit together, the *Indomitable's* lieutenant, burly and bluff, nowise disconcerted by Captain Graveling's omitting to proffer the customary hospitalities on an occasion so unwelcome to him, an omission simply caused by preoccupation of thought, unceremoniously invited himself into the cabin, and also to a flask from the spirit-locker, a receptacle which his experienced eye instantly discovered. In fact he was one of those sea-dogs in whom all the hardship and peril of naval life in the great prolonged wars of his time never impaired the natural instinct for sensuous enjoyment. His duty he always faithfully did; but duty is sometimes a dry obligation, and he was for irrigating its aridity, whensoever possible, with a fertilizing decoction of strong waters. For the cabin's proprietor there was nothing left but to play the part of the enforced host with whatever grace and alacrity were practicable. As necessary adjuncts to the flask, he silently placed tumbler and water-jug before the irrepressible guest. But excusing himself from partaking just then, [he] dismally watched the unembarrassed officer deliberately diluting his grog a little, then tossing it off in three swallows, pushing the empty tumbler away, yet not so far as to be beyond easy reach, at the same [time] settling himself in his seat and smacking his lips with high satisfaction, looking straight at the host.

These proceedings over, the Master broke the silence; and there lurked a rueful reproach in the tone of his voice; "Lieutenant, you are going to take my best man from me, the jewel of 'em."

"Yes, I know" rejoined the other, immediately drawing back the tumbler preliminary to a replenishing; "Yes, I know. Sorry."

"Beg pardon, but you don't understand, Lieutenant. See here now. Before I shipped that young fellow, my forecastle was a rat-pit of quarrels. It was black times, I tell you, aboard the '*Rights*' here. I was worried to that degree my pipe had no comfort for me. But Billy came; and it was like a Catholic priest striking peace in an Irish shindy. Not that he preached to them or said or did anything in particular; but a virtue went out of him, sugaring the sour ones. They took to him like hornets to treacle; all but the buffer of the gang, the big shaggy chap with the fire-red whiskers. He indeed out of envy, perhaps, of the newcomer, and thinking such a 'sweet and pleasant fellow,' as he mockingly designated him to the others, could hardly have the spirit of a game-cock, must needs bestir himself in trying to get up an ugly row with him. Billy forebore with him and reasoned with him in a pleasant way—he is something like myself, lieutenant, to whom aught like a quarrel is hateful—but nothing served. So, in the second dog-watch one day the Red Whiskers in presence of the others, under pretence of showing Billy just whence a sirloin steak was cut—for the fellow had once been a butcher—insultingly gave him a dig under the ribs. Quick as lightning Billy let fly his arm. I dare say he never meant to do quite as much as he did, but anyhow he gave the burly fool a terrible drubbing. It took about half a minute, I should think. And, lord bless you, the lubber was astonished at the celerity. And will you believe it, Lieutenant, the Red Whiskers now really loves Billy—loves him, or is the biggest hypocrite that ever I heard of. But they all love him. Some of 'em do his washing, darn his old trousers for him; the carpenter is at odd times making a pretty little chest of drawers for him. Anybody will do anything for Billy Budd; and it's the happy family here. But now, Lieutenant, if that young fellow goes—I know how it will be aboard the '*Rights*.' Not again very soon shall I, coming up from dinner, lean over the capstan smoking a quiet pipe—no, not very soon again, I think. Ay,

Lieutenant, you are going to take away the jewel of 'em; you are going to take away my peacemaker!" And with that the good soul had really some ado in checking a rising sob.

"Well," said the officer who had listened with amused interest to all this, and now waxing merry with his tipple; "Well, blessed are the peacemakers especially the fighting peacemakers! And such are the seventy-four beauties some of which you see poking their noses out of the port-holes of yonder war-ship lying-to for me" pointing thro' the cabin window at the *Indomitable*. "But courage! don't look so downhearted, man. Why, I pledge you in advance the royal approbation. Rest assured that His Majesty will be delighted to know that in a time when his hard tack is not sought for by sailors with such avidity as should be; a time also when some shipmasters privily resent the borrowing from them a tar or two for the service; His Majesty, I say, will be delighted to learn that *one* shipmaster at least cheerfully surrenders to the King, the flower of his flock, a sailor who with equal loyalty makes no dissent.—But where's my beauty? Ah," looking through the cabin's open door "Here he comes; and, by Jove—lugging along his chest—Apollo with his portmanteau!—My man," stepping out to him, "you can't take that big box aboard a warship. The boxes there are mostly shot-boxes. Put your duds in a bag, lad. Boot and saddle for the cavalryman, bag and hammock for the man-of-war's man."

The transfer from chest to bag was made. And, after seeing his man into the cutter and then following him down, the lieutenant pushed off from the *Rights-of-Man*. That was the merchant-ship's name; tho' by her master and crew abbreviated in sailor fashion into *The Rights*. The hard-headed Dundee owner was a staunch admirer of Thomas Paine whose book in rejoinder to Burke's arraignment of the French Revolution had then been published for some time and had gone everywhere. In christening his vessel after the title of Paine's volume the man of Dundee was something like his contemporary shipowner, Stephen Girard of Philadelphia, whose sympathies, alike with his native land and its liberal philosophers, he evinced by naming his ships after Voltaire, Diderot, and so forth.

But now, when the boat swept under the merchant-man's stern, and officer and oarsmen were noting—some bitterly and others with a grin,—the name emblazoned there; just then it was that the new recruit jumped up from the bow where the coxswain had directed him to sit, and waving [his] hat to his silent shipmates sorrowfully looking over at him from the taffrail, bade the lads a genial good-bye. Then, making a salutation as to the ship herself, "And good-bye to you too, old *Rights of Man*."

"Down, Sir!" roared the lieutenant, instantly assuming all the rigor of his rank, though with difficulty repressing a smile.

To be sure, Billy's action was a terrible breach of naval decorum.

But in that decorum he had never been instructed; in consideration of which the lieutenant would hardly have been so energetic in re-proof but for the concluding farewell to the ship. This he rather took as meant to convey a covert sally on the new recruit's part, a sly slur at impressment in general, and that of himself in especial. And yet, more likely, if satire it was in effect, it was hardly so by in-tention, for Billy tho' happily endowed with the gayety of high health, youth, and a free heart, was yet by no means of a satirical turn. The will to it and the sinister dexterity were alike wanting. To deal in double meanings and insinuations of any sort was quite foreign to his nature.

As to his enforced enlistment, that he seemed to take pretty much as he was wont to take any vicissitude of weather. Like the animals, though no philosopher, he was, without knowing it, practically a fatalist. And, it may be, that he rather liked this adventurous turn in his affairs, which promised an opening into novel scenes and martial excitements.

Aboard the *Indomitable* our merchant-sailor was forthwith rated as an able-seaman and assigned to the starboard watch of the fore-top. He was soon at home in the service, not at all disliked for his un-pretentious good looks and a sort of genial happy-go-lucky air. No merrier man in his mess: in marked contrast to certain other in-dividuals included like himself among the impressed portion of the ship's company; for these when not actively employed were some-times, and more particularly in the last dog-watch when the drawing near of twilight induced revery, apt to fall into a saddish mood which in some partook of sullenness. But they were not so young as our foretopman, and no few of them must have known a hearth of some sort, others may have had wives and children left, too probably, in uncertain circumstances, and hardly any but must have had acknowl-edged kith and kin, while for Billy, as will shortly be seen, his entire family was practically invested in himself.

2

Though our new-made foretopman was well received in the top and on the gun-decks, hardly here was he that cynosure he had pre-viously been among those minor ship's companies of the merchant marine, with which companies only had he hitherto consorted.

He was young; and despite his all but fully developed frame in aspect looked even younger than he really was, owing to a lingering adolescent expression in the as yet smooth face all but feminine in purity of natural complexion but where, thanks to his seagoing, the lily was quite suppressed and the rose had some ado visibly to flush through the tan.

To one essentially such a novice in the complexities of factitious life, the abrupt transition from his former and simpler sphere to the ampler and more knowing world of a great warship; this might well

have abashed him had there been any conceit or vanity in his composition. Among her miscellaneous multitude, the *Indomitable* mustered several individuals who however inferior in grade were of no
common natural stamp, sailors more signally susceptive of that air
which continuous martial discipline and repeated presence in battle
can in some degree impart even to the average man. As the *handsome sailor* Billy Budd's position aboard the seventy-four was something analogous to that of a rustic beauty transplanted from the
provinces and brought into competition with the highborn dames
of the court. But this change of circumstances he scarce noted. As
little did he observe that something about him provoked an ambiguous smile in one or two harder faces among the blue-jackets.
Nor less unaware was he of the peculiar favorable effect his person
and demeanor had upon the more intelligent gentlemen of the quarter-
deck. Nor could this well have been otherwise. Cast in a mould
peculiar to the finest physical examples of those Englishmen in whom
the Saxon strain would seem not at all to partake of any Norman
or other admixture, he showed in face that humane look of reposeful
good nature which the Greek sculptor in some instances gave to his
heroic strong man, Hercules. But this again was subtly modified by
another and pervasive quality. The ear, small and shapely, the arch
of the foot, the curve in mouth and nostril, even the indurated hand
dyed to the orange-tawny of the toucan's bill, a hand telling alike of
the halyards and tar-bucket; but, above all, something in the mobile
expression, and every chance attitude and movement, something suggestive of a mother eminently favored by Love and the Graces; all this
strangely indicated a lineage in direct contradiction to his lot. The
mysteriousness here, became less mysterious through a matter-of-fact
elicited when Billy at the capstan was being formally mustered into
the service. Asked by the officer, a small brisk little gentleman as it
chanced among other questions, his place of birth, he replied, "Please,
Sir, I don't know."

"Don't know where you were born?—Who was your father?"

"God knows, Sir."

Struck by the straightforward simplicity of these replies, the officer
next asked "Do you know anything about your beginning?"

"No, Sir. But I have heard that I was found in a pretty silk-lined
basket hanging one morning from the knocker of a good man's door
in Bristol[.]"

"*Found* say you? Well," throwing back his head and looking up
and down the new recruit; "Well[,] it turns out to have been a pretty
good find. Hope they'll find some more like you, my man; the fleet
sadly needs them."

Yes, Billy Budd was a foundling, a presumable bye-blow, and,
evidently, no ignoble one. Noble descent was as evident in him as in
a blood horse.

For the rest, with little or no sharpness of faculty or any trace of the wisdom of the serpent, nor yet quite a dove, he possessed that kind and degree of intelligence going along with the unconventional rectitude of a sound human creature, one to whom not yet has been proffered the questionable apple of knowledge. He was illiterate; he could not read, but he could sing, and like the illiterate nightingale was sometimes the composer of his own song.

Of self-consciousness he seemed to have little or none, or about as much as we may reasonably impute to a dog of Saint Bernard's breed.

Habitually living with the elements and knowing little more of the land than as a beach, or, rather, that portion of the terraqueous globe providentially set apart for dance-houses doxies and tapsters, in short what sailors call a "fiddlers' green," his simple nature remained unsophisticated by those moral obliquities which are not in every case incompatible with that manufacturable thing known as respectability. But are sailors, frequenters of "fiddlers'-greens," without vices? No; but less often than with landsmen do their vices, so called, partake of crookedness of heart, seeming less to proceed from viciousness than exuberance of vitality after long constraint; frank manifestations in accordance with natural law. By his original constitution aided by the cooperating influences of his lot, Billy in many respects was little more than a sort of upright barbarian, much such perhaps as Adam presumably might have been ere the urbane Serpent wriggled himself into his company.

And here be it submitted that apparently going to corroborate the doctrine of man's fall, a doctrine now popularly ignored, it is observable that where certain virtues pristine and unadulterate peculiarly characterize anybody in the external uniform of civilization, they will upon scrutiny seem not to be derived from custom or convention, but rather to be out of keeping with these, as if indeed exceptionally transmitted from a period prior to Cain's city and citified man. The character marked by such qualities has to an unvitiated taste an untampered-with flavor like that of berries, while the man thoroughly civilized even in a fair specimen of the breed has to the same moral palate a questionable smack as of a compounded wine. To any stray inheritor of these primitive qualities found, like Caspar Hauser, wandering dazed in any Christian capital of our time[,] the good-natured poet's famous invocation, near two thousand years ago, of the good rustic out of his latitude in the Rome of the Cesars, still appropriately holds:—

> "Honest and poor, faithful in word and thought
> What has thee, Fabian, to the city brought."

Though our Handsome Sailor had as much of masculine beauty as one can expect anywhere to see; nevertheless, like the beautiful woman in one of Hawthorne's minor tales, there was just one thing amiss in him. No visible blemish indeed, as with the lady; no, but an occasional liability to a vocal defect. Though in the hour of elemental uproar or peril, he was everything that a sailor should be, yet under sudden provocation of strong heart-feeling his voice otherwise singularly musical, as if expressive of the harmony within, was apt to develop an organic hesitancy, in fact more or less of a stutter or even worse. In this particular Billy was a striking instance that the arch interferer, the envious marplot of Eden still has more or less to do with every human consignment to this planet of earth. In every case, one way or another he is sure to slip in his little card, as much as to remind us—I too have a hand here.

The avowal of such an imperfection in the Handsome Sailor should be evidence not alone that he is not presented as a conventional hero, but also that the story in which he is the main figure is no romance.

3

At the time of Billy Budd's arbitrary enlistment into the *Indomitable* that ship was on her way to join the Mediterranean fleet. No long time elapsed before the junction was effected. As one of that fleet the seventy-four participated in its movements, tho' at times on account of her superior sailing qualities, in the absence of frigates, despatched on separate duty as a scout and at times on less temporary service. But with all this the story has little concernment, restricted as it is to the inner life of one particular ship and the career of an individual sailor.

It was the summer of 1797. In the April of that year had occurred the commotion at Spithead followed in May by a second and yet more serious outbreak in the fleet at the Nore. The latter is known, and without exaggeration in the epithet, as the Great Mutiny. It was indeed a demonstration more menacing to England than the contemporary manifestoes and conquering and proselyting armies of the French Directory.

To the British Empire the Nore Mutiny was what a strike in the fire-brigade would be to London threatened by general arson. In a crisis when the kingdom might well have anticipated the famous signal that some years later published along the naval line of battle what it was that upon occasion England expected of Englishmen; *that* was the time when at the mast-heads of the three-deckers and seventy-fours moored in her own roadstead—a fleet, the right arm of a Power then all but the sole free conservative one of the Old World, the blue-jackets, to be numbered by thousands [,] ran up with huzzas the British colors with the union and cross wiped out; by that cancellation transmuting the flag of founded law and freedom defined, into the enemy's red meteor of unbridled and unbounded revolt. Reasonable discontent growing out of practical grievances in the fleet had been ignited into irrational combustion as by live cinders blown across the Channel from France in flames.

The event converted into irony for a time those spirited strains of Dibdin—as a song-writer no mean auxiliary to the English Government at the European conjuncture—strains celebrating, among other things, the patriotic devotion of the British tar:

"And as for my life, 'tis the King's!"

Such an episode in the Island's grand naval story her naval historians naturally abridge; one of them (G. P. R. James)[1] candidly acknowledging that fain would he pass it over did not "impartiality forbid fastidiousness." And yet his mention is less a narration than a reference, having to do hardly at all with details. Nor are these readily to be found in the libraries. Like some other events in every age befalling states everywhere including America the Great Mutiny was of such character that national pride along with views of policy would fain shade it off into the historical background. Such events can not be ignored, but there is a considerate way of historically treating them. If a well-constituted individual refrains from blazoning aught amiss or calamitous in his family; a nation in the like circumstance may without reproach be equally discreet.

Though after parleyings between Government and the ringleaders, and concessions by the former as to some glaring abuses, the first uprising—that at Spithead—with difficulty was put down, or matters for the time pacified; yet at the Nore the unforeseen renewal of insurrection on a yet larger scale, and emphasized in the conferences that ensued by demands deemed by the authorities not only inadmissible but aggressively insolent, indicated—if the Red Flag did not sufficiently do so[—]what was the spirit animating the men. Final suppression, however, there was; but only made possible perhaps by the unswerving loyalty of the marine corps a[nd] voluntary resumption of loyalty among influential sections of the crews.

To some extent the Nore Mutiny may be regarded as analogous to the distempering irruption of contagious fever in a frame constitutionally sound, and which anon throws it off.

At all events, of these thousands of mutineers were some of the tars who not so very long afterwards—whether wholly prompted thereto by patriotism or pugnacious instinct, or by both,—helped to win a coronet for Nelson at the Nile, and the naval crown of crowns for him at Trafalgar. To the mutineers those battles and especially Trafalgar were a plenary absolution and a grand one: For all that

---

[1] Melville probably meant the British naval historian William James, author of *The Naval History of Great Britain* (London, 1860).

goes to make up scenic naval display, heroic magnificence in arms, those battles especially Trafalgar stand unmatched in human annals.

4

*Concerning "The greatest sailor since the
world began."* Tennyson

In this matter of writing, resolve as one may to keep to the main road, some by-paths have an enticement not readily to be withstood. I am going to err into such a by-path. If the reader will keep me company I shall be glad. At the least we can promise ourselves that pleasure which is wickedly said to be in sinning, for a literary sin the divergence will be.

Very likely it is no new remark that the inventions of our time have at last brought about a change in sea-warfare in degree corresponding to the revolution in all warfare effected by the original introduction from China into Europe of gunpowder. The first European fire-arm, a clumsy contrivance, was, as is well known, scouted by no few of the knights as a base implement, good enough peradventure for weavers too craven to stand up crossing steel with steel in frank fight. But as ashore knightly valor tho' shorn of its blazonry did not cease with the knights, neither on the seas though nowadays in encounters there a certain kind of displayed gallantry be fallen out of date as hardly applicable under changed circumstances, did the nobler qualities of such naval magnates as Don John of Austria, Doria, Van Tromp, Jean Bart, the long line of British Admirals and the American Decaturs of 1812 become obsolete with their wooden walls.

Nevertheless, to anybody who can hold the Present at its worth without being inappreciative of the Past, it may be forgiven, if to such an one the solitary old hulk at Portsmouth, Nelson's *Victory,* seems to float there, not alone as the decaying monument of a fame incorruptible, but also as a poetic reproach, softened by its picturesqueness, to the *Monitors* and yet mightier hulls of the European iron-clads. And this not altogether because such craft are unsightly, unavoidably lacking the symmetry and grand lines of the old battle-ships, but equally for other reasons.

There are some, perhaps, who while not altogether inaccessible to that poetic reproach just alluded to, may yet on behalf of the new order, be disposed to parry it; and this to the extent of iconoclasm, if need be. For example, prompted by the sight of the star inserted in the *Victory's* quarter-deck designating the spot where the Great Sailor fell, these martial utilitarians may suggest considerations implying that Nelson's ornate publication of his person in battle was not only unnecessary, but not military, nay, savored of foolhardiness and vanity. They may add, too, that at Trafalgar it was in effect nothing less than a challenge to death; and death came; and that but for his bravado the victorious Admiral might possibly have survived the battle, and so, instead of having his sagacious dying injunctions over-ruled by his immediate successor in command he himself when the contest was decided might have brought his shattered fleet to anchor, a proceeding which might have averted the deplorable loss of life by shipwreck in the elemental tempest that followed the martial one.

Well, should we set aside the more disputable point whether for various reasons it was possible to anchor the fleet, then plausibly enough the Benthamites of war may urge the above.

But the *might-have-been* is but boggy ground to build on. And, certainly, in foresight as to the larger issue of an encounter, and anxious preparations for it—buoying the deadly way and mapping it out, as at Copenhagen—few commanders have been so painstakingly circumspect as this same reckless declarer of his person in fight.

Personal prudence even when dictated by quite other than selfish considerations surely is no special virtue in a military man; while an excessive love of glory, impassioning a less burning impulse, the honest sense of duty, is the first. If the name *Wellington* is not so much of a trumpet to the blood as the simpler name *Nelson,* the reason for this may perhaps be inferred from the above. Alfred in his funeral ode on the victor of Waterloo ventures not to call him the greatest soldier of all time, tho' in the same ode he invokes Nelson as "the greatest sailor since the world began."

At Trafalgar Nelson on the brink of opening the fight sat down and wrote his last brief will and testament. If under the presenti-ment of the most magnificent of all victories to be crowned by his own glorious death, a sort of priestly motive led him to dress his person in the jewelled vouchers of his own shining deeds; if thus to have adorned himself for the altar and the sacrifice were indeed vainglory, then affectation and fustian is each more heroic line in the great epics and dramas, since in such lines the poet but embodies in verse those exaltations of sentiment that a nature like Nelson, the opportunity being given, vitalizes into acts.

5

Yes, the outbreak at the Nore was put down. But not every griev-ance was redressed. If the contractors, for example, were no longer permitted to ply some practices peculiar to their tribe everywhere, such as providing shoddy cloth, rations not sound, or false in the measure, not the less impressment, for one thing, went on. By custom sanctioned for centuries, and judicially maintained by a Lord Chan-cellor as late as Mansfield, that mode of manning the fleet, a mode now fallen into a sort of abeyance but never formally renounced, it was not practicable to give up in those years. Its abrogation would have crippled the indispensable fleet, one wholly under canvas, no steam-power, its innumerable sails and thousands of cannon, every-thing in short, worked by muscle alone; a fleet the more insatiate in demand for men, because then multiplying its ship[s] of all grades against contingencies present and to come of the convulsed Continent.

Discontent foreran the Two Mutinies, and more or less it lurkingly survived them. Hence it was not unreasonable to apprehend some return of trouble sporadic or general. One instance of such apprehensions: In the same year with this story, Nelson, then Vice Admiral Sir Horatio, being with the fleet off the Spanish coast, was directed by the Admiral in command to shift his pennant from the *Captain* to the *Theseus;* and for this reason: that the latter ship having newly arrived on the station from home where it had taken part in the Great Mutiny, danger was apprehended from the temper of the men; and it was thought that an officer like Nelson was the one, not indeed to terrorize the crew into base subjection, but to win them, by force of his mere presence back to an allegiance if not as enthusiastic as his own, yet as true. So it was that for a time on more than one quarter-deck anxiety did exist. At sea precautionary vigilance was strained against relapse. At short notice an engagement might come on. When it did, the lieutenants assigned to batteries felt it incumbent on them, in some instances, to stand with drawn swords behind the men working the guns.

6

But on board the seventy-four in which Billy now swung his hammock, very little in the manner of the men and nothing obvious in the demeanor of the officers would have suggested to an ordinary observer that the Great Mutiny was a recent event. In their general bearing and conduct the commissioned officers of a war-ship naturally take their tone from the commander, that is if he have that ascendancy of character that ought to be his.

Captain the Honorable Edward Fairfax Vere, to give his full title, was a bachelor of forty or thereabouts, a sailor of distinction even in a time prolific of renowned seamen. Though allied to the higher nobility his advancement had not been altogether owing to influences connected with that circumstance. He had seen much service, been in various engagements, always acquitting himself as an officer mindful of the welfare of his men, but never tolerating an infraction of discipline; thoroughly versed in the science of his profession, and intrepid to the verge of temerity, though never injudiciously so. For his gallantry in the West Indian waters as flag-lieutenant under Rodney in that Admiral's crowning victory over De Grasse, he was made a post-captain.

Ashore in the garb of a civilian scarce anyone would have taken him for a sailor, more especially that he never garnished unprofessional talk with nautical terms, and grave in his bearing, evinced little appreciation of mere humor. It was not out of keeping with these traits that on a passage when nothing demanded his paramount action, he was the most undemonstrative of men. Any landsmen observing this gentleman not conspicuous by his stature and wearing no pronounced insignia, emerging from his cabin to the open deck, and noting the silent deference of the officers retiring to leeward, might have taken him for the King's guest, a civilian aboard the King's-ship[,] some highly honorable discreet envoy on his way to an important post. But in fact this unobtrusiveness of demeanor may have proceeded from a certain unaffected modesty of manhood sometimes accompanying a resolute nature, a modesty evinced at all times not calling for pronounced action, and which shown in any rank of life suggests a virtue aristocratic in kind.

As with some others engaged in various departments of the world's more heroic activities, Captain Vere though practical enough upon occasion would at times betray a certain dreaminess of mood. Standing alone on the weather-side of the quarter deck, one hand holding by the rigging he would absently gaze off at the blank sea. At the presentation to him then of some minor matter interrupting the current of his thoughts he would show more or less irascibility; but instantly he would control it.

In the navy he was popularly known by the appellation—Starry Vere. How such a designation happened to fall upon one who whatever his sturdy qualities was without any brilliant ones was in this wise: A favorite kinsman, Lord Denton, a free-hearted fellow, had been the first to meet and congratulate him upon his return to England from his West Indian cruise; and but the day previous turning over a copy of Andrew Marvell's poems had lighted, not for the first time however, upon the lines entitled *Appleton House,* the name of one of the seats of their common ancestor, a hero in the German wars of the seventeenth century, in which poem occur the lines,

> "This 'tis to have been from the first
> In a domestic heaven nursed,
> Under the discipline severe
> Of Fairfax and the starry Vere[.]"

And so, upon embracing his cousin fresh from Rodney's great victory wherein he had played so gallant a part, brimming over with just family pride in the sailor of their house, he exuberantly exclaimed, "Give ye joy, Ed; give ye joy, my starry Vere!" This got currency, and the novel prefix serving in familiar parlance readily to distinguish the *Indomitable's* Captain from another Vere his senior, a distant relative an[d] officer of like rank in the navy, it remained permanently attached to the surname.

7

In view of the part that the commander of the *Indomitable* plays in scenes shortly to follow, it may be well to fill out that sketch of him outlined in the previous chapter.

Aside from his qualities as a sea-officer Captain Vere was an exceptional character. Unlike no few of England's renowned sailors, long and arduous service with signal devotion to it, had not resulted in absorbing and *salting* the entire man. He had a marked leaning toward everything intellectual. He loved books, never going to sea without a newly replenished library, compact but of the best. The isolated leisure, in some cases so wearisome, falling at intervals to commanders even during a war-cruise, never was tedious to Captain Vere. With nothing of that literary taste which less heeds the thing conveyed than the vehicle, his bias was towards those books to which every serious mind of superior order occupying any active post of authority in the world, naturally inclines: books treating of actual men and events no matter of what era—history, biography and unconventional writers, who, free from cant and convention, like Montaigne, honestly and in the spirit of common sense philosophize upon realities.

In this line of reading he found confirmation of his own more reasoned thoughts—confirmation which he had vainly sought in social converse, so that as touching most fundamental topics, there had got to be established in him some positive convictions, which he forefelt would abide in him essentially unmodified so long as his intelligent part remained unimpaired. In view of the troubled period in which his lot was cast this was well for him. His settled convictions were as a dyke against those invading waters of novel opinion[,] social[,] political and otherwise, which carried away as in a torrent no few minds in those days, minds by nature not inferior to his own. While other members of that aristocracy to which by birth he belonged were incensed at the innovators mainly because their theories were inimical to the privileged classes, not alone Captain Vere disinterestedly opposed them because they seemed to him incapable of embodiment in lasting institutions, but at war with the peace of the world and the true welfare of mankind.

With minds less stored than his and less earnest, some officers of his rank, with whom at times he would necessarily consort, found him lacking in the companionable quality, a dry and bookish gentleman as they deemed. Upon any chance withdrawal from their company one would be apt to say to another, something like this: "Vere is a noble fellow, Starry Vere. Spite the gazettes, Sir Horatio["] meaning him with the Lord title ["]is at bottom scarce a better seaman or fighter. But between you and me now don't you think there is a queer streak of the pedantic running thro' him? Yes, like the King's yarn in a coil of navy-rope?["]

Some apparent ground there was for this sort of confidential criticism; since not only did the Captain's discourse never fall into the jocosely familiar, but in illustrating of any point touching the stirring personages and events of the time he would be as apt to cite some historic character or incident of antiquity as that he would cite from the moderns. He seemed unmindful of the circumstance that to his bluff company such remote allusions however pertinent they might really be were altogether alien to men whose reading was mainly confined to the journals. But considerateness in such matters is not easy to natures constituted like Captain Vere's. Their honesty prescribes to them directness, sometimes far-reaching like that of a migratory fowl that in its flight never heeds when it crosses a frontier.

8

The lieutenants and other commissioned gentlemen forming Captain Vere's staff it is not necessary here to particularize, nor needs it to make any mention of any of the warrant-officers. But among the petty-officers was one who having much to do with the story, may as well be forthwith introduced. His portrait I essay, but shall never hit it. This was John Claggart, the Master-at-arms. But that sea-title may to landsmen seem somewhat equivocal. Originally doubtless that petty-officer's function was the instruction of the men in the use of arms, sword or cutlas. But very long ago, owing to the advance in gunnery making hand-to-hand encounters less frequent and giving to nitre and sulphur the preeminence over steel, that function ceased; the master-at-arms of a great war-ship becoming a sort of Chief of Police charged among other matters with the duty of preserving order on the populous lower gun-decks.

Claggart was a man about five and thirty, somewhat spare and tall, yet of no ill figure upon the whole. His hand was too small and shapely to have been accustomed to hard toil. The face was a notable one; the features all except the chin cleanly cut as those on a Greek medallion; yet the chin, beardless as Tecumseh's, had something of strange protuberant heaviness in its make that recalled the prints of the Rev. Dr. Titus Oates, the historic deponent with the clerical drawl in the time of Charles II and the fraud of the alleged Popish Plot. It served Claggart in his office that his eye could cast a tutoring glance. His brow was of the sort phrenologically associated with more than average intellect; silken jet curls partly clustering over it, making a foil to the pallor below, a pallor tinged with a faint shade of amber akin to the hue of time-tinted marbles of old. This complexion, singularly contrasting with the red or deeply bronzed visages of the sailors, and in part the result of his official seclusion from the sunlight, tho it was not exactly displeasing, nevertheless seemed to hint of something defective or abnormal in the constitution and blood. But his general aspect and manner were so suggestive of an education and career incongruous with his naval function that when not actively engaged in it he looked like a man of high quality, social and moral, who for reasons of his own was keeping incog. Nothing was known of his former life. It might be that he was an Englishman; and yet there lurked a bit of accent in his speech suggesting that possibly he was not such by birth, but through naturalization in early childhood. Among certain grizzled sea-gossips of the gun-decks and forecastle went a rumor perdue that the master-at-arms was a *chevalier* who had volunteered into the King's navy by way of compounding for some mysterious swindle whereof he had been arraigned at the King's Bench. The fact that nobody could substantiate this report was, of course, nothing against its secret currency. Such a rumor once started on the gun-decks in reference to almost anyone below the rank of a commissioned officer would, during the period assigned to this narrative, have seemed not altogether wanting in credibility to the tarry old wiseacres of a man-of-war crew. And indeed a man of Claggart's accomplishments, without prior nautical experience entering the navy at mature life, as he did, and necessarily allotted at the start to the lowest grade in it; a man too who never made allusion to his previous life ashore; these were circumstances which in the dearth of exact knowledge as to his true antecedents opened to the invidious a vague field for unfavorable surmise.

But the sailors' dog-watch gossip concerning him derived a vague plausibility from the fact that now for some period the British Navy could so little afford to be squeamish in the matter of keeping up the muster-rolls, that not only were press-gangs notoriously abroad both afloat and ashore, but there was little or no secret about another matter, namely that the London police were at liberty to capture any able-bodied suspect, any questionable fellow at large and summarily ship him to the dockyard or fleet. Furthermore, even among voluntary enlistments there were instances where the motive thereto partook neither of patriotic impulse nor yet of a random desire to experience a bit of sea-life and martial adventure. Insolvent debtors of minor grade, together with the promiscuous lame ducks of morality found in the Navy a convenient and secure refuge. Secure, because once enlisted aboard a King's-Ship, they were as much in sanctuary, as the transgressor of the Middle Ages harboring himself under the shadow of the altar. Such sanctioned irregularities, which for obvious reasons the Government would hardly think to parade at the time and which consequently, and as affecting the least influential class of mankind, have all but dropped into oblivion, lend color to something for the truth whereof I do not vouch, and hence have some scruple in stating; something I remember having seen in print though the book I can not recall; but the same thing was personally communicated to me now more than forty years ago by an old pensioner in a cocked hat with whom I had a most interesting talk on the terrace at Greenwich, a Baltimore negro, a Trafalgar man. It was to this effect: In the case of a warship short of hands whose speedy sailing was imperative, the deficient quota in lack of any other way of making it good, would be eked out by draughts culled direct from the jails. For reasons previously suggested it would not perhaps be easy at the present day directly to prove or disprove the allegation. But allowed as a verity, how significant would it be of England's straits at the time confronted by those wars which like a flight of harpies rose shrieking from the din and dust of the fallen Bastille. That era appears measurably clear to us who look back at it, and but read of it. But to the grandfathers of us graybeards, the more thoughtful of them, the genius of it presented an aspect like that of Camoen's Spirit of the Cape, an eclipsing menace mysterious and prodigious. Not America was exempt from apprehension. At the height of Napoleon's unexampled conquests, there were Americans who had fought at Bunker Hill who looked forward to the possibility that the Atlantic might prove no barrier against the ultimate schemes of this French upstart from the revolutionary chaos who seemed in act of fulfilling judgement prefigured in the Apocalypse.

But the less credence was to be given to the gun-deck talk touching Claggart, seeing that no man holding his office in a man-of-war can ever hope to be popular with the crew. Besides, in derogatory comments upon anyone against whom they have a grudge, or for any reason or no reason mislike, sailors are much like landsmen, they are apt to exaggerate or romance it.

About as much was really known to the *Indomitable's* tars of the master-at-arms' career before entering the service as an astronomer knows about a comet's travels prior to its first observable appearance in the sky. The verdict of the sea quid-nuncs has been cited only by way of showing what sort of moral impression the man made upon rude uncultivated natures whose conceptions of human wickedness were necessarily of the narrowest, limited to ideas of vulgar rascality, —a thief among the swinging hammocks during a night-watch, or the man-brokers and land-sharks of the sea-ports.

It was no gossip, however, but fact, that though, as before hinted, Claggart upon his entrance into the navy was, as a novice, assigned to the least honorable section of a man-of-war's crew, embracing the drudgery, he did not long remain there.

The superior capacity he immediately evinced, his constitutional sobriety, ingratiating deference to superiors, together with a peculiar ferreting genius manifested on a singular occasion, all this capped by a certain austere patriotism abruptly advanced him to the position of master-at-arms.

Of this maritime Chief of Police the ship's-corporals, so called, were the immediate subordinates, and compliant ones; and this, as is to be noted in some business departments ashore, almost to a degree inconsistent with entire moral volition. His place put various converging wires of underground influence under the Chief's control, capable when astutely worked thro his understrappers of operating to the mysterious discomfort[,] if nothing worse, of any of the sea-commonalty.

9

Life in the fore-top well agreed with Billy Budd. There, when not actually engaged on the yards yet higher aloft, the topmen, who as such had been picked out for youth and activity, constituted an aerial club lounging at ease against the smaller stun'sails rolled up into cushions, spinning yarns like the lazy gods, and frequently amused with what was going on in the busy world of the decks below. No wonder then that a young fellow of Billy's disposition was well content in such society. Giving no cause of offence to anybody, he was always alert at a call. So in the merchant service it had been with him. But now such a punctiliousness in duty was shown that his top-mates would sometimes good-naturedly laugh at him for it. This heightened alacrity had its cause, namely, the impression made upon him by the first formal gangway-punishment he had ever witnessed, which befell the day following his impressment. It had been in-curred by a little fellow, young, a novice[,] an after-guardsman absent from his assigned post when the ship was being put about; a derelic-tion resulting in a rather serious hitch to that manœuvre, one de-manding instantaneous promptitude in letting go and making fast. When Billy saw the culprit's naked back under the scourge gridironed with red welts, and worse; when he marked the dire expression on the liberated man's face as with his woolen shirt flung over him by the executioner he rushed forward from the spot to bury himself in the crowd, Billy was horrified. He resolved that never through remissness would he make himself liable to such a visitation or do or omit aught that might merit even verbal reproof. What then was his surprise and concern when ultimately he found himself getting into petty trouble occasionally about such matters as the stowage of his bag or some-thing amiss in his hammock, matters under the police oversight of the ship's-corporals of the lower decks, and which brought down on him a vague threat from one of them.

So heedful in all things as he was, how could this be? He could not understand it, and it more than vexed him. When he spoke to his young topmates about it they were either lightly incredulous or found something comical in his unconcealed anxiety. "Is it your bag, Billy?" said one "well, sew yourself up in it, bully boy, and then you'll be sure to know if anybody meddles with it."

Now there was a veteran aboard who because his years began to disqualify him for more active work had been recently assigned duty as main-mast-man in his watch, looking to the gear belayed at the rail roundabout that great spar near the deck. At off-times the foretopman had picked up some acquaintance with him, and now in his trouble it occurred to him that he might be the sort of person to go to for wise counsel. He was an old Dansker long anglicized in the service, of few words, many wrinkles and some honorable scars. His wizened face, time-tinted and weather-stained to the complexion of an antique parchment, was here and there peppered blue by the chance explosion of a gun-cartridge in action. He was an *Agamemnon*-man; some two years prior to the time of this story having served under Nelson when but Sir Horatio in that ship immortal in naval memory, and which[,] dismantled and in part broken up to her bare ribs[,] is seen a grand skeleton in Haydon's etching. As one of a boarding-party from the *Agamemnon* he had received a cut slantwise along one temple and cheek leaving a long pale scar like a streak of dawn's light falling athwart the dark visage. It was on account of that scar and the affair in which it was known that he had received it, as well as from his blue-peppered complexion that the Dansker went among the *Indomitable's* crew by the name of "Board-her-in-the-smoke."

Now the first time that his small weazel-eyes happened to light on Billy Budd, a certain grim internal merriment set all his ancient wrinkles into antic play. Was it that his eccentric unsentimental old sapience primitive in its kind saw or thought it saw something which in contrast with the war-ship's environment looked oddly incongruous in the handsome sailor? But after slyly studying him at intervals, the old Merlin's equivocal merriment was modified; for now when the twain would meet, it would start in his face a quizzing sort of look, but it would be but momentary and sometimes replaced by an expression of speculative query as to what might eventually befall a nature like that, dropped into a world not without some man-traps and against whose subtleties simple courage lacking experience and address and without any touch of defensive ugliness, is of little avail; and where such innocence as man is capable of does yet in a moral emergency not always sharpen the faculties or enlighten the will.

However it was the Dansker in his ascetic way rather took to Billy. Nor was this only because of a certain philosophic interest in such a character. There was another cause. While the old man's eccentricities, sometimes bordering on the ursine, repelled the juniors, Billy, undeterred thereby, revering him as a salt hero would make advances, never passing the old Agamemnon-man without a salutation marked by that respect which is seldom lost on the aged however crabbed at times or whatever their station in life.

There was a vein of dry humor, or what not, in the mast-man; and, whether in freak of patriarchal irony touching Billy's youth and athletic frame, or for some other and more recondite reason, from the first in addressing him he always substituted Baby for Billy. The

Dansker in fact being the originator of the name by which the fore-topman eventually became known aboard ship.

Well then, in his mysterious little difficulty going in quest of the wrinkled one, Billy found him off duty in a dog-watch ruminating by himself seated on a shot-box of the upper gun-deck now and then surveying with a somewhat cynical regard certain of the more swaggering promenaders there. Billy recounted his trouble, again wondering how it all happened. The salt seer attentively listened, accompanying the foretopman's recital with queer twitchings of his wrinkles and problematical little sparkles of his small ferret eyes. Making an end of his story, the foretopman asked, "And now, Dansker, do tell me what you think of it."

The old man, shoving up the front of his tarpaulin and deliberately rubbing the long slant scar at the point where it entered the thin hair, laconically said, "Baby Budd, *Jemmy Legs*" (meaning the master-at-arms) "is down on you[.]"

"*Jemmy Legs!*" ejaculated Billy his welkin eyes expanding; "what for? Why he calls me *the sweet and pleasant young fellow,* they tell me."

"Does he so?" grinned the grizzled one; then said "Ay[,] Baby Lad[,] a sweet voice has *Jemmy Legs*."

"No, not always. But to me he has. I seldom pass him but there comes a pleasant word."

"And that's because he's down upon you, Baby Budd."

Such reiteration along with the manner of it, incomprehensible to a novice, disturbed Billy almost as much as the mystery for which he had sought explanation. Something less unpleasingly oracular he tried to extract; but the old sea-Chiron thinking perhaps that for the nonce he had sufficiently instructed his young Achilles, pursed his lips, gathered all his wrinkles together and would commit himself to nothing further.

Years, and those experiences which befall certain shrewder men subordinated life-long to the will of superiors, all this had developed in the Dansker the pithy guarded cynicism that was his leading characteristic.

10

The next day an incident served to confirm Billy Budd in his incredulity as to the Dansker's strange summing up of the case submitted. The ship at noon going large before the wind was rolling on her course, and he below at dinner and engaged in some sportful talk with the members of his mess, chanced in a sudden lurch to spill the entire contents of his soup-pan upon the new scrubbed deck. Claggart, the Master-at-arms, official rattan in hand, happened to be passing along the battery in a bay of which the mess was lodged, and the greasy liquid streamed just across his path. Stepping over it, he was proceeding on his way without comment, since the matter was nothing to take notice of under the circumstances, when he happened to observe who it was that had done the spilling. His countenance changed. Pausing, he was about to ejaculate something hasty at the sailor, but checked himself, and pointing down to the streaming soup, playfully tapped him from behind with his rattan, saying in a low musical voice peculiar to him at times "Handsomely done, my lad! And handsome is as handsome did it too!" And with that passed on. Not noted by Billy as not coming within his view was the involuntary smile, or rather grimace, that accompanied Claggart's equivocal words. Aridly it drew down the thin corners of his shapely mouth. But everybody taking his remark as meant for humorous, and at which therefore as coming from a superior they were bound to laugh, "with counterfeited glee" acted accordingly; and Billy tickled, it may be, by the allusion to his being the handsome sailor, merrily joined in; then addressing his messmates exclaimed "There now, who says that Jemmy Legs is down on me!" "And who said he was, Beauty?" demanded one Donald with some surprise. Whereat the foretopman looked a little foolish recalling that it was only one person, Board-her-in-the-smoke who had suggested what to him was the smoky idea that this master-at-arms was in any peculiar way hostile to him. Meantime that functionary resuming his path must have momentarily worn some expression less guarded than that of the bitter smile, and usurping the face from the heart, some distorting expression perhaps, for a drummer-boy heedlessly frolicking along from the opposite direction and chancing to come into light collision with his person was strangely disconcerted by his aspect. Nor was the impression lessened when the official impulsively giving him a sharp cut with the rattan, vehemently exclaimed "Look where you go!"

11

What was the matter with the master-at-arms? And, be the matter what it might, how could it have direct relation to Billy Budd with whom prior to the affair of the spilled soup he had never come into any special contact official or otherwise? What indeed could the trouble have to do with one so little inclined to give offence as the merchant-ship's *peacemaker,* even him who in Claggart's own phrase was "the sweet and pleasant young fellow?["] Yes, why should *Jemmy Legs,* to borrow the Dansker's expression, be *down* on the Handsome Sailor? But, at heart and not for nothing, as the late chance encounter may indicate to the discerning, down on him, secretly down on him, he assuredly was.

Now to invent something touching the more private career of Claggart, something involving Billy Budd, of which something the latter should be wholly ignorant, some romantic incident implying that Claggart's knowledge of the young blue-jacket began at some

period anterior to catching sight of him on board the seventy-four—
all this, not so difficult to do, might avail in a way more or less interesting to account for whatever of enigma may appear to lurk in the
case. But in fact there was nothing of the sort. And yet the cause,
necessarily to be assumed as the sole one assignable, is in its very
realism as much charged with that prime element of Radcliffian romance, *the mysterious,* as any that the ingenuity of the author of the
Mysteries of Udolpho could devise. For what can more partake of the
mysterious than an antipathy spontaneous and profound such as is
evoked in certain exceptional mortals by the mere aspect of some
other mortal, however harmless he may be? if not called forth by
this very harmlessness itself.

Now there can exist no irritating juxtaposition of dissimilar per-
sonalities comparable to that which is possible aboard a great war-ship
fully manned and at sea. There, every day among all ranks almost
every man comes into more or less of contact with almost every other
man. Wholly there to avoid even the sight of an aggravating object
one must needs give it Jonah's toss or jump overboard himself. Imagine how all this might eventually operate on some peculiar human
creature the direct reverse of a saint?

But for the adequate comprehending of Claggart by a normal
nature these hints are insufficient. To pass from a normal nature to
him one must cross "the deadly space between." And this is best
done by indirection.

Long ago an honest scholar my senior, said to me in reference to
one who like himself is now no more, a man so unimpeachably respectable that against him nothing was ever openly said tho' among
the few something was whispered, "Yes, X—— is a nut not to be
cracked by the tap of a lady's fan. You are aware that I am the adher-
ent of no organized religion much less of any philosophy built into a
system. Well, for all that, I think that to try and get into X——, enter
his labyrinth and get out again, without a clue derived from some
source other than what is known as *knowledge of the world*—that were
hardly possible, at least for me."

"Why" said I, "X—— however singular a study to some, is yet
human, and knowledge of the world assuredly implies the knowledge
of human nature, and in most of its varieties."

"Yes, but a superficial knowledge of it, serving ordinary purposes.
But for anything deeper, I am not certain whether to know the world
and to know human nature be not two distinct branches of knowledge,
which while they may coexist in the same heart, yet either may exist
with little or nothing of the other. Nay, in an average man of the
world, his constant rubbing with it blunts that fine spiritual insight
indispensable to the understanding of the essential in certain exceptional characters, whether evil ones or good. In a matter of some importance I have seen a girl wind an old lawyer about her little finger.

Nor was it the dotage of senile love. Nothing of the sort. But he knew law better than he knew the girl's heart. Coke and Blackstone hardly shed so much light into obscure spiritual places as the Hebrew prophets. And who were they? Mostly recluses."

At the time my inexperience was such that I did not quite see the drift of all this. It may be that I see it now. And, indeed, if that lexicon which is based on Holy Writ were any longer popular, one might with less difficulty define and denominate certain phenomenal men. As it is, one must turn to some authority not liable to the charge of being tinctured with the Biblical element.

In a list of definitions included in the authentic translation of Plato, a list attributed to him, occurs this: "Natural Depravity: a depravity according to nature." A definition which tho' savoring of Calvinism, by no means involves Calvin's dogmas as to total mankind. Evidently its intent makes it applicable but to individuals. Not many are the examples of this depravity which the gallows and jail supply. At any rate for notable instances, since these have no vulgar alloy of the brute in them, but invariably are dominated by intellectuality, one must go elsewhere. Civilization, especially if of the austerer sort, is auspicious to it. It folds itself in the mantle of respectability. It has its certain negative virtues serving as silent auxiliaries. It never allows wine to get within its guard. It is not going too far to say that it is without vices or small sins. There is a phenomenal pride in it that excludes them from anything mercenary or avaricious. In short the depravity here meant partakes nothing of the sordid or sensual. It is serious, but free from acerbity. Though no flatterer of mankind it never speaks ill of it.

But the thing which in eminent instances signalizes so exceptional a nature is this: though the man's even temper and discreet bearing would seem to intimate a mind peculiarly subject to the law of reason, not the less in his heart he would seem to riot in complete exemption from that law[,] having apparently little to do with reason further than to employ it as an ambidexter implement for effecting the irrational. That is to say: Toward the accomplishment of an aim which in wantonness of malignity would seem to partake of the insane, he will direct a cool judgement sagacious and sound.

These men are true madmen, and of the most dangerous sort, for their lunacy is not continuous but occasional[,] evoked by some special object; it is probably secretive, which is as much to say it is self-contained, so that when moreover, most active[,] it is to the average mind not distinguishable from sanity, and for the reason above suggested that whatever its aims may be, and the aim is never declared—the method and the outward proceeding are always perfectly rational.

Now something such an one was Claggart, in whom was the mania of an evil nature, not engendered by vicious training or corrupting books or licentious living, but born with him and innate, in short "a depravity according to nature."

12

Lawyers, Experts, Clergy
An Episode

By the way, can it be the phenomenon, disowned or at least concealed, that in some criminal cases puzzles the courts? For this cause have our juries at times not only to endure the prolonged contentions of lawyers with their fees, but also the yet more perplexing strife of the medical experts with theirs?—But why leave it to them? why not subpoena as well the clerical proficients? Their vocation bringing them into peculiar contact with so many human beings, and sometimes in their least guarded hour, in interviews very much more confidential than those of physician and patient; this would seem to qualify them to know something about those intricacies involved in the question of moral responsibility; whether in a given case, say, the crime proceeded from mania in the brain or rabies of the heart. As to any differences among themselves these clerical proficients might develop on the stand, these could hardly be greater than the direct contradictions exchanged between the remunerated medical experts.

Dark sayings are these, some will say. But why? Is it because they somewhat savor of Holy Writ in its phrase "mysteries of iniquity"? If they do, such savor was far enough from being intended[,] for little will it commend these pages to many a reader of to-day.

The point of the present story turning on the hidden nature of the master-at-arms has necessitated this chapter. With an added hint or two in connection with the incident at the mess, the resumed narrative must be left to vindicate, as it may, its own credibility.

13

Pale ire, envy and despair

That Claggart's figure was not amiss, and his face, save the chin, well moulded, has already been said. Of these favorable points he seemed not insensible, for he was not only neat but careful in his dress. But the form of Billy Budd was heroic; and if his face was without the intellectual look of the pallid Claggart's, not the less was it lit, like his, from within, though from a different source. The bonfire in his heart made luminous the rose-tan in his cheek.

In view of the marked contrast between the persons of the twain, it is more than probable that when the master-at-arms in the scene last given applied to the sailor the proverb *Handsome is as handsome does;* he there let escape an ironic inkling, not caught by the young sailors who heard it, as to what it was that had first moved him against Billy, namely, his significant personal beauty.

Now envy and antipathy[,] passions irreconcilable in reason, nevertheless in fact may spring conjoined like Chang and Eng in one birth. Is Envy then such a monster? Well, though many an arraigned mortal has in hopes of mitigated penalty pleaded guilty to horrible actions, did ever anybody seriously confess to envy? Something there is in it universally felt to be more shameful than even felonious crime. And not only does everybody disown it but the better sort are inclined to incredulity when it is in earnest imputed to an intelligent man. But since its lodgement is in the heart not the brain, no degree of intellect supplies a guarantee against it. But Claggart's was no vulgar form of the passion. Nor, as directed toward Billy Budd did it partake of that streak of apprehensive jealousy that marred Saul's visage perturbedly brooding on the comely young David. Claggart's envy struck deeper. If askance he eyed the good looks, cheery health and frank enjoyment of young life in Billy Budd, it was because these [went] along with a nature that as Claggart magnetically felt, had in its simplicity never willed malice or experienced the reactionary bite of that serpent. To him, the spirit lodged within Billy, and looking out from his welkin eyes as from windows, that ineffability it was which made the dimple in his dyed cheek, suppled his joints, and dancing in his yellow curls made him preeminently the Handsome Sailor. One person excepted the master-at-arms was perhaps the only man in the ship intellectually capable of adequately appreciating the moral phenomenon presented in Billy Budd. And the insight but intensified his passion, which assuming various secret forms within him, at times assumed that of cynic disdain—disdain of innocence—To be nothing more than innocent! Yet in an æsthetic way he saw the charm of it, the courageous free-and-easy temper of it, and fain would have shared it, but he despaired of it.

With no power to annul the elemental evil in him, tho readily enough he could hide it; apprehending the good, but powerless to be it; a nature like Claggart's surcharged with energy as such natures almost invariably are, what recourse is left to it but to recoil upon itself and like the scorpion for which the Creator alone is responsible, act out to the end the part allotted it.

14

Passion, and passion in its profoundest, is not a thing demanding a palatial stage whereon to play its part. Down among the groundlings, among the beggars and rakers of the garbage, profound passion is enacted. And the circumstances that provoke it, however trivial or mean, are no measure of its power. In the present instance the stage is a scrubbed gun-deck, and one of the external provocations a man-of-war's-man's spilled soup.

Now when the Master-at-arms noticed whence came that greasy fluid streaming before his feet, he must have taken it—to some extent wilfully, perhaps—not for the mere accident it assuredly was, but for the sly escape of a spontaneous feeling on Billy's part more or less answering to the antipathy on his own. In effect a foolish demonstration he must have thought, and very harmless, like the futile kick of a heifer, which yet were the heifer a shod stallion, would not be so harmless. Even so was it that into the gall of Claggart's envy he infused the vitriol of his contempt. But the incident confirmed to him certain tell-tale reports purveyed to his ear by *Squeak*, one of his more cunning Corporals, a grizzled little man, so nicknamed by the sailors on account of his squeaky voice, and sharp visage ferreting about the dark corners of the lower decks after interlopers, satirically suggesting to them the idea of a rat in a cellar.

From his Chief's employing him as an implicit tool in laying little traps for the worriment of the Foretopman—for it was from the Master-at-arms that the petty persecutions heretofore adverted to had proceeded—the corporal having naturally enough concluded that his master could have no love for the sailor, made it his business, faithful understrapper that he was, to foment the ill blood by perverting to his Chief certain innocent frolics of the good natured Foretopman, besides inventing for his mouth sundry contumelious epithets he claimed to have overheard him let fall. The Master-at-arms never suspected the veracity of these reports, more especially as to the epithets, for he well knew how secretly unpopular may become a master-at-arms[,] at least a master-at-arms of those days zealous in his function, and how the blue-jackets shoot at him in private their raillery and wit; the nickname by which he goes among them (*Jemmy Legs*) implying under the form of merriment their cherished disrespect and dislike.

But in view of the greediness of hate for patrolmen it hardly needed a purveyor to feed Claggart's passion. An uncommon prudence is habitual with the subtler depravity, for it has everything to hide. And in case of an injury but suspected, its secretiveness voluntarily cuts it off from enlightenment or disillusion; and, not unreluctantly, action is taken upon surmise as upon certainty. And the retaliation is apt to be in monstrous disproportion to the supposed offence; for when in anybody was revenge in its exactions aught else but an inordinate usurer. But how with Claggart's conscience? For though consciences are unlike as foreheads, every intelligence, not excluding the Scriptural devils who "believe and tremble," has one. But Claggart's conscience being but the lawyer to his will, made ogres of trifles, probably arguing that the motive imputed to Billy in spilling the soup just when he did, together with the epithets alleged, these, if nothing more, made a strong case against him; nay, justified animosity into a sort of retributive righteousness. The Pharisee is the Guy Fawkes prowling in the hid chambers underlying the Claggarts. And they can really form no conception of an unreciprocated malice. Probably, the master-at-arms' clandestine persecution of Billy was started to try the temper of the man; but it had not developed any quality in him that enmity could make official use of or even pervert into plausible self-justification; so that the occurrence at the mess, petty if it were, was a welcome one to that peculiar conscience assigned to be the private mentor of Claggart; And, for the rest, not improbably it put him upon new experiments.

15

Not many days after the last incident narrated something befell Billy Budd that more gravelled him than aught that had previously occurred.

It was a warm night for the latitude; and the Foretopman, whose watch at the time was properly below, was dozing on the uppermost deck whither he had ascended from his hot hammock one of hundreds suspended so closely wedged together over a lower gun-deck that there was little or no swing to them. He lay as in the shadow of a hill-side, stretched under the lee of the booms, a piled ridge of spare spars amidships between foremast and mainmast and among which the ship's largest boat, the launch, was stowed. Alongside of three other slumberers from below, he lay near that end of the booms which approaches the foremast; his station aloft on duty as a foretopman being just over the deck-station of the forecastlemen, entitling him according to usage to make himself more or less at home in that neighborhood.

Presently he was stirred into semi-consciousness by somebody, who must have previously sounded the sleep of the others, touching his shoulder, and then as the Foretopman raised his head, breathing into his ear in a quick whisper, "Slip into the lee forechains, Billy; there is something in the wind. Don't speak. Quick, I will meet you there;" and disappeared.

Now Billy like sundry other essentially good-natured ones had some of the weaknesses inseparable from essential good nature; and among these was a reluctance, almost an incapacity of plumply saying *no* to an abrupt proposition not obviously absurd, on the face of it, nor obviously unfriendly, nor iniquitous. And being of warm blood he had not the phlegm tacitly to negative any proposition by unresponsive inaction. Like his sense of fear, his apprehension as to aught outside of the honest and natural was seldom very quick. Besides, upon the present occasion, the drowse from his sleep still hung upon him.

However it was, he mechanically rose, and sleepily wondering what could be in the wind, betook himself to the designated place, a narrow platform, one of six, outside of the high bulwarks and screened by the great dead-eyes and multiple columned lanyards of the shrouds and back-stays; and, in a great war-ship of that time, of dimensions commensurate [with the] hull's magnitude; a tarry balcony in short overhanging the sea, and so secluded that one mariner of the *Indomitable,* a non-conformist old tar of a serious turn, made it even in daytime his private oratory.

In this retired nook the stranger soon joined Billy Budd. There was no moon as yet; a haze obscured the star-light. He could not distinctly see the stranger's face. Yet from something in the outline and carriage, Billy took him to be, and correctly, for one of the afterguard.

"Hist! Billy," said the man in the same quick cautionary whisper as before; "You were impressed, weren't you? Well, so was I"; and he paused, as to mark the effect. But Billy not knowing exactly what to make of this said nothing. Then the other: "We are not the only impressed ones, Billy. There's a gang of us.—Couldn't you—help—at a pinch?["]

"What do you mean?["] demanded Billy here thoroughly shaking off his drowse.

"Hist, hist!["] the hurried whisper now growing husky, ["]see here"; and the man held up two small objects faintly twinkling in the nightlight; "see, they are yours, Billy, if you'll only—"

But Billy broke in, and in his resentful eagerness to deliver himself his vocal infirmity somewhat intruded: "D-D-Damme, I don't know what you are d-d-driving at, or what you mean, but you had better g-g-go where you belong!" For the moment the fellow, as confounded, did not stir; and Billy springing to his feet, said "If you d-don't start I'll t-t-toss you back over the r-rail!" There was no mistaking this and the mysterious emissary decamped disappearing in the direction of the mainmast in the shadow of the booms.

"Hallo, what's the matter?" here came growling from a forecastleman awakened from his deck-doze by Billy's raised voice. And as the foretopman reappeared and was recognized by him; "Ah, *Beauty,* is it you? Well, something must have been the matter for you st-st-stuttered."

"O," rejoined Billy, now mastering the impediment; "I found an afterguardsman in our part of the ship here and I bid him be off where he belongs."

"And is that all you did about it, foretopman?" gruffly demanded another, an irascible old fellow of brick-colored visage and hair, and who was known to his associate forecastlemen as *Red Pepper;* "Such sneaks I should like to marry to the gunner's daughter!" by that expression meaning that he would like to subject them to disciplinary castigation over a gun.

However, Billy's rendering of the matter satisfactorily accounted to these inquirers for the brief commotion, since of all the sections of a ship's company the forecastlemen, veterans for the most part and bigoted in their sea-prejudices, are the most jealous in resenting territorial encroachments, especially on the part of any of the afterguard, of whom they have but a sorry opinion, chiefly landsmen, never going aloft except to reef or furl the mainsail, and in no wise competent to handle a marlinspike or turn in a *dead-eye,* say.

16

This incident sorely puzzled Billy Budd. It was an entirely new experience; the first time in his life that he had ever been personally approached in underhand intriguing fashion. Prior to this encounter he had known nothing of the afterguardsman, the two men being stationed wide apart, one forward and aloft during his watch, the other on deck and aft.

What could it mean? And could they really be guineas, those two glittering objects the interloper had held up to his (Billy's) eyes? Where could the fellow get guineas? Why even spare buttons[2] are not so plentiful at sea. The more he turned the matter over, the more he was non-plussed, and made uneasy and discomforted. In his disgustful recoil from an overture which tho' he but ill comprehended he instinctively knew must involve evil of some sort, Billy Budd was like a young horse fresh from the pasture suddenly inhaling a vile whiff from some chemical factory and by repeated snortings tries to get it out of his nostrils and lungs. This frame of mind barred all desire of holding further parley with the fellow, even were it but for the purpose of gaining some enlightenment as to his design in approaching him. And yet he was not without natural curiosity to see how such a visitor in the dark would look in broad day.

He espied him the following afternoon in his first dog-watch below one of the smokers on that forward part of the upper gun deck allotted to the pipe. He recognized him by his general cut and build, more than by his round freckled face and glassy eyes of pale blue, veiled with lashes all but white. And yet Billy was a bit uncertain whether indeed it were he—yonder chap about his own age chatting and laughing in free-hearted way, leaning against a gun; a genial young fellow enough to look at, and something of a rattle-brain, to all appearance. Rather chubby too for a sailor even an afterguardsman. In short the last man in the world, one would think, to be overburthened with thoughts, especially those perilous thoughts that must needs belong to a conspirator in any serious project, or even to the underling of such a conspirator.

Altho' Billy was not aware of it, the fellow, with a side-long watchful glance had perceived Billy first, and then noting that Billy was looking at him, thereupon nodded a familiar sort of friendly recognition as to an old acquaintance, without interrupting the talk he

---

2 The manuscript reads "*buttons* spare buttons," but surely Melville intended to remove the duplication.

was engaged in with the group of smokers. A day or two afterwards chancing in the evening promenade on a gun deck, to pass Billy, he offered a flying word of good-fellowship as it were, which by its un-expectedness, and equivocalness under the circumstances so embar-rassed Billy that he knew not how to respond to it, and let it go un-noticed.

Billy was now left more at a loss than before. The ineffectual speculation into which he was led was so disturbingly alien to him that he did his best to smother [it]. It never entered his mind that here was a matter which from its extreme questionableness, it was his duty as a loyal blue-jacket to report in the proper quarter. And, probably, had such a step been suggested to him, he would have been deterred from taking it by the thought, one of novice-magnanimity, that it would savor overmuch of the dirty work of a tell-tale. He kept the thing to himself. Yet upon one occasion, he could not forbear a little disburthening himself to the old Dansker, tempted thereto perhaps by the influence of a balmy night when the ship lay becalmed; the twain, silent for the most part, sitting together on deck, their heads propped against the bulwarks. But it was only a partial and anony-mous account that Billy gave, the unfounded scruples above referred to preventing full disclosure to anybody. Upon hearing Billy's version, the sage Dansker seemed to divine more than he was told; and after a little meditation during which his wrinkles were pursed as into a point, quite effacing for the time that quizzing expression his face sometimes wore,—"Didn't I say so, Baby Budd?"

"Say what?" demanded Billy.

"Why, *Jemmy Legs* is *down* on you."

"And what" rejoined Billy in amazement, "has *Jemmy Legs* to do with that cracked afterguardsman?"

"Ho, it was an afterguardsman then. A cat's-paw, a cat's-paw!" And with that exclamation, which, whether it had reference to a light puff of air just then coming over the calm sea, or subtler relation to the afterguardsman, there is no telling, the old Merlin gave a twisting wrench with his black teeth at his plug of tobacco, vouchsafing no reply to Billy's impetuous question, tho' now repeated, for it was his wont to relapse into grim silence when interrogated in skeptical sort as to any of his sententious oracles, not always very clear ones, rather par-taking of that obscurity which invests most Delphic deliverances from any quarter.

Long experience had very likely brought this old man to that bit-ter prudence which never interferes in aught and never gives advice.

17

Yes, despite the Dansker's pithy insistence as to the Master-at-arms being at the bottom of these strange experiences of Billy on board the *Indomitable,* the young sailor was ready to ascribe them to almost anybody but the man who, to use Billy's own expression, "always had a pleasant word for him." This is to be wondered at. Yet not so much to be wondered at. In certain matters, some sailors even in mature life remain unsophisticated enough. But a young seafarer of the disposition of our athletic Foretopman, is much of a child-man. And yet a child's utter innocence is but its blank ignorance, and the innocence more or less wanes as intelligence waxes. But in Billy Budd intelligence, such as it was, had advanced, while yet his simple mindedness remained for the most part unaffected. Experience is a teacher indeed; yet did Billy's years make his experience small. Besides, he had none of that intuitive knowledge of the bad which in natures not good or incompletely so foreruns experience, and therefore may pertain, as in some instances it too clearly does pertain, even to youth.

And what could Billy know of man except of man as a mere sailor? And the old-fashioned sailor, the veritable man-before-the-mast, the sailor from boyhood up, he, tho' indeed of the same species as a landsman is in some respects singularly distinct from him. The sailor is frankness, the landsman is finesse. Life is not a game with the sailor, demanding the long head; no intricate game of chess where few moves are made in straightforwardness, and ends are attained by indirection; an oblique, tedious, barren game hardly worth that poor candle burnt out in playing it.

Yes, as a class, sailors are in character a juvenile race. Even their deviations are marked by juvenility. And this more especially holding true with the sailors of Billy's time. Then, too, certain things which apply to all sailors, do more pointedly operate here and there, upon the junior one. Every sailor, too is accustomed to obey orders without debating them; his life afloat is externally ruled for him; he is not brought into that promiscuous commerce with mankind where unobstructed free agency on equal terms—equal superficially, at least—soon teaches one that unless upon occasion he exercise a distrust keen in proportion to the fairness of the appearance, some foul turn may be served him. A ruled undemonstrative distrustfulness is so habitual, not with business-men so much, as with men who know their kind in less shallow relations than business, namely, certain men-of-the-world, that they come at last to employ it all but unconsciously; and some of them would very likely feel real surprise at being charged with it as one of their general characteristics.

18

But after the little matter at the mess Billy Budd no more found himself in strange trouble at times about his hammock or his clothes-bag or what not. While, as to that smile that occasionally sunned him, and the pleasant passing word, these were if not more frequent, yet if anything more pronounced than before.

But for all that, there were certain other demonstrations now. When Claggart's unobserved glance happened to light on belted Billy rolling along the upper gun-deck in the leisure of the second dog-watch exchanging passing broadsides of fun with other young prome-naders in the crowd; that glance would follow the cheerful sea-Hy-perion with a settled meditative and melancholy expression, his eyes strangely suffused with incipient feverish tears. Then would Claggart ook like the man of sorrows. Yes, and sometimes the melancholy ex-pression would have in it a touch of soft yearning, as if Claggart could even have loved Billy but for fate and ban. But this was an evanescence, and quickly repented of, as it were, by an immitigable look, pinching and shrivelling the visage into the momentary semblance of a wrinkled walnut. But sometimes catching sight in advance of the foretopman coming in his direction, he would, upon their nearing, step aside a little to let him pass, dwelling upon Billy for the moment with the glittering dental satire of a Guise. But upon any abrupt unforeseen encounter a red light would [flash] forth from his eye like a spark from an anvil in a dusk smithy. That quick fierce light was a strange one, darted from orbs which in repose were of a color nearest approaching a deeper violet, the softest of shades.

Tho' some of these caprices of the pit could not but be observed by their object, yet were they beyond the construing of such a nature. And the *thews* of Billy were hardly compatible with that sort of sensi-tive spiritual organisation which in some cases instinctively conveys to ignorant innocence an admonition of the proximity of the malign. He thought the Master-at-arms acted in a manner rather queer at times. That was all. But the occasional frank air and pleasant word went for what they purported to be, the young sailor never having heard as yet of the "too fair-spoken man."

Had the foretopman been conscious of having done or said any-thing to provoke the ill will of the official, it would have been differ-ent with him, and his sight might have been purged if not sharpened. As it was[,] innocence was his blinder.

So was it with him in yet another matter. Two minor officers—the Armorer and Captain of the Hold, with whom he had never ex-changed a word, his position in the ship not bringing him into contact with them; these men now for the first began to cast upon Billy when they chanced to encounter him, that peculiar glance which evidences that the man from whom it comes has been some way tampered with and to the prejudice of him upon whom the glance lights. Never did it occur to Billy as a thing to be noted or a thing suspicious, tho' he well knew the fact, that the Armorer and Captain of the Hold, with the ship's-yeoman, apothecary, and others of that grade, were by naval usage, mess-mates of the master-at-arms, men with ears convenient to his confidential tongue.

But the general popularity that our *Handsome Sailor's* manly forwardness [drew forth] upon occasion, and [his] irresistible good nature[,] indicating [indicated?] no mental superiority tending to excite an invidious feeling; this good will on the part of most of his shipmates made him the less to concern himself about such mute aspects toward him as those whereto allusion has just been made.

As to the afterguardsman, tho' Billy for reasons already given necessarily saw little of him, yet when the two did happen to meet, invariably came the fellow's off-hand cheerful recognition, sometimes accompanied by a passing pleasant word or two. Whatever that equivocal young person's original design may really have been, or the design of which he might have been the deputy, certain it was from his manner upon these occasions, that he had wholly dropped it.

It was as if his precocity of crookedness (and every vulgar villain is precocious) had for once deceived him, and the man he had sought to entrap as a simpleton had, through his very simplicity ignorantly baffled him.

But shrewd ones may opine that it was hardly possible for Billy to refrain from going up to the afterguardsman and bluntly demanding to know his purpose in the initial interview, so abruptly closed in the fore-chains. Shrewd ones may also think it but natural in Billy to set about sounding some of the other impressed men of the ship in order to discover what basis, if any, there was for the emissary's obscure suggestions as to plotting disaffection aboard. Yes, [the] shrewd may so think. But something more, or rather, something else than mere shrewdness is perhaps needful for the due understanding of such a character as Billy Budd's.

As to Claggart, the monomania in the man—if that indeed it were —as involuntarily disclosed by starts in the manifestations detailed, yet in general covered over by his self-contained and rational demeanor; this, like a subterranean fire was eating its way deeper and deeper in him. Something decisive must come of it.

19

After the mysterious interview in the fore-chains, the one so abruptly ended there by Billy, nothing especially German [germane?] to the story occurred until the events now about to be narrated.

Elsewhere it has been said that in the lack of frigates (of course better sailers than line-of-battle ships) in the English squadron up the Straits at that period, the *Indomitable* was occasionally employed not only as an available substitute for a scout, but at times on detached service of more important kind. This was not alone because of her sailing qualities, not common in a ship of her rate, but quite as much, probably, that the character of her commander, it was thought, specially adapted him for any duty where under unforeseen difficulties a prompt initiative might have to be taken in some matter demanding knowledge and ability in addition to those qualities implied in good seamanship. It was on an expedition of the latter sort, a somewhat distant one, and when the *Indomitable* was almost at her furthest remove from the fleet that in the latter part of an afternoon-watch she unexpectedly came in sight of a ship of the enemy. It proved to be a frigate. The latter perceiving thro' the glass that the weight of men and metal would be heavily against her, invoking her light heels crowded sail to get away. After a chase urged almost against hope and lasting until about the middle of the first dog-watch, she signally succeeded in effecting her escape.

Not long after the pursuit had been given up, and ere the excitement incident thereto had altogether waned away, the Master-at-Arms ascending from his cavernous sphere made his appearance cap in hand by the mainmast respectfully waiting the notice of Captain Vere then solitary walking the weather-side of the quarter-deck, doubtless somewhat chafed at the failure of the pursuit. The spot where Claggart stood was the place allotted to men of lesser grades seeking some more particular interview either with the officer-of-the-deck or the Captain himself. But from the latter it was not often that a sailor or petty-officer of those days would seek a hearing; only some exceptional cause, would, according to established custom, have warranted that.

Presently, just as the Commander absorbed in his reflections was on the point of turning aft in his promenade, he became sensible of Claggart's presence, and saw the doffed cap held in deferential expectancy. Here be it said that Captain Vere's personal knowledge of this petty-officer had only begun at the time of the ship's last sailing from home, Claggart then for the first, in transfer from a ship detained for repairs, supplying on board the *Indomitable* the place of a previous master-at-arms disabled and ashore.

No sooner did the Commander observe who it was that now deferentially stood awaiting his notice, than a peculiar expression came over him. It was not unlike that which uncontrollably will flit across the countenance of one at unawares encountering a person who though known to him indeed has hardly been long enough known for thorough knowledge, but something in whose aspect nevertheless now for the first provokes a vaguely repellent distaste. But coming to a stand, and resuming much of his wonted official manner, save that a sort of impatience lurked in the intonation of the opening word, he said "Well? what is it, Master-at-Arms?"

With the air of a subordinate grieved at the necessity of being a messenger of ill tidings, and while conscientiously determined to be frank, yet equally resolved upon shunning overstatement, Claggart at this invitation or rather summons to disburthen, spoke up. What he said, conveyed in the language of no uneducated man, was to the effect following if not altogether in these words, namely, that during the chase and preparations for the possible encounter he had seen enough to convince him that at least one sailor aboard was a dangerous character in a ship mustering some who not only had taken a guilty part in the late serious troubles, but others also who, like the man in question, had entered His Majesty's service under another form than enlistment.

At this point Captain Vere with some impatience, interrupted him: "Be direct, man; say impressed men."

Claggart made a gesture of subservience, and proceeded.

Quite lately he (Claggart) had begun to suspect that on the gun-decks some sort of movement prompted by the sailor in question was covertly going on, but he had not thought himself warranted in reporting the suspicion so long as it remained indistinct. But from what he had that afternoon observed in the man referred to the suspicion of something clandestine going on had advanced to a point less removed from certainty. He deeply felt, he added, the serious responsibility assumed in making a report involving such possible consequences to the individual mainly concerned, besides tending to augment those natural anxieties which every naval commander must feel in view of extraordinary outbreaks so recent as those which, he sorrowfully said, it needed not to name.

Now at the first broaching of the matter Captain Vere taken by surprise could not wholly dissemble his disquietude. But as Claggart went on, the former's aspect changed into restiveness under something in the witness' manner in giving his testimony. However, he refrained from interrupting him. And Claggart, continuing, concluded with this:

"God forbid, your honor, that the *Indomitable's* should be the experience of the—"

"Never mind that!" here peremptorily broke in the superior, his face altering with anger, instinctively divining the ship that the other was about to name, one in which the Nore Mutiny had assumed a singularly tragical character that for a time jeopardized the life of its commander. Under the circumstances he was indignant at the purposed allusion. When the commissioned officers themselves were on all occasions very heedful how they referred to the recent events, for a petty-officer unnecessarily to allude to them in the presence of his Captain, this struck him as a most immodest presumption. Besides, to his quick sense of self-respect, it even looked under the circumstances something like an attempt to alarm him. Nor at first was he without some surprise that one who so far as he had hitherto come under his notice had shown considerable tact in his function should in this particular evince such lack of it.

But these thoughts and kindred dubious ones flitting across his mind were suddenly replaced by an intuitional surmise which though as yet obscure in form served practically to affect his reception of the ill tidings. Certain it is, that long versed in everything pertaining to the complicated gun-deck life, which like every other form of life, has its secret mines and dubious side, the side popularly disclaimed, Captain Vere did not permit himself to be unduly disturbed by the general tenor of his subordinate's report. Furthermore, if in view of recent events prompt action should be taken at the first palpable sign of recurring insubordination, for all that, not judicious would it be, he thought, to keep the idea of lingering disaffection alive by undue forwardness in crediting an informer even if his own subordinate and charged among other things with police surveillance of the crew. This feeling would not perhaps have so prevailed with him were it not that upon a prior occasion the patriotic zeal officially evinced by Claggart had somewhat irritated him as appearing rather supersensible and strained. Furthermore, something even in the official's self-possessed and somewhat ostentatious manner in making his specifications strangely reminded him of a bandsman, a perjurous witness in a capital case before a court-martial ashore of which when a lieutenant he Captain Vere had been a member.

Now the peremptory check given to Claggart in the matter of the arrested allusion was quickly followed up by this: "You say that there is at least one dangerous man aboard. Name him."

"William Budd. A foretopman, your honor—"

"William Budd" repeated Captain Vere with unfeigned astonishment; "and mean you the man that Lieutenant Ratcliffe took from the merchantman not very long ago—the young fellow who seems to be so popular with the men—Billy, the Handsome Sailor, as they call him?["]

"The same, your honor; but for all his youth and good looks, a deep one. Not for nothing does he insinuate himself into the good will of his shipmates, since at the least all hands will at a pinch say a good word for him at all hazards. Did Lieutenant Ratcliffe happen to tell your honor of that adroit fling of Budd's, jumping up in the cutter's bow under the merchantman's stern when he was being taken off? It is even masqued by that sort of good humored air that at heart he resents his impressment. You have but noted his fair cheek. A man-trap may be under his ruddy-tipped daisies."

Now the *Handsome Sailor* as a signal figure among the crew had naturally enough attracted the Captain's attention from the first. Tho' in general not very demonstrative to his officers, he had congratulated Lieutenant Ratcliffe upon his good fortune in lighting on such a fine specimen of the genus homo, who in the nude might have posed for a statue of young Adam before the Fall.

As to Billy's adieu to the ship *Rights-of-Man*, which the boarding lieutenant had indeed reported to him but in a deferential way more as a good story than aught else, Captain Vere[,] tho mistakenly understanding it as a satiric sally, had but thought so much the better of the impressed man for it; as a military sailor, admiring the spirit that could take an arbitrary enlistment so merrily and sensibly. The fore-topman's conduct, too, so far as it had fallen under the Captain's notice had confirmed the first happy augury, while the new recruit's qualities as a *sailor-man* seemed to be such that he had thought of recommending him to the executive officer for promotion to a place that would more frequently bring him under his own observation, namely, the captaincy of the mizzen-top, replacing there in the star-board watch a man not so young whom partly for that reason he deemed less fitted for the post. Be it parenthesized here that since the mizzen-top-men having not to handle such breadths of heavy canvas as the lower sails on the main-mast and fore-mast, a young man if of the right stuff not only seems best adapted to duty there, but in fact is generally selected for the captaincy of that top, and the company under him are light hands and often but striplings. In sum, Captain Vere had from the beginning deemed Billy Budd to be what in the naval parlance of the time was called a *"King's bar-gain*[,]*"* that is to say, for His Britannic Majesty's navy a capital investment at small outlay or none at all.

After a brief pause during which the reminiscences above mentioned passed vividly through his mind and he weighed the import of Claggart's last suggestion conveyed in the phrase "pitfall under the clover,"[3] and the more he weighed it the less reliance he felt in the informer's good faith. Suddenly he turned upon him and in a low voice: "Do you come to me, master-at-arms[,] with so foggy a tale? As to Budd, cite me an act or spoken word of his confirmatory of what you in general charge against him. Stay," drawing nearer to him[,] "heed what you speak. Just now, and in a case like this, there is a yard-arm-end for the false-witness."

"Ah, your honor!" sighed Claggart mildly shaking his shapely head as in sad deprecation of such unmerited severity of tone. Then, bridling—erecting himself as in virtuous self-assertation, he circumstantially alleged certain words and acts, which collectively, if credited, led to presumptions mortally inculpating Budd. And for some of these averments, he added, substantiating proof was not far.

With gray eyes impatient and distrustful essaying to fathom to the bottom Claggart's calm violet ones, Captain Vere again heard him out; then for the moment stood ruminating. The mood he evinced, Claggart—himself for the time liberated from the other's scrutiny—steadily regarded with a look difficult to render,—a look curious of the operation of his tactics, a look such as might have been that of the spokesman of the envious children of Jacob deceptively

---

[3] The phrase Claggart had used three paragraphs previously was "A man-trap . . . under his ruddy-tipped daisies." Melville surely would have corrected the discrepancy.

imposing upon the troubled patriarch the blood-dyed coat of young Joseph.

Though something exceptional in the moral quality of Captain Vere made him, in earnest encounter with a fellow-man, a veritable touch-stone of that man's essential nature, yet now as to Claggart and what was really going on in him his feeling partook less of in-tuitional conviction than of strong suspicion clogged by strange dubieties. The perplexity he evinced proceeded less from aught touch-ing the man informed against—as Claggart doubtless opined—than from considerations how best to act in regard to the informer. At first indeed he was naturally for summoning that substantiation of his allegations which Claggart said was at hand. But such a proceed-ing would result in the matter at once getting abroad, which in the present stage of it, he thought, might undesirably affect the ship's company. If Claggart was a false witness,—that closed the affair. And therefore before trying the accusation, he would first practically test the accuser; and he thought this could be done in a quiet undemon-strative way.

The measure he determined upon involved a shifting of the scene, a transfer to a place less exposed to observation than the broad quarter-deck. For although the few gun-room officers there at the time had, in due observance of naval etiquette, withdrawn to leeward the moment Captain Vere had begun his promenade on the deck's weather-side; and tho' during the colloquy with Claggart they of course ventured not to diminish the distance; and though through-out the interview Captain Vere's voice was far from high, and Clag-gart's silvery and low; and the wind in the cordage and the wash of the sea helped the more to put them beyond ear-shot; nevertheless, the interview's continuance already had attracted observation from some topmen aloft and other sailors in the waist or further forward.

Having determined upon his measures, Captain Vere forthwith took action. Abruptly turning to Claggart he asked[,] "Master-at-arms, is it now Budd's watch aloft?"

"No, your honor." Whereupon, "Mr. Wilkes!" summoning the nearest midshipman, "tell Albert to come to me." Albert was the Captain's hammock-boy, a sort of sea-valet in whose discretion and fidelity his master had much confidence. The lad appeared. "You know Budd the foretopman?"

"I do, Sir."

"Go find him. It is his watch off. Manage to tell him out of ear-shot that he is wanted aft. Contrive it that he speaks to nobody. Keep him in talk yourself. And not till you get well aft here, not till then let him know that the place where he is wanted is my cabin. You understand. Go.—Master-at-Arms, show yourself on the decks below, and when you think it time for Albert to be coming with his man, stand by quietly to follow the sailor in."

20

Now when the foretopman found himself closeted there, as it were, in the cabin with the Captain and Claggart, he was surprised enough. But it was a surprise unaccompanied by apprehension or distrust. To an immature nature essentially honest and humane, forewarning intimations of subtler danger from one's kind come tardily if at all. The only thing that took shape in the young sailor's mind was this: Yes, the Captain, I have always thought, looks kindly upon me. Wonder if he's going to make me his coxswain. I should like that. And maybe now he is going to ask the master-at-arms about me.

"Shut the door there, sentry," said the commander; "stand without, and let nobody come in.—Now, master-at-arms, tell this man to his face what you told of him to me;" and stood prepared to scrutinize the mutually confronting visages.

With the measured step and calm collected air of an asylum-physician approaching in the public hall some patient beginning to show indications of a coming paroxysm, Claggart deliberately advanced within short range of Billy, and mesmerically looking him in the eye, briefly recapitulated the accusation.

Not at first did Billy take it in. When he did, the rose-tan of his cheek looked struck as by white leprosy. He stood like one impaled and gagged. Meanwhile the accuser's eyes removing not as yet from the blue dilated ones, underwent a phenomenal change, their wonted rich violet color blurring into a muddy purple. Those lights of human intelligence losing human expression, gelidly protruding like the alien eyes of certain uncatalogued creatures of the deep. The first mesmeric glance was one of serpent fascination; the last was as the hungry lurch of the torpedo-fish.

"Speak, man!" said Captain Vere to the transfixed one struck by his aspect even more than by Claggart's, "Speak! defend yourself." Which appeal caused but a strange dumb gesturing and gurgling in Billy; amazement at such an accusation so suddenly sprung on inexperienced nonage; this, and, it may be horror of the accuser, serving to bring out his lurking defect and in this instance for the time intensifying it into a convulsed tongue-tie; while the intent head and entire form straining forward in any agony of ineffectual eagerness to obey the injunction to speak and defend himself, gave an expression to the face like that of a condemned Vestal priestess in the moment of being buried alive, and in the first struggle against suffocation.

Though at the time Captain Vere was quite ignorant of Billy's liability to vocal impediment, he now immediately divined it, since vividly Billy's aspect recalled to him that of a bright young schoolmate of his whom he had once seen struck by much the same startling impotence in the act of eagerly rising in the class to be foremost in response to a testing question put to it by the master. Going close up to the young sailor, and laying a soothing hand on his shoulder, he said[:] "There is no hurry, my boy. Take your time, take your time." Contrary to the effect intended, these words so fatherly in tone, doubtless touching Billy's heart to the quick, prompted yet more violent efforts at utterance—efforts soon ending for the time in confirming the paralysis, and bringing to his face an expression which was as a crucifixion to behold. The next instant, quick as the flame from a discharged cannon at night, his right arm shot out, and Claggart dropped to the deck. Whether intentionally or but owing to the young athlete's superior height, the blow had taken effect full upon the forehead, so shapely and intellectual-looking a feature in the master-at-arms; so that the body fell over lengthwise, like a heavy plank tilted from erectness. A gasp or two, and he lay motionless.

"Fated boy," breathed Captain Vere in tone so low as to be almost a whisper, "what have you done! But here, help me."

The twain raised the felled one from the loins up into a sitting position. The spare form flexibly acquiesced, but inertly. It was like handling a dead snake. They lowered it back. Regaining erectness Captain Vere with one hand covering his face stood to all appearance as impassive as the object at his feet. Was he absorbed in taking in all the bearings of the event and what was best not only now at once to be done, but also in the sequel? Slowly he uncovered his face; and the effect was as if the moon emerging from eclipse should reappear with quite another aspect than that which had gone into hiding. The father in him, manifested towards Billy thus far in the scene, was replaced by the military disciplinarian. In his official tone he bade the foretopman retire to a state-room aft, (pointing it out) and there remain till thence summoned. This order Billy in silence mechanically obeyed. Then going to the cabin-door where it opened on the quarter-deck, Captain Vere said to the sentry without, "Tell somebody to send Albert here." When the lad appeared his master so contrived it that he should not catch sight of the prone one. "Albert," he said to him, "tell the Surgeon I wish to see him. You need not come back till called." When the Surgeon entered—a self-poised character of that grave sense and experience that hardly anything could take him aback,—Captain Vere advanced to meet him, thus unconsciously intercepting his view of Claggart and interrupting the other's wonted ceremonious salutation, said, "Nay, tell me how it is with yonder man," directing his attention to the prostrate one.

The Surgeon looked, and for all his self-command, somewhat started at the abrupt revelation. On Claggart's always pallid complexion, thick black blood was now oozing from nostril and ear. To

the gazer's professional eye it was unmistakably no living man that
he saw.

"Is it so then?["] said Captain Vere intently watching him. "I
thought it. But verify it." Whereupon the customary tests confirmed
the Surgeon's first glance, who now looking up in unfeigned concern, cast a look of intense inquisitiveness upon his superior. But
Captain Vere, with one hand to his brow, was standing motionless.
Suddenly, catching the Surgeon's arm convulsively, he exclaimed,
pointing down to the body—"It is the divine judgement on Ananias!
Look!"

Disturbed by the excited manner he had never before observed in
the *Indomitable's* Captain, and as yet wholly ignorant of the affair,
the prudent Surgeon nevertheless held his peace, only again looking
an earnest interrogation as to what it was that had resulted in such
a tragedy.

But Captain Vere was now again motionless standing absorbed
in thought. But again starting, he vehemently exclaimed—"Struck
dead by an angel of God! Yet the angel must hang!["]

At these passionate interjections, mere incoherences to the listener
as yet unapprised of the antecedents, the Surgeon was profoundly
discomposed. But now as recollecting himself, Captain Vere in less
harsh tone briefly related the circumstances leading up to the event.

["]But come; we must despatch" he added. ["]Help me to remove
him (meaning the body) to yonder compartment,["] designating one
opposite that where the foretopman remained immured. Anew disturbed by a request that as implying a desire for secrecy, seemed
unaccountably strange to him, there was nothing for the subordinate
to do but comply.

"Go now" said Captain Vere with something of his wonted manner—["]Go now. I shall presently call a drum-head court. Tell the
lieutenants what has happened, and tell Mr. Mordant," meaning the
captain of marines, "and charge them to keep the matter to themselves."

21

Full of disquietude and misgiving the Surgeon left the cabin. Was
Captain Vere suddenly affected in his mind, or was it but a transient
excitement, brought about by so strange and extraordinary a happening? As to the drum-head court, it struck the Surgeon as impolitic,
if nothing more. The thing to do, he thought, was to place Billy
Budd in confinement and in a way dictated by usage, and postpone
further action in so extraordinary a case, to such time as they should
rejoin the squadron, and then refer it to the Admiral. He recalled the
unwonted agitation of Captain Vere and his excited exclamations
so at variance with his normal manner. Was he unhinged? But assuming that he is, it is not so susceptible of proof. What then can

he do? No more trying situation is conceivable than that of an officer subordinate under a Captain whom he suspects to be, not mad indeed, but yet not quite unaffected in his intellect. To argue his order to him would be insolence. To resist him would be mutiny.

In obedience to Captain Vere he communicated what had happened to the lieutenants & captain of marines; saying nothing as to the Captain's state. They fully shared his own surprise and concern. Like him too they seemed to think that such a matter should be referred to the Admiral.

22

Who in the rainbow can draw the line where the violet tint ends and the orange tint begins? Distinctly we see the difference of the colors, but where exactly does the one first blendingly enter into the other? So with sanity and insanity. In pronounced cases there is no question about them. But in some supposed cases, in various degrees supposedly less pronounced, to draw the exact line of demarkation few will undertake tho for a fee some professional experts will. There is nothing namable but that some men will undertake to do it for pay.

Whether Captain Vere, as the Surgeon professionally and privately surmised, was really the sudden victim of any degree of aberration, one must determine for himself by such light as this narrative may afford.

[That] the unhappy event which has been narrated could not have happened at a worse juncture was but too true. For it was close on the heel of the suppressed insurrections, an aftertime very critical to naval authority, demanding from every English sea-commander two qualities not readily interfusable—prudence and rigor. Moreover there was something crucial in the case.

In the jugglery of circumstances preceding and attending the event on board the *Indomitable* and in the light of that martial code whereby it was formally to be judged, innocence and guilt personified in Claggart and Budd in effect changed places. In a legal view the apparent victim of the tragedy was he who had sought to victimize a man blameless; and the indisputable deed of the latter, navally regarded, constituted the most heinous of military crimes. Yet more. The essential right and wrong involved in the matter, the clearer that might be, so much the worse for the responsibility of a loyal sea-commander inasmuch as he was not authorized to determine the matter on that primitive basis.

Small wonder then that the *Indomitable's* Captain[,] though in general a man of rapid decision, felt that circumspectness not less than promptitude was necessary. Until he could decide upon his course, and in each detail; and not only so, but until the concluding measure was upon the point of being enacted, he deemed it advisable, in view of all the circumstances to guard as much as possible against publicity. Here he may or may not have erred. Certain it is however that subsequently in the confidential talk of more than one or two gun-rooms and cabins he was not a little criticized by some officers, a fact imputed by his friends and vehemently by his cousin Jack Denton to professional jealousy of *Starry Vere*. Some imaginative ground for invidious comment there was. The maintenance of secrecy in the matter, the confining all knowledge of it for a time to the place where the homicide occurred, the quarter-deck cabin; in these particulars lurked some resemblance to the policy adopted in those tragedies of the palace which have occurred more than once in the capital founded by Peter the Barbarian.

The case indeed was such that fain would the *Indomitable's* captain have deferred taking any action whatever respecting it further than to keep the foretopman a close prisoner till the ship rejoined the squadron and then submitting the matter to the judgement of his Admiral.

But a true military officer is in one particular like a true monk. Not with more of self-abnegation will the latter keep his vows of monastic obedience than the former his vows of allegiance to martial duty.

Feeling that unless quick action was taken on it, the deed of the foretopman, so soon as it should be known on the gun-decks would tend to awaken any slumbering embers of the Nore among the crew, a sense of the urgency of the case overruled in Captain Vere every other consideration. But tho' a conscientious disciplinarian he was no lover of authority for mere authority's sake. Very far was he from embracing opportunities for monopolizing to himself the perils of moral responsibility[,] none at least that could properly be referred to an official superior or shared with him by his official equals or even subordinates. So thinking[,] he was glad it would not be at variance with usage to turn the matter over to a summary court of his own officers, reserving to himself as the one on whom the ultimate accountability would rest, the right of maintaining a supervision of it, or formally or informally interposing at need. Accordingly a drum-head court was summarily convened, he electing the individuals composing it, the First Lieutenant, the Captain of marines, and the Sailing Master.

In associating an officer of marines with the sea-lieutenants in a case having to do with a sailor the Commander perhaps deviated from general custom. He was prompted thereto by the circumstance that he took that soldier to be a judicious person, thoughtful, and not altogether incapable of grappling with a difficult case unprecedented in his prior experience. Yet even as to him he was not without some latent misgiving, for withal he was an extremely good-natured man, an enjoyer of his dinner, a sound sleeper, and inclined to obesity. [A] man who tho' he would always maintain his manhood in battle might not prove altogether reliable in a moral dilemma involving aught of the tragic. As to the First Lieutenant and the Sailing Master Captain Vere could not but be aware that though honest natures, of approved gallantry upon occasion[,] their intelligence was mostly confined to the matter of active seamanship and the fighting demands of their profession. The court was held in the same cabin where the unfortunate affair had taken place. This cabin, the Commander's, embraced the entire area under the poop-deck. Aft, and on either side[,] was a small state-room[;] the one room temporarily a jail & the other a dead-house[,] and a yet smaller compartment leaving a space between, expanding forward into a goodly oblong of length coinciding with the ship's beam. A skylight of moderate dimension was overhead and at each end of the oblong space were two sashed port-hole windows easily convertible back into embrasures for short carronades.

All being quickly in readiness, Billy Budd was arraigned, Captain Vere necessarily appearing as the sole witness in the case, and as such temporarily sinking his rank, though singularly maintaining it in a matter apparently trivial, namely, that he testified from the ship's weather-side[,] with that object having caused the court to sit on the lee-side. Concisely he narrated all that had led up to the catastrophe, omitting nothing in Claggart's accusation and deposing as to the manner in which the prisoner had received it. At this testimony the three officers glanced with no little surprise at Billy Budd, the last man they would have suspected either of the mutinous design alleged by Claggart or the undeniable deed he himself had done.

The First Lieutenant[,] taking judicial primacy and turning toward the prisoner, said, "Captain Vere has spoken. Is it or is it not as Captain Vere says?" In response came syllables not so much impeded in the utterance as might have been anticipated. They were these: "Captain Vere tells the truth. It is just as Captain Vere says, but it is not as the Master-at-Arms said. I have eaten the King's bread and I am true to the King."

"I believe you, my man" said the witness[,] his voice indicating a suppressed emotion not otherwise betrayed.

"God will bless you for that, Your Honor!" not without stammering said Billy, and all but broke down. But immediately was recalled to self-control by another question, to which with the same emotional difficulty of utterance he said[,] "No, there was no malice between us. I never bore malice against the Master-at-arms. I am sorry that he is dead. I did not mean to kill him. Could I have used my tongue I would not have struck him. But he foully lied to my face and in presence of my Captain, and I had to say something, and I could only say it with a blow, God help me!"

In the impulsive above-board manner of the frank one[,] the court saw confirmed all that was implied in words that just previously had perplexed them[,] coming as they did from the testifier to the tragedy and promptly following Billy's impassioned disclaimer of mutinous intent—Captain Vere's words, "I believe you, my man."

Next it was asked of him whether he knew of or suspected aught savoring of incipient trouble (meaning mutiny, tho' the explicit term was avoided) going on in any section of the ship's company.

The reply lingered. This was naturally imputed by the court to the same vocal embarrassment which had retarded or obstructed previous answers. But in main it was otherwise here; the question immediately recalling to Billy's mind the interview with the after-guardsman in the fore-chains. But an innate repugnance to playing a part at all approaching that of an informer against one's own ship-mates—the same erring sense of uninstructed honor which had stood in the way of his reporting the matter at the time though as a loyal man-of-war-man it was incumbent on him[,] and failure so to do if charged against him and proven, would have subjected him to the heaviest of penalties; this, with the blind feeling now his, that nothing really was being hatched, prevailed with him. When the answer came it was a negative.

"One question more," said the officer of marines now first speaking and with a troubled earnestness, "You tell us that what the Master-at-arms said against you was a lie. Now why should he have so lied, so maliciously lied, since you declare there was no malice between you?"

At that question unintentionally touching on a spiritual sphere wholly obscure to Billy's thoughts, he was nonplussed, evincing a confusion indeed that some observers, such as can readily be imagined, would have construed into involuntary evidence of hidden guilt. Nevertheless he strove some way to answer, but all at once relinquished the vain endeavor, at the same time turning an appealing glance towards Captain Vere as deeming him his best helper and friend. Captain Vere who had been seated for a time rose to his feet, addressing the interrogator. "The question you put to him comes naturally enough. But how can he rightly answer it? or anybody else? unless indeed it be he who lies within there" designating the compartment where lay the corpse. "But the prone one there will not rise to our summons. In effect, tho', as it seems to me, the point you make is hardly material. Quite aside from any conceivable motive actuating the Master-at-arms, and irrespective of the provocation to the blow, a martial court must needs in the present case confine its attention to the blow's consequence, which consequence justly is to be deemed not otherwise than as the striker's deed."

This utterance the full significance of which it was not at all likely that Billy took in, nevertheless caused him to turn a wistful interrogative look toward the speaker, a look in its dumb expressiveness not unlike that which a dog of generous breed might turn upon his master seeking in his face some elucidation of a previous gesture ambiguous to the canine intelligence. Nor was the same utterance without marked effect upon the three officers, more especially the soldier. Couched in it seemed to them a meaning unanticipated, involving a prejudgement on the speaker's part. It served to augment a mental disturbance previously evident enough.

The soldier once more spoke; in a tone of suggestive dubiety addressing at once his associates and Captain Vere: "Nobody is present —none of the ship's company, I mean, who might shed lateral light, if any is to be had, upon what remains mysterious in this matter."

"That is thoughtfully put[,]" said Captain Vere; "I see your drift. Ay, there is a mystery; but, to use a Scriptural phrase, it is 'a mystery of iniquity,' a matter for psychologic theologians to discuss. But what has a military court to do with it? Not to add that for us any possible investigation of it is cut off by the lasting tongue-tie of—him—in yonder," again designating the mortuary state-room. ["]The prisoner's deed,—with that alone we have to do."

To this, and particularly the closing reiteration, the marine soldier knowing not how aptly to reply, sadly abstained from saying aught. The First Lieutenant who at the outset had not unnaturally assumed primacy in the court, now overrulingly instructed by a glance from Captain Vere, a glance more effective than words, resumed that primacy. Turning to the prisoner, "Budd," he said, and scarce in equable tones, "Budd, if you have aught further to say for yourself, say it now."

Upon this the young sailor turned another quick glance toward Captain Vere; then, as taking a hint from that aspect, a hint confirming his own instinct that silence was now best, replied to the Lieutenant[,] "I have said all, Sir."

The marine—the same who had been the sentinel without the cabin-door at the time that the foretopman followed by the master-at-arms, entered it—he, standing by the sailor throughout these judicial proceedings, was now directed to take him back to the after compartment originally assigned to the prisoner and his custodian. As the twain disappeared from view, the three officers as partially liberated from some inward constraint associated with Billy's mere presence, simultaneously stirred in their seats. They exchanged looks of troubled indecision, yet feeling that decide they must and without long delay. As for Captain Vere, he for the time stood unconsciously with his back toward them, apparently in one of his absent fits, gazing out from a sashed port-hole to windward upon the monotonous blank of the twilight sea. But the court's silence continuing, broken only at moments by brief consultations in low earnest tones, this seemed to arm him and energize him. Turning, he to-and-fro paced the cabin athwart; in the returning ascent to windward, climbing the slant deck in the ship's lee roll; without knowing it symbolizing thus in his action a

mind resolute to surmount difficulties even if against primitive instincts strong as the wind and the sea. Presently he came to a stand
before the three. After scanning their faces he stood less as mustering
his thoughts for expression, than as one inly deliberating how best
to put them to well-meaning men not intellectually mature, men with
whom it was necessary to demonstrate certain principles that were
axioms to himself. Similar impatience as to talking is perhaps one
reason that deters some minds from addressing any popular assemblies.

When speak he did, something both in the substance of what he
said and his manner of saying it, showed the influence of unshared
studies modifying and tempering the practical training of an active
career. This, along with his phraseology now and then was suggestive
of the grounds whereon rested that imputation of a certain pedantry
socially alleged against him by certain naval men of wholly practical
cast, captains who nevertheless would frankly concede that His Majesty's navy mustered no more efficient officer of their grade than
Starry Vere.

What he said was to this effect: "Hitherto I have been but the witness, little more; and I should hardly think now to take another
tone, that of your coadjutor, for the time, did I not perceive in you,
—at the crisis too—a troubled hesitancy, proceeding, I doubt not from
the clash of military duty with moral scruple—scruple vitalized by
compassion. For the compassion how can I otherwise than share it.
But, mindful of paramount obligations I strive against scruples that
may tend to enervate decision. Not, gentlemen, that I hide from myself that the case is an exceptional one. Speculatively regarded, it well
might be referred to a jury of casuists. But for us here acting not as
casuists or moralists, it is a case practical, and under martial law
practically to be dealt with.

"But your scruples: do they move as in a dusk? Challenge them.
Make them advance and declare themselves. Come now: do they
import something like this: If, mindless of palliating circumstances,
we are bound to regard the death of the Master-at-arms as the prisoner's deed, then does that deed constitute a capital crime whereof
the penalty is a mortal one. But in natural justice is nothing but the
prisoner's overt act to be considered? How can we adjudge to summary and shameful death a fellow-creature innocent before God, and
whom we feel to be so?—Does that state it aright? You sign sad assent.
Well, I too feel that, the full force of that. It is Nature. But do these
buttons that we wear attest that our allegiance is to Nature? No, to
the King. Though the ocean, which is inviolate Nature primeval,
tho' this be the element where we move and have our being as sailors,
yet as the King's officers lies our duty in a sphere correspondingly
natural? So little is that true, that in receiving our commissions we in
the most important regards ceased to be natural free-agents. When
war is declared are we the commissioned fighters previously con-

sulted? We fight at command. If our judgements approve the war, that is but coincidence. So in other particulars. So now. For suppose condemnation to follow these present proceedings. Would it be so much we ourselves that would condemn as it would be martial law operating through us? For that law and the rigour of it, we are not responsible. Our vowed responsibility is in this: That however pitilessly that law may operate, we nevertheless adhere to it and administer it.

["]But the exceptional in the matter moves the hearts within you. Even so too is mine moved. But let not warm hearts betray heads that should be cool. Ashore in a criminal case will an upright judge allow himself off the bench to be waylaid by some tender kinswoman of the accused seeking to touch him with her tearful plea? Well the heart here denotes the feminine in man is as that piteous woman, and hard tho' it be[,] she must here be ruled out."

He paused, earnestly studying them for a moment; then resumed.

"But something in your aspect seems to urge that it is not solely the heart that moves in you, but also the conscience, the private conscience. But tell me whether or not, occupying the position we do, private conscience should not yield to that imperial one formulated in the code under which alone we officially proceed?"

Here the three men moved in their seats, less convinced than agitated by the course of an argument troubling but the more the spontaneous conflict within.

Perceiving which, the speaker paused for a moment; then abruptly changing his tone, went on.

"To steady us a bit, let us recur to the facts.—In war-time at sea a man-of-war's-man strikes his superior in grade, and the blow kills. Apart from its effect the blow itself is, according to the Articles of War, a capital crime. Furthermore—"

"Ay, Sir," emotionally broke in the officer of marines, "in one sense it was. But surely Budd purposed neither mutiny nor homicide."

"Surely not, my good man. And before a court less arbitrary and more merciful than a martial one, that plea would largely extenuate. At the Last Assizes it shall acquit. But how here? We proceed under the law of the Mutiny Act. In feature no child can resemble his father more than that Act resembles in spirit the thing from which it derives—War. In His Majesty['s] service—in this ship indeed—there are Englishmen forced to fight for the King against their will. Against their conscience, for aught we know. Tho' as their fellow-creatures some of us may appreciate their position, yet as navy officers, what reck we of it? Still less recks the enemy. Our impressed men he would fain cut down in the same swath with our volunteers. As regards the enemy's naval conscripts, some of whom may even share our own abhorrence of the regicidal French Directory, it is the same on our side. War looks but to the frontage, the appearance. And the Mutiny

Act, War's child, takes after the father. Budd's intent or non-intent is nothing to the purpose.

["]But while, put to it by those anxieties in you which I can not but respect, I only repeat myself—while thus strangely we prolong proceedings that should be summary—the enemy may be sighted and an engagement result. We must do; and one of two things must we do—condemn or let go."

"Can we not convict and yet mitigate the penalty?" asked the junior Lieutenant here speaking, and falteringly, for the first.

"Lieutenant, were that clearly lawful for us under the circumstances consider the consequences of such clemency. The people" (meaning the ship's company) "have native-sense; most of them are familiar with our naval usage and tradition; and how would they take it? Even could you explain to them—which our official position forbids—they, long moulded by arbitrary discipline have not that kind of intelligent responsiveness that might qualify them to comprehend and discriminate. No, to the people the foretopman's deed however it be worded in the announcement will be plain homicide committed in a flagrant act of mutiny. What penalty for that should follow, they know. But it does not follow. *Why?* they will ruminate. You know what sailors are. Will they not revert to the recent outbreak at the Nore? Ay. They know the well-founded alarm—the panic it struck throughout England. Your clement sentence they would account pusillanimous. They would think that we flinch, that we are afraid of them—afraid of practising a lawful rigor singularly demanded at this juncture lest it should provoke new troubles. What shame to us such a conjecture on their part, and how deadly to discipline. You see then, whither prompted by duty and the law I steadfastly drive. But I beseech you, my friends, do not take me amiss. I feel as you do for this unfortunate boy. But did he know our hearts, I take him to be of that generous nature that he would feel even for us on whom in this military necessity so heavy a compulsion is laid."

With that, crossing the deck he resumed his place by the sashed port-hole, tacitly leaving the three to come to a decision. On the cabin's opposite side the troubled court sat silent. Loyal lieges, plain and practical, though at bottom they dissented from some points Captain Vere had put to them, they were without the faculty, hardly had the inclination to gainsay one whom they felt to be an earnest man, one too not less their superior in mind than in naval rank. But it is not improbable that even such of his words as were not without influence over them, less came home to them than his closing appeal to their instinct as sea-officers in the forethought he threw out as to the practical consequences to discipline, considering the unconfirmed tone of the fleet at the time, should a man-of-war's-man['s] violent killing at sea of a superior in grade be allowed to pass for aught else than a capital crime demanding prompt infliction of the penalty.

Not unlikely they were brought to something more or less akin to that harassed frame of mind which in the year 1842 actuated the commander of the U.S. brig-of-war *Somers* to resolve, under the so-called Articles of War, Articles modelled upon the English Mutiny Act, to resolve upon the execution at sea of a midshipman and two petty-officers as mutineers designing the seizure of the brig. Which resolution was carried out though in a time of peace and within not many days sail of home. An act vindicated by a naval court of inquiry subsequently convened ashore. History, and here cited without comment. True, the circumstances on board the *Somers* were different from those on board the *Indomitable*. But the urgency felt, well-warranted or otherwise, was much the same.

Says a writer whom few know, "Forty years after a battle it is easy for a non-combatant to reason about how it ought to have been fought. It is another thing personally and under fire to direct the fighting while involved in the obscuring smoke of it. Much so with respect to other emergencies involving considerations both practical and moral, and when it is imperative promptly to act. The greater the fog the more it imperils the steamer, and speed is put on tho' at the hazard of running somebody down. Little ween the snug card-players in the cabin of the responsibilities of the sleepless man on the bridge."

In brief, Billy Budd was formally convicted and sentenced to be hung at the yard-arm at the early morning-watch, it being now night. Otherwise, as is customary in such cases, the sentence would forthwith have been carried out. In war-time on the field or in the fleet, a mortal punishment decreed by a drum-head court—on the field sometimes decreed by but a nod from the General—follows without delay on the heel of conviction without appeal.

23

It was Captain Vere himself who of his own motion communicated the finding of the court to the prisoner; for that purpose going to the compartment where he was in custody and bidding the marine there to withdraw for the time.

Beyond the communication of the sentence what took place at this interview was never known. But in view of the character of the twain briefly closeted in that state-room, each radically sharing in the rarer qualities of our nature—so rare indeed as to be all but incredible to average minds however much cultivated—some conjectures may be ventured.

It would have been in consonance with the spirit of Captain Vere should he on this occasion have concealed nothing from the condemned one—should he indeed have frankly disclosed to him the part he himself had played in bringing about the decision, at the same time revealing his actuating motives. On Billy's side it is not improbable that such a confession would have been received in much the same spirit that prompted it. Not without a sort of joy indeed he might have appreciated the brave opinion of him implied in his Captain making such a confidant of him. Nor, as to the sentence itself could he have been insensible that it was imparted to him as to one not afraid to die. Even more may have been. Captain Vere in [the] end may have developed the passion sometimes latent under a[n] exterior stoical or indifferent. He was old enough to have been Billy's father. The austere devotee of military duty letting himself melt back into what remains primeval in our formalized humanity may in [the] end have caught Billy to his heart even as Abraham may have caught young Isaac on the brink of resolutely offering him up in obedience to the exacting behest. But there is no telling the sacrament, seldom if in any case revealed to the gadding world wherever under circumstances at all akin to those here attempted to be set forth two of great Nature's nobler order embrace. There is privacy at the time, inviolable to the survivor, and holy oblivion the sequel to each diviner magnanimity, providentially covers all at last.

The first to encounter Captain Vere in act of leaving the compartment was the senior Lieutenant. The face he beheld, for the moment one expressive of the agony of the strong, was to that officer, tho' a man of fifty, a startling revelation. That the condemned one suffered less than he who mainly had effected the condemnation was apparently indicated by the former's exclamation in the scene soon perforce to be touched upon.

24

Of a series of incidents within a brief term rapidly following each other, the adequate narration may take up a term less brief, especially if explanation or comment here and there seem requisite to the better understanding of such incidents. Between the entrance into the cabin of him who never left it alive, and him who when he did leave it left it as one condemned to die; between this and the closeted interview just given less than an hour and a half had elapsed. It was an interval long enough however to awaken speculations among no few of the ship's company as to what it was that could be detaining in the cabin the master-at-arms and the sailor; for a rumor that both of them had been seen to enter it and neither of them had been seen to emerge, this rumor had got abroad upon the gun-decks and in the tops; the people of a great warship being in one respect like villagers taking microscopic note of every outward movement or non-movement going on. When therefore in weather not at all tempestuous all hands were called in the second dog-watch, a summons under such circumstances not usual in those hours, the crew were not wholly unprepared for some announcement extraordinary, one having connection too with the continued absence of the two men from their wonted haunts.

There was a moderate sea at the time; and the moon, newly risen and near to being at its full, silvered the white spar-deck wherever not blotted by the clear-cut shadows horizontally thrown of fixtures and moving men. On either side the quarter-deck the marine guard under arms was drawn up; and Captain Vere standing in his place surrounded by all the ward-room officers, addressed his men. In so doing his manner showed neither more nor less than that property pertaining to his supreme position aboard his own ship. In clear terms and concise he told them what had taken place in the cabin; that the master-at-arms was dead; that he who had killed him had been already tried by a summary court and condemned to death; and that the execution would take place in the early morning watch. The word *mutiny* was not named in what he said. He refrained too from making the occasion an opportunity for any preachment as to the maintenance of discipline, thinking perhaps that under existing circumstances in the navy the consequence of violating discipline should be made to speak for itself.

Their captain's announcement was listened to by the throng of standing sailors in a dumbness like that of a seated congregation of believers in hell listening to the clergyman's announcement of his Calvinistic text.

At the close, however, a confused murmur went up. It began to wax. All but instantly, then, at a sign, it was pierced and suppressed by shrill whistles of the Boatswain and his Mates piping down one watch.

To be prepared for burial Claggart's body was delivered to certain petty-officers of his mess. And here, not to clog the sequel with lateral matters, it may be added that at a suitable hour, the Master-at-arms was committed to the sea with every funeral honor properly belonging to his naval grade.

In this proceeding as in every public one growing out of the tragedy strict adherence to usage was observed. Nor in any point could it have been at all deviated from, either with respect to Claggart or Billy Budd[,] without begetting undesirable speculations in the ship's company, sailors, and more particularly men-of-war's men, being of all men the greatest sticklers for usage.

For similar cause, all communication between Captain Vere and the condemned one ended with the closeted interview already given, the latter being now surrendered to the ordinary routine preliminary to the end. This transfer under guard from the Captain's quarters was effected without unusual precautions—at least no visible ones.

If possible not to let the men so much as surmise that their officers anticipate aught amiss from them is the tacit rule in a military ship.

And the more that some sort of trouble should really be apprehended the more do the officers keep that apprehension to themselves; tho' not the less unostentatious vigilance may be augmented.

In the present instance the sentry placed over the prisoner had strict orders to let no one have communication with him but the Chaplain. And certain unobtrusive measures were taken absolutely to insure this point.

25

In a seventy-four of the old order the deck known as the upper gun-deck was the one covered over by the spar-deck which last though not without its armament was for the most part exposed to the weather. In general it was at all hours free from hammocks; those of the crew swinging on the lower gun-deck, and berth-deck, the latter being not only a dormitory but also the place for the stowing of the sailors' bags, and on both sides lined with the large chests or movable pantries of the many messes of the men.

On the starboard side of the *Indomitable's* upper gun-deck, behold Billy Budd under sentry lying prone in irons in one of the bays formed by the regular spacing of the guns comprising the batteries on either side. All these pieces were of the heavier calibre of that period. Mounted on lumbering wooden carriages they were hampered with cumbersome harness of breeching and strong side-tackles for running them out. Guns and carriages, together with the long rammers and shorter lintstocks lodged in loops overhead—all these, as customary, were painted black; and the heavy hempen breechings tarred to the same tint, wore the like livery of the undertakers. In contrast with the funereal hue of these surroundings the prone sailor's exterior apparel, white *jumper* and white duck trousers, each more or less soiled, dimly glimmered in the obscure light of the bay like a patch of discolored snow in early April lingering at some upland cave's black mouth. In effect he is already in his shroud or the garments that shall serve him in lieu of one. Over him but scarce illuminating him, two battle-lanterns swing from two massive beams of the deck above. Fed with the oil supplied by the war-contractors (whose gains, honest or otherwise, are in every land an anticipated portion of the harvest of death) with flickering splashes of dirty yellow light they pollute the pale moonshine[,] all but ineffectually struggling in obstructed flecks thro the open ports from which the tompioned cannon protrude. Other lanterns at intervals serve but to bring out somewhat the obscurer bays which like small confessionals or side-chapels in a cathedral branch from the long dim-vistaed broad aisle between the two batteries of that covered tier.

Such was the deck where now lay the Handsome Sailor. Through the rose-tan of his complexion, no pallor could have shown. It would have taken days of sequestration from the winds and the sun to have brought about the effacement of that. But the skeleton in the cheek-bone at the point of its angle was just beginning delicately to be defined under the warm-tinted skin. In fervid hearts self-contained some brief experiences devour our human tissue as secret fire in a ship's hold consumes cotton in the bale.

But now lying between the two guns, as nipped in the vice of fate, Billy's agony, mainly proceeding from a generous young heart's virgin experience of the diabolical incarnate and effective in some men—the tension of that agony was over now. It survived not the something healing in the closeted interview with Captain Vere. Without movement, he lay as in a trance. That adolescent expression previously noted as his, taking on something akin to the look of a slumbering child in the cradle when the warm hearth-glow of the still chamber at night plays on the dimples that at whiles mysteriously form in the cheek, silently coming and going there. For now and then in the gyved one's trance a serene happy light born of some wandering reminiscence or dream would diffuse itself over his face, and then wane away only anew to return.

The Chaplain coming to see him and finding him thus, and perceiving no sign that he was conscious of his presence, attentively regarded him for a space, then slipping aside, withdrew for the time, peradventure feeling that even he the minister of Christ tho' receiving his stipend from Mars had no consolation to proffer which could result in a peace transcending that which he beheld. But in the small hours he came again. And the prisoner now awake to his surroundings noticed his approach and civilly, all but cheerfully, welcomed him. But it was to little purpose that in the interview following the good man sought to bring Billy Budd to some godly understanding that he must die, and at dawn. True, Billy himself freely referred to his death as a thing close at hand; but it was something in the way that children will refer to death in general, who yet among their other sports will play a funeral with hearse and mourners.

Not that like children Billy was incapable of conceiving what death really is. No, but he was wholly without irrational fear of it, a fear more prevalent in highly civilized communities than those so-called barbarous ones which in all respects stand nearer to unadulterate Nature. And, as elsewhere said, a barbarian Billy radically was; as much so, for all the costume, as his countrymen the British captives, living trophies, made to march in the Roman triumph of Germanicus. Quite as much so as those later barbarians, young men probably, and picked specimens among the earlier British converts to Christianity, at least nominally such and taken to Rome (as today converts from lesser isles of the sea may be taken to London) of whom the Pope of that time, admiring the strangeness of their personal beauty so unlike the Italian stamp, their clear ruddy complexion and curled flaxen locks, exlaimed, "Angles" (meaning *English* the modern derivative) "Angles do you call them? And is it because they look so like angels?" Had it been later in time one would think that the Pope had in mind Fra Angelico's seraphs some of whom, plucking apples in gardens of the Hesperides have the faint rose-bud complexion of the more beautiful English girls.

If in vain the good Chaplain sought to impress the young barbarian with ideas of death akin to those conveyed in the skull, dial, and cross-bones on old tombstones; equally futile to all appearance were his efforts to bring home to him the thought of salvation and a Saviour. Billy listened, but less out of awe or reverence perhaps than from a certain natural politeness; doubtless at bottom regarding all that in much the same way that most mariners of his class take any discourse abstract or out of the common tone of the work-a-day world. And this sailor-way of taking clerical discourse is not wholly unlike the way in which the pioneer of Christianity full of transcendent miracles was received long ago on tropic isles by any superior *savage* so called—a Tahitian say of Captain Cook's time or shortly after that time. Out of natural courtesy he received, but did not appropriate. It was like a gift placed in the palm of an outstretched hand upon which the fingers do not close.

But the *Indomitable's* Chaplain was a discreet man possessing the good sense of a good heart. So he insisted not in his vocation here. At the instance of Captain Vere, a lieutenant had apprised him of pretty much everything as to Billy; and since he felt that innocence was even a better thing than religion wherewith to go to Judgement, he reluctantly withdrew; but in his emotion not without first performing an act strange enough in an Englishman, and under the circumstances yet more so in any regular priest. Stooping over, he kissed on the fair cheek his fellow-man, a felon in martial law, one who though on the confines of death he felt he could never convert to a dogma; nor for all that did he fear for his future.

Marvel not that having been made acquainted with the young sailor's essential innocence (an irruption of heretic thought hard to suppress) the worthy man lifted not a finger to avert the doom of such a martyr to martial discipline. So to do would not only have been as idle as invoking the desert, but would also have been an audacious transgression of the bounds of his function, one as exactly prescribed to him by military law as that of the boatswain or any other naval officer. Bluntly put, a chaplain is the minister of the Prince of Peace serving in the host of the God of War—Mars. As such, he is as incongruous as that musket of Blücher etc. at Christmas. Why then is he there? Because he indirectly subserves the purpose attested by the cannon; because too he lends the sanction of the religion of the meek to that which practically is the abrogation of everything but brute Force.

26

The night so luminous on the spar-deck but otherwise on the cavernous ones below, levels so like the tiered galleries in a coal-mine—the luminous night passed away. But, like the prophet in the chariot disappearing in heaven and dropping his mantle to Elisha, the withdrawing night transferred its pale role to the breaking day. A meek shy light appeared in the East, where stretched a diaphanous fleece of white furrowed vapor. That light slowly waxed. Suddenly *eight bells* was struck aft, responded to by one louder metallic stroke from forward. It was four o'clock in the morning. Instantly the silver whistles were heard summoning all hands to witness punishment. Up through the great hatchways rimmed with racks of heavy shot, the watch below came pouring overspreading with the watch already on deck the space between the mainmast and foremast including that occupied by the capacious *launch* and the black booms tiered on either side of it, boat and booms making a summit of observation for the powder-boys and younger tars. A different group comprising one watch of topmen leaned over the rail of that sea-balcony, no small one in a seventy-four, looking down on the crowd below. Man or boy none spake but in whisper, and few spake at all. Captain Vere—as before, the central figure among the assembled commissioned officers—stood nigh the break of the poop-deck facing forward. Just below him on the quarter-deck the marines in full equipment were drawn up much as at the scene of the promulgated sentence.

At sea in the old time, the execution by halter of a military sailor was generally from the fore-yard. In the present instance, for special reasons the main-yard was assigned. Under an arm of that lee yard[4] the prisoner was presently brought up, the Chaplain attending him. It was noted at the time and remarked upon afterwards, that in this final scene the good man evinced little or nothing of the perfunctory. Brief speech indeed he had with the condemned one, but the genuine Gospel was less on his tongue than in his aspect and manner towards him. The final preparations personal to the latter being speedily brought to an end by two boatswain's-mates, the consummation impended. Billy stood facing aft. At the penultimate moment, his words, his only ones, words wholly unobstructed in the utterance were these—"God bless Captain Vere!" Syllables so unanticipated coming from one with the ignominious hemp about his neck—a conventional felon's benediction directed aft towards the quarters of honor;

---

[4] In the manuscript Melville wrote the words "weather or lee" above this line, evidently intending to make his decision later.

syllables too delivered in the clear melody of a singing-bird on the point of launching from the twig, had a phenomenal effect, not un-enhanced by the rare personal beauty of the young sailor spiritualized now thro' late experiences so poignantly profound.

Without volition as it were, as if indeed the ship's populace were but the vehicles of some vocal current electric, with one voice from alow and aloft came a resonant sympathetic echo—"God bless Captain Vere!" And yet at that instant Billy alone must have been in their hearts, even as he was in their eyes.

At the pronounced words and the spontaneous echo that volu-minously rebounded them, Captain Vere, either thro stoic self-control or a sort of momentary paralysis induced by emotional shock, stood erectly rigid as a musket in the ship-armorer's rack.

The hull deliberately recovering from the periodic roll to lee-ward was just regaining an even keel, when the last signal[,] a precon-certed dumb one[,] was given. At the same moment it chanced that the vapory fleece hanging low in the East, was shot thro with a soft glory as of the fleece of the Lamb of God seen in mystical vision[,] and simultaneously therewith, watched by the wedged mass of up-turned faces, Billy ascended; and, ascending, took the full rose of the dawn.

In the pinioned figure, arrived at the yard-end, to the wonder of all no motion was apparent[,] none save that created by the ship's mo-tion, in moderate weather so majestic in a great ship ponderously can-noned.

End of Chapter

27

A digression

When some days afterward in reference to the singularity just men-tioned, the Purser a rather ruddy rotund person more accurate as an accountant than profound as a philosopher, said at mess to the Surgeon, "What testimony to the force lodged in will-power[,]" the latter—saturnine spare and tall, one in whom a discreet causticity went along with a manner less genial than polite, replied, "Your pardon, Mr. Purser. In a hanging scientifically conducted—and under special orders I myself directed how Budd's was to be effected—any movement following the completed suspension and originating in the body suspended, such movement indicates mechanical spasm in the muscular system. Hence the absence of that is no more attributable to will-power as you call it than to horse-power—begging your pardon."

"But this muscular spasm you speak of, is not that in a degree more or less invariable in these cases?["]

"Assuredly so, Mr. Purser."

"How then, my good sir, do you account for its absence in this instance?"

"Mr. Purser, it is clear that your sense of the singularity in this matter equals not mine. You account for it by what you call will-power[,] a term not yet included in the lexicon of science. For me I do not, with my present knowledge pretend to account for it at all. Even should we assume the hypothesis that at the first touch of the halyards the action of Budd's heart, intensified by extraordinary emotion at its climax, abruptly stopt—much like a watch when in carelessly winding it up you strain at the finish, thus snapping the chain—even under that hypothesis how account for the phenomenon that followed.[?]"

"You admit then that the absence of spasmodic movement was phenomenal."

["]It was phenomenal, Mr. Purser, in the sense that it was an appearance the cause of which is not immediately to be assigned."

["]But tell me, my dear Sir,["] pertinaciously continued the other, "was the man's death effected by the halter, or was it a species of euthanasia?["]

"*Euthanasia*, Mr. Purser, is something like your *will-power*: I doubt its authenticity as a scientific term—begging your pardon again. It is at once imaginative and metaphysical,—in short, Greek. But[,]" abruptly changing his tone[,] "there is a case in the sick-bay that I do not care to leave to my assistants. Beg your pardon, but excuse me." And rising from the mess he formally withdrew.

28

The silence at the moment of execution and for a moment or two continuing thereafter, a silence but emphasized by the regular wash of the sea against the hull or the flutter of a sail caused by the helmsman's eyes being tempted astray, this emphasized silence was gradually disturbed by a sound not easily to be verbally rendered. Whoever has heard the freshet-wave of a torrent suddenly swelled by pouring showers in tropical mountains, showers not shared by the plain; whoever has heard the first muffled murmur of its sloping advance through precipitous woods, may form some conception of the sound now heard. The seeming remoteness of its source was because of its murmurous indistinctness since it came from close-by, even from the men massed on the ship's open deck. Being inarticulate, it was dubious in significance further than it seemed to indicate some capricious revulsion of thought or feeling such as mobs ashore are liable to, in the present instance possibly implying a sullen revocation on the men's part of their involuntary echoing of Billy's benediction. But ere the murmur had time to wax into clamor it was met by a strategic command, the more telling that it came with abrupt unexpectedness.

"Pipe down the starboard watch[,] Boatswain, and see that they go."

Shrill as the shriek of the sea-hawk the whistles of the Boatswain and his Mates pierced that ominous low sound, dissipating it; and yielding to the mechanism of discipline the throng was thinned by one half. For the remainder most of them were set to temporary employments connected with trimming the yards and so forth, business readily to be got up to serve occasion by any officer-of-the-deck.

Now each proceeding that follows a mortal sentence pronounced at sea by a drum-head court is characterised by promptitude not perceptibly merging into hurry, tho bordering that. The hammock, the one which had been Billy's bed when alive, having already been ballasted with shot and otherwise prepared to serve for his canvas coffin, the last offices of the sea-undertakers, the Sail-Maker's Mates, were now speedily completed. When everything was in readiness a second call for all hands made necessary by the strategic movement before mentioned was sounded and now to witness burial.

The details of this closing formality it needs not to give. But when the tilted plank let slide its freight into the sea, a second strange human murmur was heard, blended now with another inarticulate sound proceeding from certain larger sea-fowl whose attention having been attracted by the peculiar commotion in the water resulting from the heavy sloped dive of the shotted hammock into the sea, flew screaming to the spot. So near the hull did they come, that the stridor or bony creak of their gaunt double-jointed pinions was audible. As the ship under light airs passed on, leaving the burial-spot astern, they still kept circling it low down with the moving shadow of their outstretched wings and the croaked requiem of their cries.

Upon sailors as superstitious as those of the age preceding ours, men-of-war's men too who had just beheld the prodigy of repose in the form suspended in air and now foundering in the deeps; to such mariners the action of the sea-fowl tho' dictated by mere animal greed for prey, was big with no prosaic significance. An uncertain movement began among them, in which some encroachment was made. It was tolerated but for a moment. For suddenly the drum beat to quarters, which familiar sound happening at least twice every day, had upon the present occasion a signal peremptoriness in it. True martial discipline long continued superinduces in average man a sort of impulse [of] docility whose operation at the official sound of command much resembles in its promptitude the effect of an instinct.

The drum-beat dissolved the multitude, distributing most of them along the batteries of the two covered gun-decks. There, as wont, the guns' crews stood by their respective cannon erect and silent. In due course the First Officer, sword under arm and standing in his place on the quarter-deck[,] formally received the successive reports of the sworded Lieutenants commanding the sections of batteries below; the

last of which reports being made[,] the summed report he delivered
with the customary salute to the Commander. All this occupied time,
which in the present case, was the object of beating to quarters at an
hour prior to the customary one. That such variance from usage was
authorized by an officer like Captain Vere, a martinet as some deemed
him, was evidence of the necessity for unusual action implied in what
he deemed to be temporarily the mood of his men. "With mankind[,]"
he would say[,] "forms, measured forms are everything; and that is the
import couched in the story of Orpheus with his lyre spell-binding
the wild denizens of the wood." And this he once applied to the disruption of forms going on across the Channel and the consequences
thereof.

At this unwonted muster at quarters, all proceeded as at the regular hour. The band on the quarter-deck played a sacred air. After
which the Chaplain went thro' the customary morning service. That
done, the drum beat the retreat, and toned by music and religious rites
subserving the discipline & purpose of war, the men in their wonted
orderly manner, dispersed to the places allotted them when not at the
guns.

And now it was full day. The fleece of low-hanging vapor had
vanished, licked up by the sun that late had so glorified it. And the
circumambient air in the clearness of its serenity was like smooth
white marble in the polished block not yet removed from the marble-
dealer's yard.

29

The symmetry of form attainable in pure fiction can not so readily
be achieved in a narration essentially having less to do with fable than
with fact. Truth uncompromisingly told will always have its ragged
edges; hence the conclusion of such a narration is apt to be less finished than an architectural finial.

How it fared with the Handsome Sailor during the year of the
Great Mutiny has been faithfully given. But tho' properly the story
ends with his life, something in way of sequel will not be amiss. Three
brief chapters will suffice.

In the general re-christening under the Directory of the craft originally forming the navy of the French monarchy, the *St. Louis* line-of-
battle ship was named the *Athéiste*. Such a name, like some other
substituted ones in the Revolutonary fleet while proclaiming the in-
fidel audacity of the ruling power was yet, tho' not so intended to be,
the aptest name, if one consider it, ever given to a war-ship; far more
so indeed than the *Devastation,* the *Erebus* (the *Hell*) and similar
names bestowed upon fighting-ships.

On the return-passage to the English fleet from the detached cruise
during which occurred the events already recorded, the *Indomitable*

fell in with the *Athéiste*. An engagement ensued; during which Captain Vere in the act of putting his ship alongside the enemy with a view of throwing his boarders across her bulwarks, was hit by a musket-ball from a port-hole of the enemy's main cabin. More than disabled he dropped to the deck and was carried below to the same cock-pit where some of his men already lay. The senior Lieutenant took command. Under him the enemy was finally captured and though much crippled was by rare good fortune successfully taken into Gibraltar, an English port not very distant from the scene of the fight. There, Captain Vere with the rest of the wounded was put ashore. He lingered for some days, but the end came. Unhappily he was cut off too early for the Nile and Trafalgar. The spirit that spite its philosophic austerity may yet have indulged in the most secret of all passions, ambition, never attained to the fulness of fame.

Not long before death while lying under the influence of that magical drug which soothing the physical frame mysteriously operates on the subtler element in man, he was heard to murmur words inexplicable to his attendant—"Billy Budd, Billy Budd." That these were not the accents of remorse, would seem clear from what the attendant said to the *Indomitable's* senior officer of marines who[,] as the most reluctant to condemn of the members of the drum-head court, too well knew[,] tho' here he kept the knowledge to himself, who Billy Budd was.

30

Some few weeks after the execution, among other matters under the head of *News from the Mediterranean,* there appeared in a naval chronicle of the time, an authorized weekly publication, an account of the affair. It was doubtless for the most part written in good faith, tho' the medium, partly rumor, through which the facts must have reached the writer, served to deflect and in part falsify them. The account was as follows:—

"On the tenth of the last month a deplorable occurrence took place on board H.M.S. *Indomitable.* John Claggart, the ship's master-at-arms, discovering that some sort of plot was incipient among an inferior section of the ship's company, and that the ring-leader was one William Budd; he, Claggart[,] in the act of arraigning the man before the Captain[,] was vindictively stabbed to the heart by the suddenly drawn sheath-knife of Budd.

["]The deed and the implement employed, sufficiently suggest that tho' mustered into the service under an English name the assassin was no Englishman, but one of those aliens adopting English cognomens whom the present extraordinary necessities of the Service have caused to be admitted into it in considerable numbers.

["]The enormity of the crime and the extreme depravity of the criminal, appear the greater in view of the character of the victim, a middle-aged man respectable and discreet, belonging to that minor official grade, the petty-officers, upon whom, as none know better than the commissioned gentlemen, the efficiency of His Majesty's navy so largely depends. His function was a responsible one; at once onerous & thankless and his fidelity in it the greater because of his strong patriotic impulse. In this instance as in so many other instances in these days, the character of this unfortunate man signally refutes, if refutation were needed, that peevish saying attributed to the late Dr. Johnson, that patriotism is the last refuge of a scoundrel.

["]The criminal paid the penalty of his crime. The promptitude of the punishment has proved salutary. Nothing amiss is now apprehended aboard H.M.S. *Indomitable*."

The above, appearing in a publication now long ago superannuated and forgotten[,] is all that hitherto has stood in human record to attest what manner of men respectively were John Claggart and Billy Budd[.]

31

Everything is for a term remarkable in navies. Any tangible object associated with some striking incident of the service is converted into a monument. The spar from which the Foretopman was suspended, was for some few years kept trace of by the bluejackets. Their knowledge followed it from ship to dock-yard and again from dock-yard to ship, still pursuing it even when at last reduced to a mere dock-yard boom. To them a chip of it was as a piece of the Cross. Ignorant tho' they were of the secret facts of the tragedy, and not thinking but that the penalty was somehow unavoidably inflicted from the naval point of view, for all that they instinctively felt that Billy was a sort of man as incapable of mutiny as of wilful murder. They recalled the fresh young image of the Handsome Sailor, that face never deformed by a sneer or subtler vile freak of the heart within. Their impression of him was doubtless deepened by the fact that he was gone, and in a measure mysteriously gone. At the time on the gun decks of the *Indomitable* the general estimate of his nature and its unconscious simplicity eventually found rude utterance from another foretopman[,] one of his own watch[,] gifted, as some sailors are, with an artless poetic temperament; the tarry hands made some lines which after circulating among the shipboard crew for a while, finally got rudely printed at Portsmouth as a ballad. The title given to it was the sailor's.

Billy in the Darbies

Good of the Chaplain to enter Lone Bay
And down on his marrow-bones here and pray
For the likes just o' me, Billy Budd.—But look:

Through the port comes the moon-shine astray!
It tips the guard's cutlas and silvers this nook;
But 'twill die in the dawning of Billy's last day.
A jewel-block they'll make of me tomorrow,
Pendant pearl from the yard-arm-end
Like the ear-drop I gave to Bristol Molly—
O, 'tis me, not the sentence they'll suspend.
Ay, Ay, all is up; and I must up too
Early in the morning, aloft from alow.
On an empty stomach, now, never it would do.
They'll give me a nibble—bit o' biscuit ere I go.
Sure, a messmate will reach me the last parting cup;
But, turning heads away from the hoist and the belay,
Heaven knows who will have the running of me up!
No pipe to those halyards.—But aren't it all sham?
A blur's in my eyes; it is dreaming that I am.
A hatchet to my hawser? all adrift to go?
The drum roll to grog, and Billy never know?
But Donald he has promised to stand by the plank;
So I'll shake a friendly hand ere I sink.
But—no! It is dead then I'll be, come to think.—
I remember Taff the Welshman when he sank.
And his cheek it was like the budding pink[.]
But me they'll lash me in hammock, drop me deep.
Fathoms down, fathoms down, how I'll dream fast asleep.
I feel it stealing now. Sentry, are you there?
Just ease these darbies at the wrist, and roll me over fair,
I am sleepy, and the oozy weeds about me twist.

END OF BOOK

April 19th 1891

The Critics

1. FIVE EARLY VIEWS

From Raymond M. Weaver (1921)*

. . . .

The novel, *Billy Budd*, is built around the character of Jack Chase, the "Handsome Sailor." In the character of Billy Budd, Melville attempts to portray the native purity and nobility of the uncorrupted man. Melville spends elaborate pains in analysing "the mystery of iniquity," and in celebrating by contrast the god-like beauty of body and spirit of his hero. Billy Budd, by his heroic guilelessness is, like an angel of vengeance, precipitated into manslaughter; and for his very righteousness he is hanged. *Billy Budd*, finished within a few months before the end of Melville's life, would seem to teach that though the wages of sin is death, that sinners and saints alike toil for a common hire. In *Billy Budd* the orphic sententiousness is gone, it is true. But gone also is the brisk lucidity, the sparkle, the verve. Only the disillusion abided with him to the last.[381]. . . .

From John Middleton Murry (1924)†

. . . .

With the mere fact of the long silence in our minds we could not help regarding "Billy Budd" as the last will and spiritual testament of a man of genius. We could not help expecting this, if we have any imagi-

* From R. M. Weaver, *Herman Melville, Mariner and Mystic,* Introduction by Mark Van Doren (New York: Pageant Books Inc., 1960), by permission of the publisher.

† From "Herman Melville's Silence," *Times Literary Supplement,* No. 1173 (July 10, 1924), p. 433, by permission of The Times Publishing Company Limited. All Rights Reserved. (C).

native understanding. Of course, if we are content to dismiss in our minds, if not in our words, the man of genius as mad, there is no need to trouble. Some one is sure to have told us that "Billy Budd," like "Pierre," is a tissue of naivety and extravagance: that will be enough. And, truly, "Billy Budd" is like "Pierre"—startlingly like. Once more Melville is telling the story of the inevitable and utter disaster of the good and trying to convey to us that this must be so and ought to be so—chronometrically and horologically. He is trying, as it were with his final breath, to reveal the knowledge that has been haunting him —that these things must be so and not otherwise.

Billy Budd is a foretopman, pressed out of the merchant service into the King's Navy in the year of the Nore mutiny. He is completely good, not with the sickly goodness of self-conscious morality, but as one born into earthly paradise—strong, young, manly, loyal, brave, unsuspecting, admired by his officers and adored by his shipmates. And he is hated by the master-at-arms, the policeman of the lower deck. Claggart hates him, simply because he is Billy Budd, with the instinctive hatred of the evil for the good. Melville is careful to explain that there is no reason whatever for his hatred; he puts it deliberately before us as naked and elemental—the clash of absolutes. Claggart is subtle and cool, he works quietly, and he is also a man of courage. He involves Billy Budd in the thin semblance of revolutionary mutiny. The master-at-arms deliberately risks his own life in order to destroy his enemy's. He risks it, and loses it, for in the privacy of his own cabin the captain confronts the accuser with his victim, and in a flash of anger Budd strikes the master-at-arms dead. The moment in the story is unearthly. But Billy is doomed: he has killed his officer in time of war. The captain who understands and loves him presides over the court-martial, and Budd is condemned to be hanged at dawn. . . . ["Billy Budd"] was Melville's final word, worthy of him, indisputably a passing beyond the nihilism of "Moby Dick" to what may seem to some simple and childish, but will be to others wonderful and divine.[433]

From John Freeman (1926)*

. . . .

Like *Moby-Dick* this late and pure survival of Melville's genius has a double interest, the interest of story and the interest of psy-

* From John Freeman, *Herman Melville* (New York: The Macmillan Co., 1926), by permission of the publisher.

chology. *Billy Budd* is the narrative of one who, like Pierre, is un-practiced in the ways of life and the hates of other men; guilelessness is a kind of genius and the better part of innocence in this handsome young sailor[131]. . . .

Exaltation of spirit redeems such a scene [as the hanging scene] from burdens which otherwise might appear too painful to be borne. And beyond this, it is innocence that is vindicated, more conspicuously in death than it could be in life. . . . The ultimate opposition is shown clearly . . . in this public vindication of the law, and the superior assertion at the very moment of death of the nobility of pure human spirit. *Moby-Dick* ends in darkness and desolation, for the challenge of Ahab's pride is rebuked by the physical power and the un-humanness of Nature; but *Billy Budd* ends in a brightness of escape, such as the apostle saw when he exclaimed, "Death, where is thy sting!"

Finished but a few months before the author's death and only lately published, *Billy Budd* shows the imaginative faculty still secure and powerful, after nearly forty years' supineness, and the not less striking security of Melville's inward peace. . . . In his last days he re-enters an Eden-like sweetness and serenity . . . and sets his brief, appealing tragedy for witness that evil is defeat and natural goodness invincible in the[135] affections of man. In this, the simplest of stories, told with but little of the old digressive vexatiousness, and based upon recorded incidents, Herman Melville uttered his everlasting yea, and died before a soul had been allowed to hear him.[136]

From Raymond M. Weaver (1928)*

. . . .

Just as some theologians have presented the fall of man as evidence of the great glory of God, in similar manner Melville studies the evil in Claggart in vindication of the innocence of Billy Budd. For, primarily, Melville wrote *Billy Budd* in witness to his ultimate faith that evil is defeat and natural goodness invincible in the affections of man. *Billy Budd*, as *Pierre*, ends in disaster and death; in each case in-experience and innocent and seraphic impulse are wrecked against the malign forces of darkness that seem to preside[1] over external hu-

* From "Introduction," *The Shorter Novels of Herman Melville* (New York: Liveright Publishing Corp., 1928), 1–li, by permission of Sidney A. Burrell.

man destiny. In *Pierre*, Melville had hurled himself into a fury of vituperation against the world; with *Billy Budd* he would justify the ways of God to man. Among the many parallels of contrast between these two books, each is a tragedy (as was Melville's life), but in opposed senses of the term. For tragedy may be viewed not as being essentially the representation of human misery, but rather as the representation of human goodness or nobility. All of the supremest art is tragic: but the tragedy is, in Aristotle's phrase, "the representation of Eudaimonia," or the highest kind of happiness. There is, of course, in this type of tragedy, with its essential quality of encouragement and triumph, no flinching of any horror of tragic life, no shirking of the truth by a feeble idealism, none of the compromises of the so-called "happy ending." The powers of evil and horror must be granted their fullest scope; it is only thus we can triumph over them. Even though in the end the tragic hero finds no friends among the living or dead, no help in God, only a deluge of calamity everywhere, yet in the very intensity of his affliction he may reveal the splendour undiscoverable in any gentler fate. Here he has reached, not the bottom, but the crowning peak of fortune—something which neither suffering nor misfortune can touch. Only when worldly disaster has worked its utmost can we realize that there remains something in man's soul which is for ever beyond the grasp of the accidents of existence, with power in its own right to make life beautiful. Only through tragedy of this type could Melville affirm his everlasting yea. The final great revelation—or great illusion—of his life, he uttered in *Billy Budd*.[11]

From Lewis Mumford (1929)*

. . . .
Billy Budd, his final novel, is not a full-bodied story: there is statement, commentary, illustration, just statement, wise commentary, apt illustration: what is lacking is an independent and living creation. The epithets themselves lack body and colour: Billy Budd has nothing to compare with the description of boiling whale oil in Moby Dick—"a wild Hindoo odour, like the left wing of the Day of Judgement."
Billy Budd . . . lacks the fecundity and energy of White Jacket:

---

* From *Herman Melville* by Lewis Mumford, copyright, 1929, by Harcourt, Brace and Company, Inc.; renewed, 1957, by Lewis Mumford. Reprinted by permission of the publishers.

the story itself takes place on the sea, but the sea itself is missing, and even the principal characters are not primarily men: they are actors and symbols.[353] The story gains something by this concentration, perhaps: it is stripped for action, and even Melville's deliberate digressions do not halt it. Each of the characters has a Platonic clarity of form. . . .[354]

Billy Budd is the story of three men in the British Navy; it is also the story of the world, the spirit, and the devil. Melville left a note, crossed out in the original manuscript, "Here ends a story not unwarranted by what happens in this incongruous world of ours—innocence and infirmity, spiritual depravity and fair respite." The meaning is so obvious that one shrinks from underlining it. Good and evil exist in the nature of things, each forever itself, each doomed to war with the other. In the working out of human institutions, evil has a place as well as the good: Vere is contemptuous of Claggart, but cannot do without him: he loves Budd as a son and must condemn him to the noose: justice dictates an act abhorrent to his nature, and only his inner magnanimity keeps it from being revolting. These are the fundamental ambiguities of life: so long as evil exists, the agents that intercept it will also be evil, whilst we accept the world's conditions: the universal articles of war on which our civilizations rest. Rascality may be punished; but beauty and innocence will suffer in that process far more. There is no comfort, in the perpetual Calvary[356] of the spirit, to find a thief nailed on either side. Melville had been harried by these paradoxes in Pierre. At last he was reconciled. He accepted the situation as a tragic necessity; and to meet that tragedy bravely was to find peace, the ultimate peace of resignation, even in an incongruous world. As Melville's own end approached, he cried out with Billy Budd: God Bless Captain Vere! In this final affirmation Herman Melville died. . . .[357]

2. *BILLY BUDD* AS TESTAMENT

MELVILLE'S TESTAMENT OF ACCEPTANCE*

E. L. Grant Watson

. . . .

The style of this product of Melville's last years is strikingly different from the exuberant and highly-colored prose of that great period of more ardent creation (1850–1852) which produced *Mardi, Moby-Dick,* and *Pierre*. Though it lacks that fine extravagance of the earlier books, which laid on the color with prodigality, *Billy Budd* is as rich, or even richer, in Melville's peculiar and elaborate symbolism; and this symbolism becomes all the more effective for being presented in a dry and objective manner. The fine flourishes, the purple patches, which scintillate brilliantly in *Moby-Dick,* and the deep sombre melancholy of *Pierre* are not here. The grandiloquence of youth which tempted Stevenson's very partial appreciation is here transformed into the dignity of an achieved detachment. The story develops simply, always unhurried, yet never lagging. Each character is described with the patience which the complex intention of the theme demands—the color of the eyes, the clothes, the complexion, the color of the skin, of the blood under the skin, the past, the present—these are hints at a deep and[319] solemn purpose, one no less ambitious than to portray those ambiguities of good and evil as the mutually dependent opposites, between which the world of realization finds its being.

The title *Billy Budd* is not without significance, and would strike some readers in its crude simplicity as proof that Melville was lacking in a sense of humor. How could any man, they would argue, write a tragedy and call it *Billy Budd?* But a sense of humor, like almost everything else, is relative. Melville certainly lacked it in the crude form; but he was always conscious of those occasions when he might seem, to a superficial view, to be wanting it. He is particularly con-

---

* From *The New England Quarterly,* VI (June, 1933), 319–327, by permission of the publisher.

scious of the obvious, but not in the obvious manner; and when he uses such a name as Billy Budd to set as the hub round which his own philosophy of life must revolve, he does so consciously, choosing the obvious to carry the transcendental. "I have ever found the plain things, the knottiest of all," he has written; and so he has made the simple man, the every-day Billy, the handsome sailor, the hero of a tragedy. Humor is appreciated most easily when larger things contract suddenly to smaller things—as when a man slips on a piece of orange-peel, thus converting his intention of going about his business to the abrupt act of falling on his back-side. Yet a more imaginative intelligence might, with a sense of humor just as true, see in the fall, the destiny of man, with full chorus of pities and ironic spirits. The easy contraction will seem to the sophisticated too facile to provoke a smile, a larger humor is found in the reverse process, namely in a filling in, in an exaggeration from the particular to the[320] general. With such an added pinch of imagination, the obvious thing becomes the centre of mystery. And so, with a sense of humor which perceived both the obvious and the peculiar quality of the name, Melville deliberately chose "Billy Budd." Moreover, he made the hero of this, his gospel story (as it might well be called), a foundling of uncertain parentage, whose "entire family was practically invested in himself."

It is a mistake for critics to try to tell stories which authors must have told better in their texts. The critic's function is rather to hint at what lies beneath—hidden, sometimes, under the surface. Melville called his story "an inside narrative," and though it deals with events stirring and exciting enough in themselves, it is yet more exciting because it deals with the relation of those principles which constitute life itself. A simple-mindedness unaffected by the shadow of a doubt, a divine innocence and courage, which might suggest a Christ not yet conscious of His divinity, and a malice which has lost itself in the unconscious depths of mania—the very mystery of iniquity—these opposites here meet, and find their destiny. But Melville's theme is even larger. All the grim setting of the world is in the battleship *Indomitable;* war and threatened mutiny are the conditions of her existence. Injustice and inhumanity are implicit, yet Captain Vere, her commander, is the man who obeys the law, and yet understands the truth of the spirit. It is significant of Melville's development since the writing of *Moby-Dick* and *Pierre,* that he should create this naval captain—wholly pledged to the unnaturalness of the law, but sufficiently touched, at the same time, by the divine difference from ordinary sanity[321] (he goes by the nick-name of "Starry Vere"), as to live the truth *within* the law, and yet, in the cruel process of that very obedience, to redeem an innocent man from the bitterness of death imposed by the same law. A very different ending this from the despairing acts of dissolution which mar the conclusions of the three earlier books: *Mardi, Moby-Dick,* and *Pierre.*

Melville is no longer a rebel. It should be noted that Billy Budd has not, even under the severest provocation, any element of rebellion in him; he is too free a soul to need a quality which is a virtue only in slaves. His nature spontaneously accepts whatever may befall. When impressed from the merchant-ship, the *Rights of Man,* he makes no demur to the visiting lieutenant's order to get ready his things for trans-shipment. The crew of the merchant-ship are surprised and reproachful at his uncomplaining acquiescence. Once aboard the battle-ship, the young sailor begins to look around for the advantages of chance and adventure. Such simple power to accept gives him the buoyancy to override troubles and irritations which would check inferior natures.

Yet his complete unconsciousness of the attraction, and consequent repulsion, that his youthful beauty and unsophisticated good-fellowship exercise on Claggart, makes it only easier for these qualities to turn envy into hatred. His very virtue makes him the target from the shaft of evil, and his quality of acceptance provokes to action its complementary opposite, the sense of frustration that can not bear the consciousness of itself, and so has to find escape in mania. Thus there develops the conflict between unconscious virtue (not even aware of[322] its loss of Eden and unsuspecting of the presence of evil) and the bitter perversion of love which finds its only solace in destruction.

And not only Billy Budd is marked by this supreme quality of acceptance. Captain Vere, also, possesses it, but with full consciousness, and weighted with the responsibility of understanding the natural naturalness of man's volition and the unnatural naturalness of the law. . . . In Captain Vere we find a figure which may interestingly be compared to Pontius Pilate. Like Pilate, he condemns the just man to a shameful death, knowing him to be innocent, but, unlike Pilate, he does not wash his hands, but manfully assumes the full responsibility, and in such a way as to take the half, if not more than the half, of the bitterness of the execution upon himself. We are given to suppose that there is an affinity, a[323] spiritual understanding between Captain Vere and Billy Budd, and it is even suggested that in their partial and separate existence they contribute two essential portions of that larger spirit which is man. . . . There are darker hints: those deep, far-away things in Vere, those occasional flashings-forth of intuition—short, quick probings to the very axis of reality. Though the book be read many times, the student may still remain baffled by Melville's significant arrangement of images. The story is so solidly filled out as to suggest dimensions in all directions. As soon as the mind fastens upon one subject, others flash into being.

Melville reported in *Pierre* how he fished his line into the deep sea of childhood, and there, as surely as any modern psychoanalyst, discovered all the major complexes that have since received baptism at the hands of Freudians. He peered as deep as any into the origins of sensuality, and in conscious understanding he was the equal of any modern psychologist; in poetic divination he has the advantage of most. No doubt the stresses of his own inner life demanded this exceptional awareness. In this book of his old age, the images which he chose for the presentation of his final wisdom, move between the antinomies of love and hate, of innocence and malice. From behind —from far behind the main pageant of the story—there seem to fall suggestive shadows of primal, sexual simplicities. In so conscious a symbolist as Melville, it would be surprising if there should be no meaning or half-meaning in the spilling of Billy's soup towards the homosexually-disposed[324] Claggart, in the impotence of Billy's speech in the presence of his accuser, in his swift and deadly answer, or the likening of Claggart's limp, dead body to that of a snake.

It is possible that such incidents might be taken as indications of some unresolved problem in the writer himself. This may be, but when we remember how far Melville had got in the process of self-analysis in *Pierre,* and when we have glanced at the further analysis that is obvious in the long narrative poem *Clarel,* it seems likely that this final book, written nearly forty years after *Pierre,* should contain a further, deeper wisdom. And as the philosophy in it has grown from that of rebellion to that of acceptance, as the symbolic figures of unconscious forces have become always more concrete and objective, so we may assume that these hints are intentional, and that Melville was particularly conscious of what he was doing.

But let no one suppose that he would ever pin an image to his scale of value, as an entomologist would pin an insect to his board; there is always in his interpretation a wide spaciousness. He lifts some familiar object, holding it to his light, that it may glow and illumine some portion of what must always remain vast and unknown. For his suggestive use of words, and the special values he gives them, and the large implication he can in this way compress into a sentence, the passage which tells how Billy Budd was hanged from the main yard-arm of the battle-ship *Indomitable* is a good example: . . . . [Last part of Chapter 26][325] Here is Melville at his very best, at his deepest, most poetic, and therefore at his most concentrated, most conscious. Every image has its significant implication: the very roll of the heavily-cannoned ship so majestic in moderate weather—the musket in the ship-armourer's rack; and Billy's last words are the triumphant seal of[326] his acceptance, and they are more than that, for in this supreme passage a communion between personality at its purest, most God-given form, and character, hard-hammered from the imperfect material of life on the battleship *Indomitable,* is here suggested, and one feels that the souls of Captain Vere and Billy are at that moment strangely one.

In this short history of the impressment and hanging of a handsome sailor-boy, are to be discovered problems almost as profound as those which puzzle us in the pages of the Gospels. *Billy Budd* is a book to be read many times, for at each reading it will light up, as do the greater experiences of life, a beyond leading always into the unknown.[327]

BILLY BUDD: TESTAMENT OF RESISTANCE*

Phil Withim

When E. L. G. Watson wrote his famous article, "Melville's Testament of Acceptance," he made no attempt to prove his view. All he attempted, all he achieved, was to suggest a way of looking at the story. "Melville," said Watson, "is no longer a rebel." He has come to accept the presence of evil, and he has ceased to blame God for its existence. Other critics began to write on *Billy Budd* in the same vein. Their positions varied somewhat, but the tenor, the direction of the viewpoint was always the same: Melville had mellowed, he was resigned, as Freeman says, to the recognition of necessity.[1] In F. O. Matthiessen's words, "He has come to respect necessity.... Melville could now face incongruity; he could accept the existence of both good and evil...." Or as Willard Thorp remarks, "In the end Melville called the truce."

There was, however, some dissent; both Alfred Kazin and Richard Chase indicated dissatisfaction with the "testament of acceptance" theory. In 1950 Joseph Schiffman, in an article which reviewed all these interpretations as well as those of Mumford, Weir, and Sedgwick, put forth a suggestion, which he credited to Gay Wilson Allen, "that *Billy Budd* might best be understood as a work of irony." Since this article appeared, a number of other critics have also objected to the "testament of acceptance" theory or have supported an ironic interpretation; sometimes they have done both.

---

* From *Modern Language Quarterly*, XX (June, 1959), 115–127, by permission of publisher and author.

1 F. Barron Freeman, ed., *Melville's Billy Budd* (Cambridge, 1948), p. 115. All page references to *Billy Budd* are from this edition and will be inserted in parentheses directly following the quotations. [Page references to *Billy Budd* in the present volume are in square brackets.]

This paper is another step in this same direction. It accepts the point of view that *Billy Budd* was written in a basically ironic style: it will attempt to establish a thesis in harmony with all of the parts of[115] the story and to demonstrate that the "testament of acceptance" theory is essentially self-contradictory.

The body of the story is concerned with the relationships of three men: Billy Budd, John Claggart, and Captain Vere. Whatever arguments may rage concerning other elements of the story, there is general agreement as to the character and significance of Billy Budd and John Claggart. Billy Budd is the Handsome Sailor uniting "strength and beauty," whose moral nature is not "out of keeping with the physical make" (p. [4] 135). Claggart is Billy's reverse. He is pale and unhealthy looking; his visage seems to hint of something defective or abnormal in the constitution and blood. This contrasts with the conjunction in Billy of beauty and goodness. Claggart had an "evil nature, not engendered by vicious training or corrupting books or licentious living, but born with him and innate, in short 'a depravity according to nature'" (p. [26–27] 187).

Melville is explicit about his desire to have Billy and Claggart taken as types of good and bad, and this, I think, is the chief argument against those who, like Matthiessen and Freeman, consider homosexualism an aspect of the problem. For if Melville had desired to hint at homosexualism, he would not have denied its possibility; when speaking of Claggart's peculiar nature, he says, "In short the depravity here meant partakes nothing of the sordid or sensual" (p. [26] 186). And speaking of Billy, he says he was "preëminently the Handsome Sailor" (p. [28] 192) who, as Melville has told us in the opening pages of the book, typifies strength united to beauty. In those descriptions of Billy emphasizing his delicate color and the fine detail of his features, the point is to impress us with his purity, his aristocratic heritage, not his femininity. Melville takes care to remind the reader that Billy had thrashed the bully, Red Whiskers (p. [6] 139).

But it is around the third figure, Captain Vere, that the greatest disagreement has arisen. This suggests that a detailed examination of his character and function is essential to any understanding of the novel. He is described as apparently the best type of British naval man:

always acquitting himself as an officer mindful of the welfare of his men, but never tolerating an infraction of discipline; thoroughly versed in the science of his profession, and intrepid to the verge of temerity, though never injudiciously so. (p. [15] 160)

He loves to read, particularly those books "treating of actual men and events no matter of what era—history, biography and unconventional writers, who, free from cant and convention, like Montaigne, honestly, and in the spirit of common sense philosophize upon realities" (pp. [17] 163–64). In the reading he found

confirmation of his own more reserved thoughts—confirmation which he had vainly sought in social converse, so that as touching most fundamental topics, there had got to be established in him some positive convictions which he forefelt would abide in him essentially unmodified so long as his intelligent part remained unimpaired. (p. [17] 164)[116]

This particular sentence creates a question as to Melville's meaning. Does he suggest here that the only result of Vere's reading is that his mind becomes more and more firmly fixed on his earliest opinions, that no author can ever modify them, either because he will not let their ideas penetrate or because he never reads books that do not agree with him; or does Melville imply that Vere's opinions are instinctively right and that all the books in Vere's library, "compact, but of the best" (p. [17] 163) agree with him unfailingly? But it is as yet too early to decide. Melville continues to describe Vere as one whose "settled convictions were as a dyke against those invading waters of novel opinion social political and otherwise" (p. [17] 164) and as one who opposed these novel opinions because they seemed to him not only "incapable of embodiment in lasting institutions, but at war with the peace of the world and the true welfare of mankind" (p. [17] 164). This last phrase sounds suspiciously like cant, like sarcasm. Vere's reasons here are such terribly stock arguments that it is hard to accept them at face value.

The possibility arises that the reader is expected to understand that Vere's reasoning is presented without comment because it is simply and transparently a rationalization of an uninformed and bigoted man who reads only those authors who reinforce his views. But if this possibility is to be accepted as fact, the reader must find other implied criticism of Vere, and, indeed, it does not take much searching. Melville, for example, goes to the trouble of devoting several pages to Nelson, the greatest of English captains,[2] pointing out with approval that Nelson challenged death by his brilliant apparel.

---

[2] Wendell Glick, in his article "Expediency and Absolute Morality in *Billy Budd*," *PMLA*, LXVIII (1953), 103–10, devotes much attention to the Nelson episode, equating Nelson not with Vere but with Billy, and discovers both to be heroic. This may be true, although the differences in station, occasion, and motivation seem to be unsurmountable obstacles to such an interpretation. On the other hand, it seems natural to compare Nelson with Vere: both are captains of ships in time of war, both are asked to deal with mutiny. An additional difficulty with Glick's article lies in the fact that his defense is built on the following unsupported statement: "[Melville] agreed with the Captain that justice to the individual is not the ultimate loyalty in a complex culture; the stability of the culture has the higher claim, and when the two conflict, justice to the individual must be abrogated to keep the order of society intact" (p. 104). Since this is exactly the point in question, so far as any interpretation of the meaning of *Billy Budd* is concerned, it seems facile to present it as axiomatic.

Personal prudence even when dictated by quite other than selfish consideration is surely no special virtue in a military man; while an excessive love of
glory, impassioning a less burning impulse the honest sense of duty, is the
first. (p. [14] 157)

Nelson, of course, dies a soldier's death, while Vere dies drugged and
ashore before ever reaching fame. Nelson is a fighter in direct contact
with the enemy; but Vere, in the encounter described in *Billy Budd,*
does not have an opportunity to catch the opposing ship. Vere is frequently used for diplomatic missions, the very opposite of a captain's
usual job; Vere, says Melville, though a man of "sturdy qualities
was without brilliant ones" (p. [16] 162). Nelson is asked to take command[117] of a ship recently involved in the Great Mutiny, for "it was
thought that an officer like Nelson was the one, *not indeed to terrorize
the crew into base subjection,* but to win them, by force of his mere
presence back to an allegiance if not as enthusiastic as his own, yet as
true" (p. [15] 159; italics mine). Vere, in a similar situation, hangs
Billy, "thinking perhaps that under existing circumstances in the
navy the consequence of violating discipline should be made to speak
for itself" (p. [55] 254).

It is clear that this comparison is not favorable to Captain Vere,
and if we look back to earlier descriptions, we find that they apparently
contain an implied criticism: "ever mindful of the welfare of his men,
but never tolerating an infraction of discipline"; "intrepid to the verge
of temerity, though never injudiciously so." The second half of each
statement could merely qualify the virtue mentioned in the first half,
or it could cancel the virtue completely.[3]

---

3 Cf. James E. Miller, Jr., *"Billy Budd:* The Catastrophe of Innocence," *MLN,*
LXXIII (1958), 168–76. Miller uses the quotations I have just cited to demonstrate
the opposite of my point, namely, that Vere, as opposed to both Billy (all heart)
and Claggart (all mind), "is the man of moderation with heart and intellect in
ideal balance," who recognizes the "wide and necessary separation of heavenly wisdom and earthly wisdom and the 'impossibility' of the application of the one in the
province of the other." In this interpretation Vere becomes a "Hero of Humanity"
who shields society from the cataclysmic consequences of Billy's "nakedly spontaneous and raw innocence."

Apparently Miller does not take the quotations in question ironically, whereas I
do. But how does one know when to read any line ironically? The answer, I suppose,
must be: when such a reading is suggested by and found to be consistent with the total context. In this article, I have tried to submit my own reading to such a test, but
I do not find that Miller has. Rather, pretty much abandoning *Billy Budd,* he retreats
to *Pierre,* to the Plinlimmon pamphlet, to its famous distinction between heavenly
and earthly truth and to its call for a "virtuous expediency." Unfortunately, this
pamphlet is not the clearest of Melville's work, and in Willard Thorp's words, "the
critics will argue its significance perpetually."

It would seem, therefore, an invalid critical procedure to attempt to explain
the uncertain meanings of *Billy Budd* by an appeal to the uncertain meanings of
Pierre. Even if Melville's intentions, ironic or otherwise, in *Pierre* were crystal clear,
which they are not, there is no guarantee that *Billy Budd* embodies them, forty
years later.

After Claggart accuses Billy of projected mutiny, Vere decides to confront the two men with each other in his cabin. There Billy, infuriated by the charge, confused and frustrated by his stammer, strikes Claggart dead. Apparently Vere's purpose in bringing them together is to find out the truth.[4] But how does he expect the interview to accomplish this? Claggart would have accused, and Billy would have denied. There seems to be no relevant reason for Vere's decision. Claggart had suggested that there was substantiating evidence not far away, but Vere had not sent for it, since he wished to keep the affair secret because he was afraid of the crew. In short, Vere's decision is based on the single element of prudence, and he ignores all other[118] elements inherent in the situation. Now Claggart is dead. As Vere looks on, he cries, " 'Struck dead by an angel of God. Yet the Angel must hang' " (p. [44] 229). Vere must have acute perception, indeed, to see so quickly to the heart of so complex a situation. He realizes instantly that there is no alternative to Billy's death.

Vere calls a court-martial, reserving, however, "to himself as the one on whom the ultimate accountability would rest, the right of maintaining a supervision of it, or formally or informally interposing at need" (p. [46] 236). During the trial the members of the court seem reluctant to hang Billy, and the Captain has to talk them into it. But it is hard to understand why Vere called the court at all. What purpose does it serve? Was it called to guide him to a right decision? But Vere had already made his decision. In any case the court did not guide him; he guided the court. Perhaps he thought the court would overrule him and free the boy. But Vere had reserved for himself the right of supervising and interfering at need. Apparently all Vere wants is to have on record a trial agreeing with his decision.

Vere begins his argument (pp. [50–52] 244–48) by saying that he would not interfere with their deliberations, but that he sees them at a crisis proceeding " 'from the clashing of military duty with moral scruple.' " He advises them to " 'strive against scruples that may tend to enervate decision.' " When the men look startled, he explains thus:

"How can we adjudge to summary and shameful death a fellow-creature innocent before God, and whom we feel to be so?—Does that state it aright? You sign sad assent. Well, I too feel that, the full force of that. It is Nature. But do these buttons that we wear attest that our allegiance is to Nature? No, to the King."

This is the main basis of his argument: we do not serve nature but the king.

---

[4] This point is taken from Lawrance Thompson's *Melville's Quarrel with God* (Princeton, 1952), a book which has been widely and deservedly criticized as totaling somewhat less than the sum of its parts; yet many of those parts are valuable for their detailed analyses and suggestive insights.

"We fight at command. If our judgments approve the war, that is but coincidence. So in other particulars.... Would it be so much we ourselves that would condemn as it would be martial law operating through us? For that law and the rigor of it, we are not responsible. Our vowed responsibility is in this: That however pitilessly that law may operate, we nevertheless adhere to it and administer it."

The officer of marines points out that Budd "proposed neither mutiny nor homicide." Vere agrees with him, saying that, after all, " 'At the Last Assizes it shall acquit,' " but not now. " 'War looks but to the frontage, the appearance. And the Mutiny Act, War's child, takes after the father. Budd's intent or non-intent is nothing to the purpose.' "

No one at any time questions his argument. No one suggests that the king's law should be in harmony with nature's law, or that if there is disagreement between them, the allegiance must be to the higher and the more universal law of nature. No one asks Vere to support his peculiar thesis; it is merely slipped in, so to speak, with the analogy of the buttons: because the men wear the king's buttons, they[119] are to violate natural laws. Even though Vere has admitted that the Mutiny Act looks only to frontage, to the appearance, no one suggests that the point of justice is to see through appearance to reality. But the reason that no one questions Vere's arguments is that no one understands them. "Loyal lieges, plain and practical ... they were without the faculty, hardly had the inclination to gainsay one whom they felt to be an earnest man, one too not less their superior in mind than in naval rank" (pp. [52] 248–49).

Vere, however, soon gives them an argument they can understand, for when the junior lieutenant asks why, if they must convict, they cannot mitigate the sentence, Vere replies that they cannot because the crew " 'will ruminate. You know what sailors are. Will they not revert to the recent outbreak at the Nore.... Your clement sentence they would account pusillanimous. They would think that we flinch, that we are afraid of them.' " And this is the only argument the court really understands, for, as Melville says, "it is not improbable that even such of his words as were not without influence over them, less came home to them than his closing appeal to their instincts as sea-officers...." So for all the finely spun thought, the issue is decided by fear. When subtle arguments fail, Vere calls on, not a rational argument, but an emotional one: an appeal to fear.

Another clue to Vere's thinking comes after Billy has been hanged. The men are put to work at various tasks; they are swept into the routine as fast as possible. Melville writes of this:

"With mankind" he would say "forms, measured forms are everything; and that is the import couched in the story of Orpheus with his lyre spellbinding the wild denizens of the woods." And this [Vere] once applied to the disruption of forms going on across the Channel and the consequences thereof. (p. [63] 272)

Stripped of verbiage, Vere is saying that men cannot think for themselves, that form and habit can control men as if they were no more than beasts. Vere, in an earlier passage, had thought to himself that Billy was a " 'King's bargain,' that is to say, for His Britannic Majesty's navy a capital investment at small outlay or none at all" (p. [40] 220). In this light, Vere, far from being a wise man, balanced in his judgments and fair in his attitudes, is discovered to be narrow, literal, prejudiced, completely circumscribed by the needs of the navy, less compassionate than his officers, and lastly, guilty of that worst of naval sins, over-prudence.

The core of Vere's argument is that we must bow to necessity; " 'For that law and the rigor of it, we are not responsible. Our vowed responsibility is in this: That however pitilessly that law may operate, we nevertheless adhere to it and administer it' " (pp. [51] 245–46). A logical extension of this argument is that man should abdicate responsibility for unjust law and enforce it mechanically. Man should not try to change that which is wrong, but merely accept injustice and tyranny and lie supinely beneath them; man is to stand by and watch[120] the innocent as indiscriminately ground under the heel of unresisted law as are the evil.

Melville makes his opposition to this view clear by dedicating the book to Jack Chase, his companion years before on the frigate *United States*. It was this voyage that became the story of *White-Jacket*, the novel that cried out so eloquently against impressment, flogging, the captain's tyranny. Jack Chase is here mentioned by name and is referred to as "a stickler for the Rights of Man and the liberties of the world." It would be ironic indeed to dedicate *Billy Budd* to such a man if the novel was devoted to submission. However, the preface (pp. [3] 131–32) helps to make clear the direction of the book. In it, Melville speaks of the French Revolution as an expression of "the Spirit of that Age [which] involved the rectification of the Old World's hereditary wrongs." He points out that, although the revolution had in its turn become an oppressor, the outcome was "a political advance along nearly the whole line for Europeans," and he concludes by saying,

in a way analogous to the operation of the Revolution at large the Great Mutiny, though by Englishmen naturally deemed monstrous at the time, doubtless gave the first latent prompting to most important reforms in the British Navy.

In short, tyranny can be successfully resisted.

We can now be sure of the direction of the theme of *Billy Budd*. In local context it suggests that it is wrong to submit to unjust law. Those in power, such as Vere, should do all they can to resist the evil inherent in any institution or government. All men are flawed, but not all men are depraved; and we must not let those institutions designed to control the evil destroy the good. In a larger context, man should not resign himself to the presence of evil but must always strive against it. It is possible to check the validity of this view by making sure that the various incidents, descriptions, and points reinforce it, and that they also contradict the "testament of acceptance" theory.

Observe that Vere dies drugged and on shore before he has "attained to the fullness of fame" (p. [64] 275). In other words, Vere's end is suitable to one who did not deserve such renown as the daring and imprudent Nelson, a man capable, as Vere is not, of inspiring his men to loyalty, of substituting persuasion for coercion.

Observe that Claggart is characterized as civilized and intellectual:

the man's even temper and discreet bearing would seem to intimate a mind peculiarly subject to the law of reason, not the less in his heart he would seem to riot in complete exemption from that law having apparently little to do with reason further than to employ it as an ambidexter implement for effecting the irrational. (p. [26] 186)

But such men, continues Melville,

are true madmen, and of the most dangerous sort, for their lunacy is not continuous[121] but occasional evoked by some special object; it is probably secretive which is as much to say it is self contained, so that when moreover, most active it is to the average mind not distinguishable from sanity.... (p. [26] 187)

This material comes into sharper focus when considered in relationship to Vere. He, like Claggart, is civilized; he, like Claggart, is intellectual; and he, like Claggart, uses reason to a bad end. Melville had suggested that Claggart was mad, and yet in Chapter 21, the surgeon, after seeing Claggart's body and hearing Vere say that the boy must hang, cannot banish this treasonable thought: "Was Captain Vere suddenly affected in his mind ... ? Was he unhinged?" (p. [44] 231). The surgeon reports, as instructed by Vere, to the lieutenants and the captain of the marines. "They fully stared at him in surprise and concern. Like him they seemed to think that such a matter should be reported to the Admiral" (p. [45] 232). Melville pushes further; in the next chapter he says,

Who in the rainbow can draw the line where the violet tint ends and the orange tint begins?... So with sanity and insanity.... Whether Captain Vere, as the Surgeon professionally and primarily surmised, was really the sudden victim of any degree of aberration, one must determine for himself by such light as this narrative can afford. (p. [45] 233)

Observe that Billy was removed from a ship called the *Rights of Man* by a lieutenant named Ratcliffe.

Observe that, although Vere was "solicitous of his men's welfare," yet the day after Billy was impressed, the captain flogged "a little fellow, young, a novice an after-guardsman absent from his assigned post when the ship was being put about ..." (p. [21] 174). It is useful to remember here that, when Melville was a novice, he was almost flogged for the same reason, but was saved by the interference of Jack Chase.

Observe that white is not used to portray innocence, as Matthiessen suggests; on the contrary, it is used as Melville had used it in *Moby-Dick:* to imply terror and possibly evil. For example, Claggart is described as pale in visage; Billy, when accused of treachery, appears "struck as by white leprosy" (p. [42] 225); the young man who tries to persuade Billy to join a mutiny had "glassy eyes of pale blue, veiled with lashes all but white" (p. [32] 202); Claggart's voice is silvery and low; the whistles used to pipe the men to witness the punishment of Billy are silver whistles; the moon that shines at midnight as Vere tells the men about Billy's sentence silvers the white spar-deck (p. [55] 254) as, in the ballad also, it silvers the bay where Billy lies shackled, awaiting death. In this light the whiteness of Billy's clothes may not be a sign of his purity but of the evil which is successfully destroying him; and the "circumambient air in the clearness of its serenity ... like smooth white marble" (p. [63] 273), which surrounds him as he hangs from the yardarm, may be more concerned with all-conquering evil than with submissive purity.[122]

Observe that Vere appears at the court-martial as the sole witness, "and as such temporarily sinking his rank, though singularly maintaining it in a matter apparently trivial, namely, that he testified from the ship's weather-side with that object having caused the court to sit on the lee-side" (p. [47] 238). Vere thus chooses the side which puts him literally and metaphorically above the court and gives him, in the slang meaning of the term, the advantage.

Vere, when preparing to address the court, that is, to persuade it to his opinion, paces the cabin,

in the returning ascent to windward, climbing the slant deck in the ship's lee roll; without knowing it symbolizing thus in his action a mind resolute to surmount difficulties even if against primitive instincts strong as the wind and the sea. (p. [49–50] 243)

But Melville has suggested already that the instincts of the untutored barbarian are sounder than the civilized intellect.

Observe that this is corroborated in the very next paragraph. "When speak he did, something both in the substance of what he said and his manner of saying it, showed the influence of unshared studies modifying and tempering the practical training of an active career" (p. [50] 243). But practicality is exactly what is called for. Vere never refers to these qualities, preferring instead to weave a complex skein of thought which none of his court, though thoroughly competent, can follow.

Even the governing circumstance of the entire story, namely, the recent mutinies and the consequent peril hovering over the fleet, does not go unchallenged by Melville. For at the conclusion of Vere's speech, just after his appeal to the fear of a new revolt, Melville describes the court's frame of mind as akin to that

which in the year 1842 actuated the commander of the U.S. brig-of-war *Somers* to resolve, under the so-called Articles of War, Articles modelled upon the English Mutiny Act, to resolve upon the execution at sea of a midshipman and two petty-officers as mutineers designing the seizure of the brig. Which resolution was carried out though in a time of peace and within not many days sail of home. An act vindicated by a naval court of inquiry subsequently convened ashore. History, and here cited without comment. True, the circumstances on board the *Somers* were different from those on board the *Indomitable*. But the urgency felt, well-warranted or otherwise, was much the same. (p. [53] 249)

Thus, Melville introduces a case whose justice had been considered extremely dubious and which, after forty years, was still being debated in the papers. Melville does not stop here; the last two[123] sentences state that the circumstances are not the same, and that perhaps the need for swift action on the *Indomitable* is urgent and perhaps it is not. Thus even the circumstance responsible for Vere's basic motive is undermined.

It should be pointed out that the adherents of the "testament of acceptance" theory have to deal not only with the unsuitability of Captain Vere as a spokesman for Melville, but they also have to explain away the presence of a number of contradictions which arise in the story solely as a result of their position. For example, if the story concerns the acceptance of necessary evil, then why does Melville continue beyond the death of Billy, where, and only where, an emotional equilibrium favorable to such an acceptance is attained? Vere's untimely death would be a poor reward for so faithful a servant and in the "acceptance" context would be meaningless, for the point is made and the tale ended with Billy's death. Only an ironical reversing of the point would justify continuation of the story.

It is even possible to bring into question the tone of the hanging scene. Joseph Schiffman, B. R. McElderry, and Harry Campbell have each noted contradictions in this scene that arise only if the story is interpreted as an "acceptance." Schiffman points out that, even though the crew echoes Billy's cry, "God bless Captain Vere," they are not thinking of the captain, for, in Melville's words, "yet at that instant Billy alone must have been in their hearts, even as he was in their eyes" (p. [60] 265).

B. R. McElderry demonstrates that Billy's cry is not unprecedented in the literature of the sea; he cites two plays and a novel by Marryat which have similar scenes. Thus Billy's cry is

what Melville said it was: "a conventional felon's benediction directed aft towards the quarters of honor..." It is the traditional ritual of the condemned man forgiving the official who is duty bound to order his death.

If this episode is taken ironically, then it fits the rest of the story as so far interpreted and acquires tremendous power. For Billy is willing to die as Isaac or as Christ was willing; he accepts all the captain's arguments, but it is Billy alone who is noble. The captain suffers and wishes he could avoid this duty, but he has no nobility and above all no trust in man. Yet Billy's very acceptance of his role is the evidence that proves man can be trusted, that man can rise above the need for forms.

Harry Campbell has analyzed the hanging scene and perceives therein an attempt on Melville's part to strike a balance between the sacrificial religious aspect and the aspect of the scene as sheer injustice, as an execution. For example, Melville says that "Billy ascended;[124] and ascending, took the full rose of the dawn." But he ascends only to the yardarm, where he remains a pinioned figure. Campbell also notes that the reading of the early *Baby Budd, Sailor* for "rosy dawn" was the powerful religious term "shekinah" (p. 339) and that the "silence accompanying the ascension" (p. 340) later becomes "The silence at the moment of execution" (p. 269). This last change, particularly, suggests that Melville wants us to realize that Billy's death, though noble, is still unjust. If Vere had had such nobility and strength, Billy need not have died. As Kark Zink has said, "The lesson is not that Billy learns to accept the necessary harshness of the forms, but that in their high impersonality there is a dangerous lack of discrimination—dangerous to the individual and to the social structure itself."

Another contradiction inherent in the "acceptance" theory lies in Melville's argument that barbarians with their instincts and warm hearts have sounder values than civilized men with their intricate intellects and their rabied hearts. Would it not be contradictory for Melville to suggest this not once, but twice, and then have Vere, Melville's foremost spokesman, weave a complex intellectual argument? Would it not be contradictory for Melville to have Billy die bravely, crying "God bless Captain Vere," and then have Vere say directly that mankind is a denizen of the forest and must be controlled by form and routine?

Would it not be contradictory, in the "testament of acceptance" framework, for Melville to use for the captain's name a word which at first glance suggests *veritas* "truth," but on second glance can as easily suggest *veritus* "fear," or on third glance, *vir* "man"?

Would it not be contradictory for him to use as symbols of evil flogging, impressment, arbitrary hanging, when these evils had been corrected by the time that he wrote this story, partly through his own writing?

Would it not be contradictory for Melville to use Vere as a symbol of the proper recognition of necessary evil: a man who had opposed the French Revolution and all its new social and political doctrines which since have changed the globe and reduced tyranny, injustice, poverty, and disease? Might it not be argued that, since Vere was wrong in his judgment of these attempts to change existing evils, he might also be wrong about the case in hand?

Would it not be contradictory for Melville to have a captain who is intelligent and widely read in both the ancients and the moderns, who does not apply this breadth of experience, who sees no larger context than the immediate needs of the navy?

Again, would it not be contradictory for Melville to represent Billy as inarticulate, nonthinking, naïve, emotionally adolescent, and morally undeveloped, and then expect the reader to accept his cry, "God[125] bless Captain Vere," as indicative of full understanding, instinctive or otherwise?

And finally, is not the "acceptance" theory contradictory to all that Melville stood for and fought for throughout his entire life? He had been a seaman and had witnessed at first hand the floggings and the tyrannies of the captains. He had never approved of such practices, and in *White-Jacket* he thundered against them from every angle.

No matter, then, what may be the consequences of its abolition; no matter if we have to dismantle our fleets, and our unprotected commerce should fall a prey to the spoiler, the awful admonitions of justice and humanity demand that abolition without procrastination; in a voice that is not to be mistaken, demand that abolition to-day. It is not a dollar-and-cent question of expediency; it is a matter of *right and wrong*. And if any man can lay his hand on his heart, and solemnly say that this scourging is right, let that man but once feel the lash on his own back, and in his agony you will hear the apostate call the seventh heavens to witness that it is *wrong*. And, in the name of immortal manhood, would to God that every man who upholds this thing were scourged at the gangway till he recanted.

Melville was a fighter, he was stubborn, he never accepted the easy way out. Would it not then be contradictory for him, after a lifetime of resisting practical evil in the world at large and metaphysical evil in his novels, at the very end to discover that he had been wrong all along and that his duty had always been to lie down and accept evil as unavoidable?

It is now possible to review the story swiftly. It begins with a cue from a narrator; a rebellion, like the French Revolution or the Spithead Mutiny, may result in good, although in the beginning it may not seem so. Thus, rebellion is justified in the first pages, the implication being that evil can and perhaps should be resisted. We have seen how the various characteristics of the three main actors are clues to the working out of this theme. Claggart is evil through and through; he possesses the perverted intelligence of a serpent, an intelligence used for irrational purposes. Billy Budd, on the contrary, is pure innocence, acting and judging on instinct alone. When Vere is introduced, his central characteristic is his intellection, by means of which he can justify or rationalize an over-prudence that leads to injustice. The chapter on Nelson reminds us that Vere's kind of caution and Vere's way of preventing possible mutiny are not admirable.

It may be argued that, while both Vere and Claggart possess intelligence, Vere uses his wisely and justly. But this argument collapses when it is perceived that Vere does not do what reason would suggest in so dubious a case, i.e., jail Billy until they reach land. The real point is, of course, that Vere does not act on reason and intelligence at all, but on fear; his intelligence, instead of being a guide, is a perverted instrument. Such scenes as the confusion of the officers and the doubt of the surgeon concerning Vere's sanity make sense only when regarded as putting into issue Vere's stature and ability.

It may also be argued that such episodes are intended to demonstrate[126] that Vere and only Vere has the intelligence and insight to perceive the deeper issues. But this explanation falls to the ground when it is realized that Vere's whole argument is irrational and that his final appeal is to brute force. The ballad at the end becomes particularly rich in this context. Billy is to be sacrificed, but unjustly and unnecessarily so. The ballad, written by one of his comrades who does not understand the issues but who feels obscurely the truth of the matter in spite of a calumnious official report, speaks of Billy as unafraid but sad. Billy, being innocence personified, does not fear death; but as an unjust sacrifice, he is pictured as alone and unhappy. He longs for companionship and affection and thinks wistfully of his friends; in the end he contemplates with a melancholy resignation his death:

> Fathoms down, fathoms down, how I'll dream fast asleep.
> I feel it stealing now. Sentry, are you there?
> Just ease these darbies at the wrist,
> And roll me over fair.
> I am asleep, and the oozy weeds about me twist.
> (p. [66] 281)

Thus, Billy's cry, "God Bless Captain Vere," is the crowning irony and really the climax of the story, for he was hanged unjustly. Melville says here that a harsh truth of this harsh world is that good folk can be misled, that they can be abused by the evil simply because they are trusting. Thus Melville reminds us that we must keep up the good fight: evil must not remain uncontested. And he does so not by a call to arms but by demonstrating the consequences of unresisting acquiescence.[127]

3. MAJOR READINGS

Billy Budd as Spiritual Autobiography

MELVILLE'S *BILLY BUDD* AS "AN INSIDE NARRATIVE"*

William Braswell

As with *Moby-Dick* and many other classics, it is possible to find different meanings in *Billy Budd,* complementary rather than con-flicting, by reading it on different levels. One way of reading it which seems to me worthy of further exploration is as "an inside narrative," which Melville himself called it in a subtitle in parentheses. This phrase may obviously be interpreted in various ways. It may be taken merely to imply that the story is restricted to the inner life of a single ship. It may also be taken as a hint that the story is "inside" in a family sense, on account of the part played in the *Somers* affair by Melville's cousin Guert Gansevoort. But it seems to me that Melville intended the subtitle in still another sense. I believe that *Billy Budd* may justi-fiably and profitably be considered as an inside narrative about a tragic conflict in Melville's own spiritual life. The *Indomitable,* which may be regarded merely as a man-of-war, or, on another plane, as the world of Christendom, appears to me acceptable also as a microcosm, the world of an individual—specifically, the world of Herman Melville—and the story of what happened aboard the *Indomitable,* the symboli-cal projection of a personal crisis and the resolution of it. This is not to say that *Billy Budd* is an allegory, nor to argue that its symbols have fixed, rigidly restricted meanings throughout the narrative; in fact, the shifting similitudes and the rich allusiveness suggest new truths every time one reads the novel. Still, a general symbolical pattern may be discerned.

* From *American Literature,* XXIX (May, 1957), 133–146, by permission of publisher and author.

I

With the *Indomitable* a microcosm representing Melville, certain aspects of his being are dramatized in Captain Vere, Billy Budd, and Claggart. The divine, or semidivine, origin of Melville's being is suggested in the fact that Vere is of noble lineage and that Billy and Claggart, although their origin is uncertain, are reputed to have noblemen's blood in their veins. The King is a symbol of the Deity: [133] he does not physically appear in the story, but he is the supreme authority under whose law the ship operates.

Billy Budd and Claggart are contrasting symbols. Billy, the handsome, strong, lovable sailor, represents the good tendencies, the tendencies often designated as "the heart," and the epithet "welkin-eyed"[1] suggests a celestial quality. During his service aboard the *Rights of Man* it is said that a virtue goes out of him, sugaring the sour members of the crew. He is innocent as Adam before the fall. After he has been impressed for duty aboard the *Indomitable,* he is so unsuspecting and so unfamiliar with the ways of evil that at first he thinks Claggart likes him. Later he is horrified by the false charges that Claggart brings against him. He strikes his accuser the fatal blow only because an impediment in speech prevents him from defending himself orally.

Billy's character arouses pity, but so does Claggart's. In defining Claggart's evil nature, Melville suggests analogies between him and Milton's Satan, especially Satan's being cast into hell for his plot against the Deity and his part in bringing about the fall.[2] Claggart's history is obscure, but it is rumored that he "was a *chevalier* who had volunteered into the King's navy by way of compounding for some mysterious swindle whereof he had been arraigned at the King's Bench."[3] His pallor is "in part the result of his official seclusion from the sunlight."[4] While his office keeps him below decks, "welkin-eyed" Billy is a man of the top. At an unforeseen encounter of the two "a red light" flashes forth from Claggart's violet eyes "like a spark from an anvil in a dusk smithy."[5] Yet, looking on Billy before he brings about his downfall, Claggart is filled with sadness, like Satan looking on Adam in the Garden of Eden. Claggart's lifeless body is compared to a dead snake. His depravity, like Billy's goodness, is according to na-

---

1 *Melville's Billy Budd,* ed. F. Barron Freeman (Cambridge, Mass., 1948), pp. [4, 28] 136, 192. References throughout are to this edition, as corrected by the *Corrigenda* published by the same press. [Page references to the present volume are in square brackets.]

2 Norman Holmes Pearson, "Billy Budd: 'The King's Yarn,'" *American Quarterly,* III, 99–114 (Summer, 1951), contains provocative discussion of Milton's influence on *Billy Budd.*

3 *Billy Budd,* p. [19] 169.

4 *Ibid.,* p. [18] 168.

5 *Ibid.,* p. [35] 208.

ture. He is the only person aboard with the exception of Vere who is "intellectually" capable of realizing the moral phenomenon of Billy's character; yet, "apprehending the good, but powerless to be it," a nature such as Claggart's[134] has no recourse left but "to recoil upon itself and like the scorpion for which the Creator alone is responsible, act out to the end the part allotted it."[6] With freedom of will denied him, Claggart is doomed to the role he plays.

He has further symbolical significance. As Billy symbolizes the heart, so Claggart roughly symbolizes "the head." His brow is "of the sort phrenologically associated with more than average intellect."[7] A significant comparison of the two men points out that if Billy's "face was without the intellectual look of the pallid Claggart's, not the less was it lit, like his, from within, though from a different source. The bonfire in his heart made luminous the rose-tan in his cheek."[8] The intellectual Claggart's bleached complexion suggests that he is sicklied o'er with the pale cast of thought. The contrasting symbolism of the two men is subtly indicated also in the fatal scene in Vere's quarters when Billy is confronted with Claggart's charges against him. Billy's impediment in speech here becomes a superb figure for the inarticulateness of the heart. Captain Vere's soothing words, instead of calming Billy, touch his "heart to the quick," so that, still unable to speak, he strikes Claggart a powerful blow upon "the forehead, so shapely and intellectual-looking a feature in the master-at-arms...."[9] A line not used in the final version, as transcribed by Freeman, describes Billy's blow as "electrically energized by the inmost spasm of his heart."[10] The blow comes then, in effect, directly from the heart to the head.* And as a result of it, Captain Vere is confronted by a crisis.

But this terrific blow of Billy's, this lashing out of the heart at the evil represented by Claggart—is there anything comparable to it, symbolically, in Melville's own life? I believe that there is. It seems to me that the part of the narrative leading up to the dramatic scene in Vere's quarters may be said to represent the early part of Melville's spiritual life.

---

6 *Ibid.*, p. [28] 192.

7 *Ibid.*, p. [18] 168.

8 *Ibid.*, p. [27] 190.

9 *Ibid.*, p. [43] 226.

10 *Ibid.*, p. 228, n. 45.

* Author's additional note (1960): A student who read this article, and who accepted Billy and Claggart as symbols of heart and head respectively, asked me what Captain Vere symbolizes. I regretted then not having been so explicit as to say that Captain Vere symbolizes the will: he is the final authority on all matters aboard ship and he determines the ship's course of action; he has the ultimate responsibility of choosing between right and wrong. The psychology of the soul as Melville presents it in *Billy Budd* is relatively simplified; he was more elaborate and involved in dramatizing aspects of the soul in *Mardi* and *Pierre*, as I attempted to show in Chap. VI, *Melville's Religious Thought* (Durham, 1943).

With ruddy-cheeked, welkin-eyed Billy sauntering on the deck in the sunshine, joking with friends, and with the pallid, scheming Claggart slyly promoting his own interests below deck, but still not openly asserting himself, Captain Vere has no problem out of the ordinary to contend with. The relationship between heart and head[135] in Melville's early life seems to have been, on the whole, well-balanced, with the heart somewhat predominant. There are signs of a dichotomy between heart and head at the end of *Mardi*, where all the travelers except Taji are converted to the religion of the heart practiced on the island of Serenia, but Taji sails out into the open sea in pursuit of the ultimate truth. Melville's next two books, *Redburn* and *White-Jacket*, show his compassionate heart in their fervent preaching of Christian charity, but there is ample evidence that during the period in which he wrote these novels he continued assiduously to cultivate the head.

Moby-Dick is predominantly an expression of the heart, but with a difference that sets it off from the earlier books. In addition to the compassion for mankind, there is now an impassioned hatred for the source of man's grief. In the early pages of the novel, when preparing for the entrance of Captain Ahab, Melville writes with admiration for the type of pageant character who has a "globular brain" and a "ponderous heart."[11] However one may feel about Ahab's brain, he is a man of greater heart than some critics apparently have realized. There has been a tendency of late in certain quarters to interpret *Moby-Dick* too much in the manner of a Sunday School pamphlet in which the sad fate of wicked, crazy old Ahab is intended to illustrate for Everyman-Ishmael what will happen to him if he is not a good boy. Obviously Ahab's intention is insane, as he himself admits, and from the beginning it is clear that he is doomed; but despite the tyranny with which his madness makes him drive his crew, he is a noble character with a capacity for great love. On an early appearance he is pictured, in a way to remind one of Christ, as standing before his men "with a crucifixion in his face";[12] and the Iron Crown of Lombardy which he wears was made partly of nails used in the crucifixion. He has one of those great hearts capable of feeling in one pang the sum total of pains diffused through feebler men's whole lives. He feels as though he "were Adam, staggering beneath the piled centuries since Paradise."[13] In a letter to Hawthorne, Melville said that "the reason the mass of men fear God, and *at bottom dislike* Him, is because they rather distrust His heart, and fancy Him all brain like a

---

11 *Moby-Dick*, ed. Luther S. Mansfield and Howard P. Vincent (New York, 1952), p. 73.
12 *Ibid.*, p. 122.
13 *Ibid.*, p. 535.

watch."[14] Ahab says that he himself[136] only feels, feels, feels; God alone has the right to think. His hostility toward God is based on his conception that God is without love for mankind. The plight of crazy Pip makes him exclaim, "There can be no hearts above the snowline."[15] In the last days of the voyage the despairing Starbuck shows sound perception in addressing Ahab as "grand old heart," "noble heart."[16]

At first glance it may seem incredible that there should be a symbolical relationship between Captain Ahab and Billy Budd. Ahab, of course, is a much more complex character than Billy; and, in fact, it would be possible to point out similarities between him and both Vere and Claggart. But the parallels between him and Billy seem especially significant. Consider the conflicts in which the two men become embroiled. On the one hand, there are Ahab and Billy, symbols of man's naturally good heart outraged by evil, and, on the other hand, their adversaries, Moby Dick and Claggart, symbols of evil (to Ahab, Moby Dick symbolizes "all evil").[17] One may smile at the suggestion that in the whiteness of the whale and the pallor of Claggart there is a subtle tie between the adversaries of Ahab and Billy. More important, Moby Dick is an "agent"[18] of the Deity, to use Ahab's label, and Claggart, a petty officer in His Majesty's Navy, is likewise symbolically an agent of the Deity. Thus both Ahab and Billy rebel, in effect, against the highest authority: Ahab's "blasphemy" in harpooning Moby Dick is matched by Billy's "mutiny" in striking the master-at-arms during war. In both fables the symbol of the heart, when injured, strikes back in retaliation. It might be argued with some justice that Ahab brought his injury on himself, but as Billy incurred Claggart's enmity while going about routine duties aboard ship, so Ahab was on a routine whaling cruise when he first encountered Moby Dick. Melville uses the same figure, a firing cannon, to express the terrific feeling of the two men against their opponents. Billy's blow against Claggart's pallid brow is explosive, from "the heart": "quick as the flame from a discharged cannon at night, his right arm shot out, and Claggart dropped to the deck."[19] And Ahab's chest is compared to a mortar which bursts his "hot heart's shell"[20] upon the White Whale.

The hero of Melville's next book, *Pierre*, is quite as violent as Ahab and Billy in his ultimate reaction to evil. Highly idealistic[137] and full of love for mankind, Pierre vows in the beginning that he will

---

14 Julian Hawthorne, *Nathaniel Hawthorne and His Wife: A Biography* (Boston, 1885), I, 404.

15 *Moby-Dick*, p. 514.

16 *Ibid.*, pp. 535, 558.

17 *Ibid.*, p. 181.

18 *Ibid.*, p. 162.

19 *Billy Budd*, p. [43] 226.

20 *Moby-Dick*, p. 181.

be ruled by the heart. His preference for heart over head is shown in his exclamation that "the brains grow maggoty without a heart; but the heart's the preserving salt itself, and can keep sweet without the head."[21] Pierre's following the dictates of the heart, however, his attempt to live according to the ideals of Christ, leads to such maddening entanglements that his love turns to hate. He fires his pistols point-blank at his chief antagonist in the evil world closing in about him. In prison he reflects on the joy he might have known had he been "heartless," but realizing that now he must endure hell in both this world and the next, he cries out his defiance of the Deity: "Well, be it hell. I will mould a trumpet of the flames, and, with my breath of flame, breathe back my defiance!"[22]

There is no doubt that Pierre, Ahab, and Billy all had Melville's deepest sympathy. "I stand for the heart. To the dogs with the head!"[23] Melville wrote to Hawthorne. But he ultimately realized that a rebellious heart could bring him to disaster—in fact, threatened to do so.

It is generally recognized that *Pierre,* a book of overwrought emotion, of indignation, represents a climax of some sort in Melville's life. It is one of the most baffling and most terrifying books ever written. Not long after it was published Melville's nervousness and strange behavior alarmed some of his family to the point of their having him examined for insanity. He was pronounced sane, but it is well known that he suffered much anguish during this period.

His condition soon after writing *Pierre* is symbolized, I believe, by the tragic situation aboard the *Indomitable* just after Billy has struck Claggart. The fact that the crisis in *Billy Budd* comes during a time of war when there is grave danger of mutiny suggests symbolically how critical matters were with Melville himself. Aboard the *Indomitable* decisive action is necessary to prevent possible anarchy. I believe that the action of Captain Vere in regard to Billy indicates symbolically how Melville, with his faculties threatening mutiny, resolved his own greatest personal crisis.

II

Before going into more detail about the symbolism, however, it is necessary to analyze the role of Captain Vere, because on whatever[138] plane one reads the novel, he is the key figure. The good-hearted Billy Budd and the evil Claggart have inspired relatively little dissent among critics: one is inescapably good as the other is inescapably evil. The crux of the problem is what to make of their commanding officer, who alone sees and understands the situation, and yet, knowing Billy to be essentially innocent, summarily has him hanged for

21 *Pierre; or, The Ambiguities,* ed. Henry A. Murray (New York, 1949), p. 377.
22 *Ibid.,* p. 424.
23 Julian Hawthorne, *op. cit.,* I, 404.

striking the blow that accidentally kills the master-at-arms. Most criticism of the novel treats Vere sympathetically, as a conscientious man who does his duty as he sees it. But some of the later criticism pictures him as a monstrous villain—a depraved martinet who enforces ironclad laws regardless of whether they violate individual rights. He is charged with overweening personal ambition, hypocrisy, and the abuse of confidence. His part in the trial scene is denounced as odious.[24]

Melville himself makes no explicit judgment on Vere's part in having Billy hanged. In one very important sentence he puts it up to the reader himself to judge the reasonableness of Captain Vere's actions. Just after Vere has told the Surgeon that a drumhead court is to be convened immediately to determine Billy's fate, the Surgeon reflects: Why such haste? Should not Billy be confined and the case later be referred to the Admiral? Was Vere mentally unhinged? Melville says that the line of demarcation between sanity and insanity is as difficult to draw as the line between two merging colors in a rainbow, and then adds: "Whether Captain Vere, as the Surgeon professionally and primarily surmised, was really the sudden victim of any degree of aberration, one must determine for himself by such light as this narrative may afford."[25]

Though Melville is ostensibly noncommittal, the way in which he narrates the story reveals something of his attitude toward Vere. Lawrance Thompson is alone, so far as I know, in assuming that the narrative passages in the novel as distinguished from the dramatic passages, to use his phraseology, are related by a stupid narrator whose admiration for Vere should not be attributed to Melville.[26] Unless more convincing argument than Thompson's is advanced, there is no reason for doubting that Melville intended himself to be[139] thought of as the narrator. As such, he uses a shifting point of view, looking now into the mind of one character, now into the mind of another, making general comments from time to time, and presenting scenes of dramatic action, but also shutting himself off from a scene entirely when he chooses.

He portrays Vere as both an admirable man and an excellent officer. Though not brilliant, Vere has a superior mind and a marked liking for books by authors who "in the spirit of common sense philosophize upon realities."[27] He has won distinction as an intrepid

---

[24] For derogatory comments on Vere, see, for instance, Joseph Schiffman, "Melville's Final Stage, Irony: A Re-examination of *Billy Budd* Criticism," *American Literature*, XXII, 128–136 (May, 1950); "Letter from E. M. Forster," *The Griffin*, I, 4–6 (1951); and Lawrance Thompson, *Melville's Quarrel with God* (Princeton, 1952), chap. xi.

[25] *Billy Budd*, p. [45] 233.

[26] Thompson, *op. cit.*, pp. 359–360.

[27] *Billy Budd*, p. [17] 164.

fighter. He runs a taut ship, but he has always acquitted himself as "an officer mindful of the welfare of his men."[28] In view of his role in the trial, his concern for the welfare of his men should be especially noted.

Vere is a man of firm principles, and Melville says it is well that he is, since he lives in the tempestuous era of the French Revolution. "His settled convictions were as a dyke against those invading waters of novel opinion[,] social[,] political[,] and otherwise, which carried away as in a torrent no few minds in those days, minds by nature not inferior to his own." He disinterestedly opposed the theories not only "because they seemed to him incapable of embodiment in lasting institutions, but at war with the peace of the world and the true welfare of mankind."[29]

It is impossible to appreciate Vere's actions without relating them to the world he lives in. Except in regard to the one particular allusion to it, the case of Captain MacKenzie and the three executions aboard the United States brig *Somers* during peacetime in 1842 should perhaps best be forgotten when one is attempting to analyze the character of Captain Vere, because in spite of what the historical incident may possibly have contributed to Melville's imaginative creation, what he tells about Vere is another story, about another man, at another time. There is particular significance in the choice of 1797 as the time for the action of the story. England is at war with France, now in the excesses of the Revolution; and England herself has lately been rocked by mutinies at Spithead and the Nore. The first of the mutinies was comparatively mild: the sailors complained about undesirable conditions and were granted concessions. But the Great Mutiny, which occurred the following month, was more "menacing to England than the contemporary manifestoes[140] and conquering and proselyting armies of the French Directory." To the British Empire it was "what a strike in the fire-brigade would be to London threatened by general arson." Melville's vivid figures leave no doubt as to the devastating effect upon Christendom which Vere and other loyal Englishmen feared was imminent unless rigid control were maintained:

that was the time when at the mast-heads of the three-deckers and seventy-fours moored in her own roadstead—a fleet, the right arm of a Power then all but the sole free conservative one of the Old World, the blue-jackets, to be numbered by thousands ran up with huzzas the British colors with the union and cross wiped out; by that cancellation transmuting the flag of founded law and freedom defined, into the enemy's red meteor of unbridled and unbounded revolt. Reasonable discontent growing out of practical grievances

---

[28] *Ibid.*, p. [15] 160.
[29] *Ibid.*, p. [17] 164.

in the fleet had been ignited into irrational combustion as by live cinders blown across the Channel from France in flames.[30]

After the mutiny had been quelled, it was feared that there would be further uprisings. To illustrate the precautionary measures taken at sea against such hazards, Melville points out that, with the fleet off the Spanish coast, Nelson was transferred to a ship just arrived from the Nore, with the hope that his presence would win back the loyalty of the late mutineers. Engagements with the enemy might take place at any hour. When they did occur, officers assigned to batteries felt it necessary at times to stand with drawn swords behind the gunners.

It is clear that Billy's fatal blow could not have been struck at a worse time. Though Vere would rather confine Billy and submit his case later to the Admiral, he feels it incumbent on him, as an officer responsible for the efficiency of a fighting unit, to act on the case immediately. Ironically, with Claggart lying dead on the deck, the essentially innocent man and the bearer of false witness have in effect changed places, so that Claggart, legally viewed, appears the victim of "the most heinous of military crimes. Yet more. The essential right and wrong involved in the matter, the clearer that might lie, so much the worse for the responsibility of a loyal sea-commander inasmuch as he was not authorized to determine the matter on that primitive basis."[31]

Vere advises the court that Billy's intent is not to be considered,[141] that the court must confine itself to the consequence of the blow. He knows, of course, that this is a hard doctrine for the young officers to accept:

How can we adjudge to summary and shameful death a fellow-creature innocent before God, and whom we feel to be so?—Does that state it aright? You sign sad assent. Well, I too feel that, the full force of that. It is Nature. But do these buttons that we wear attest that our allegiance is to Nature? No, to the King. Though the ocean, which is inviolate Nature primeval, though this be the element where we move and have our being as sailors, yet as the King's officers lies our duty in a sphere correspondingly natural? So little is that true, that in receiving our commissions we in the most important regards ceased to be natural free-agents. When war is declared are we the commissioned fighters previously consulted? We fight at command. If our judgements approve the war, that is but coincidence. So in other particulars. So now. For suppose condemnation to follow these present proceedings. Would it be so much we ourselves that would condemn as it would be martial law operating through us? For that law and the rigour of it, we are not responsible. Our vowed responsibility is in this: That how-

---

30 *Ibid.*, pp. [11–12] 150–151.
31 *Ibid.*, pp. [45] 234–235.

ever pitilessly that law may operate, we nevertheless adhere to it and administer it.[32]

To convict and yet mitigate the penalty would have a disastrous effect on the ship's company. Long accustomed to arbitrary discipline, the crew would be bewildered, Vere reasons, by seeing clemency granted a seaman who had murdered the master-at-arms: such a disposition of the case would be virtually an invitation to further mutiny.

Vere's speech to the court is the hardest thing in the book for readers to accept. E. M. Forster's and Eric Crozier's "tidying up" Vere in the trial scene of the libretto they wrote for Benjamin Britten's music resulted in Vere's not counseling the court.[33] But as Melville wrote the novel, there is no denying that Vere alone is ultimately responsible for the execution of Billy.

Billy Budd does not condemn Captain Vere. When Vere privately tells Billy of the verdict, what takes place between the two is not revealed, but with "each radically sharing in the rarer qualities of our nature—so rare indeed as to be all but incredible to average[142] minds however cultivated"[34]—Billy understands and approves what Vere has done. His final words, uttered just before his execution, are, "God bless Captain Vere!"[35] It has been suggested that this remark is ironical, but Billy, we are explicitly told, is incapable of conscious irony, and nobody has yet presented convincing argument that Melville meant the remark to be taken so.

Vere is portrayed as suffering more than Billy. The relationship between the two, suggestive as it is of the relationship between Abraham and Isaac, and between God the Father and the Son, apparently enables Billy to understand that Vere's role is necessitated by his adherence to forms which he holds dearer than life itself—forms for which Vere ultimately gives his own life. "With mankind," Vere believes, "forms, measured forms, are everything; and that is the story of Orpheus with his lyre spellbinding the wild denizens of the wood."[36] In an ideal world, Billy would not be punished; but in the tense man-of-war world of which the *Indomitable* is a part, forms dictate the execution of a murderer if anarchy is not to prevail. The "union and cross" on the British flag—symbols torn off by the mutineers—represent "founded law and freedom defined" as against "unbridled and unbounded revolt." Vere agonizingly perceives the injustice effected at times by adhering to forms, but he sets imperfect

---

32 *Ibid.,* pp. [50–51] 244–246.

33 See Forster on their feeling it necessary to "tidy up" Vere ("Letter from E. M. Forster," *op. cit.,* pp. 4–6). Their libretto was published by Boosey & Hawkes (London, 1951).

34 *Billy Budd,* p. [53] 251.

35 *Ibid.,* p. [59] 264.

36 *Ibid.,* p. [63] 272.

order above anarchic disorder. After each of the incidents which emotionally upset the ship's company—the announcement of the verdict, the execution, and the burial—Vere maintains discipline through enforcement of forms, issuing routine orders that he knows the men will obey.

The chief reason for immediate action on Billy's case is that an encounter with the enemy might take place at any time, and any weakening of discipline might result in defection that would mean defeat. Soon after the execution, and before the *Indomitable* rejoins the Mediterranean fleet, there is an engagement with the enemy. The well-disciplined British sailors fight valiantly and win the victory. Vere himself is fatally wounded fighting for his beloved forms.

The internal evidence as a whole shows, it seems to me, that Melville looked upon Vere as a sympathetic character. There is also a bit of external evidence on Melville's attitude toward the tragically involved commander. On the back of the dedication page of the[143] novel, Melville wrote the following annotation: "Both directly and indirectly the era lent emphasis to the difficulties professional and moral falling on Captain Vere by reason of the tragic event just recounted; difficulties not adequately to be estimated by the sea-officers of our time; and still less by landsmen."[37] If readers of today, whether military or civilian, cannot adequately estimate the moral and professional difficulties that fell on Captain Vere, are they qualified to pass judgment on his resolution of the difficulties? The implication appears to be that Melville himself does not condemn Vere. The reader, of course, as Melville remarked, is free to judge Vere for himself.

III

As an inside narrative, *Billy Budd* reveals Melville telling his own story as objectively as he could, not with self-pity, but with self-respect. Instead of being called his "Testament of Acceptance," it might perhaps better be called his apologia. In the character of Billy Budd he presents, one may say, the dominant tendencies of his young manhood; in Captain Vere he presents in essence the later Melville. The name *Budd* suggests youth; in a manuscript line not used in the final version Billy, who is also called Baby Budd, is referred to as "a flower of masculine strength and beauty, a flower, scarce yet released from the bud."[38] The name *Vere* brings to mind the Latin word for man, *vir*. The crucial point in Melville's development came when he realized the necessity for curbing the wild, rebellious spirit manifested in *Moby-Dick* and *Pierre*. The fact that the rebelliousness

---

37 *Ibid.*, p. 234, n. 12.
38 *Ibid.*, p. 219, n. 88.

was inspired, in part at least, by the highest idealism was no justification for its being tolerated, especially since it threatened to destroy his whole being.

Nearly forty years before Melville wrote *Billy Budd,* he developed the theme, most notably in Plinlimmon's tract in *Pierre,* that the heavenly wisdom of Christ is not in accord with the wisdom of this earth, and that anyone who attempts to live strictly by heavenly ideals is likely to become involved in "strange, *unique* follies and sins."[39] At the time of writing *Pierre* Melville was so wrapped up in his idealistic young hero that he presented the coldly rational Plinlimmon in a very satirical manner. It is worth remembering that although Pierre proceeds to his downfall, he does not throw[144] away Plinlimmon's pamphlet, but carries it about unknowingly in the lining of his overcoat—tucked away in his subconscious, as it were. The passing years brought about a change in Melville's attitude toward the teachings of the pamphlet. In writing *Billy Budd* he was sympathetic toward not only the Christlike Billy but also the philosophical Vere.

When Vere tells the court that in administering the laws of His Majesty's Navy they are restricted to considering the act alone, not the intent or nonintent, when he says that they are not responsible for the severity of the laws they administer, one should recall that as the King symbolizes the Deity, the laws in effect in His Majesty's Navy are symbolically the universal laws to which man must adapt himself, no matter what his personal opinion of them may be. It is only natural that Vere and his officers should be moved with pity for the essentially innocent sailor, but as commissioned officers their allegiance, as Vere points out, is not to Nature, but to the King, or God. The *Indomitable* proves its loyalty to the King by observing his rigid laws and by defeating the enemy ship, significantly named the *Athéiste.* Though this loyalty symbolizes Melville's realization that man must accept his place in the universal scheme decreed by God, one should not overlook the fact that the loyalty is based more on a sense of duty—in fact, of necessity—than on love. On the *Indomitable* it is Billy Budd rather than the King who is loved: the men preserve bits of the spar from which Billy was hanged as though they were chips from the Cross, and Vere's final words, uttered not with remorse, but with poignancy, are, "Billy Budd, Billy Budd."

At Melville's death there was found among his manuscripts together with *Billy Budd* a sketch entitled "Daniel Orme." Though it is too slight to have much value as literature, it is important as a brief symbolical self-portrait, and particularly so, in my opinion, since its kindred imagery and symbolism confirm much of what has

---

[39] *Pierre,* p. 250.

been said here about *Billy Budd*.[40] There are striking parallels in the experiences of Orme and Vere.

Both men spend most of their lives at sea aboard battleships, and though Orme, retired at the end, has not been in command of a ship,[145] he has been a "captain of the top." Both men are respected by their shipmates, but both remain somewhat apart. Vere is suspected by the Surgeon of suffering mental aberrations, and, similarly, Orme is suspected by some of his shipmates of piracy, which here, as in "I and My Chimney," symbolizes insanity. Orme, like Vere, is wounded fighting for "forms." Across the crucifix tattooed over his heart he bears a scar, which it is intimated he received repelling boarders; and Vere, under the flag of the "union and cross," is fatally wounded fighting the *Athéiste*. In his last days Orme frequently contemplates his scarred image of the crucifixion, and Vere dies murmuring of the crucified Billy Budd. In view of Melville's sea-and-land symbolism, with the sea representing abstract truth and the land empirical truth, it is important that both men die in port: Orme is found dead near a battery of rusty guns on a cliff looking seaward; Vere dies not aboard the *Indomitable* but on the gun-studded Rock of Gibraltar. Both men die calmly, with no apparent remorse.

It is not surprising that in these two symbolical narratives the image of the crucifixion figures so prominently. For Melville it had long been an image of human life, more suggestive of man's suffering than of man's hope. Men are "Cross-bearers all," to quote a phrase from *Clarel*.[41] In *Billy Budd* he develops the theme in all its magnitude; and for those who read the "inside narrative" he tells how he bore his own cross.[146]

---

40 On "Daniel Orme" as a self-portrait see William Braswell, *Melville's Religious Thought* (Durham, 1943), pp. 124–126. Richard Chase, *Herman Melville: A Critical Study* (New York, 1949), p. 298, and Newton Arvin, *Herman Melville* (New York, 1950), p. 288, both consider the sketch a self-portrait.

41 *Clarel* (London, 1924), IV, xxxiv.

EXPEDIENCY AND ABSOLUTE MORALITY IN *BILLY BUDD**

Wendell Glick

"Resolve as one may to keep to the main road," Melville wrote in *Billy Budd,* "some bypaths have an enticement not readily to be withstood. Beckoned by the genius of Nelson, knowingly, I am going to err in such a bypath."[1] With these words of caution to the reader who might object to the "literary sin" of digression, the author of *Moby Dick* launched into a spirited encomium upon the heroism of Lord Nelson, defending the Admiral against any "martial utilitarians" and "Benthamites of war" who might interpret his acts of "bravado" at Trafalgar which had resulted in his death to have been foolhardy and vain. For what reason, the question arises, did Melville feel that the eulogy on Nelson could justifiably be included in *Billy Budd?* What is the meaning of the attack upon Benthamites and utilitarians? This was no pot-boiler which required padding; surely his inclusion of the highly emotional defense of Nelson is significant for other reasons than that the chapter makes "more understandable Melville's hearty interest in martial exploits, sayings, and songs."[2]

At the time Melville was writing and revising *Billy Budd* he was in no mood to trifle with peccadilloes. "My vigor sensibly declines," he had written to Archibald MacMechan on 5 December 1889: "What little of it is left I husband for certain matters yet incomplete, and which indeed, may never be completed."[3] He could hardly have been husbanding his strength to communicate his "hearty interest in martial exploits"; his digression away from his narrative in order to

---

* From *PMLA,* LXVIII (March, 1953), 103–110, by permission of the publisher and author.

[1] Herman Melville, *Billy Budd,* ed. F. Barron Freeman (Cambridge, Mass., 1948), p. [13] 154 n. Citations to *Billy Budd* in the text of this article are to this, the best critical edition so far available. [Page references to the present volume are in square brackets.]

[2] For this reason, Freeman suggests, the digressions on Nelson are "important" (p. 42).

[3] Leon Howard, *Herman Melville* (Berkeley, 1951), p. 328.

praise Nelson must have served in his mind the more serious purpose of clarifying one of the "truths" for which, as he pointed out, *Billy Budd* was but the vehicle. The purpose of this article is to call attention to an aspect of one of these truths, heretofore unnoticed. Although it is much more, *Billy Budd* is the cogent fruition of a lifetime of observation and study of the eternal conflict between absolute morality and social expediency; and the digression on Nelson, though it intrudes upon the plot, is central to an understanding of Melville's final resolution of this crucial problem.

In writing *Billy Budd,* Melville made clear at the outset of his novel, he was writing no "romance"; he would not be bound, consequently, in[103] his delineation of the "Handsome Sailor," by any of the conventions usually followed in depicting a romantic hero. Nor would he be bound to refrain from digressing if digression served his purposes. His interest was less in art than in "Truth uncompromisingly told" (pp. [11, 63] 149 and 274). He was quite willing, he asserted, to sacrifice "the symmetry of form attainable in pure fiction" and to risk "ragged edges" on his final work if by so doing he could tell a story "having less to do with fable than with fact" (p. [63] 274). Thus relieved both from the conventional restrictions usually imposed by art and from the financial exigencies which had dictated the content of some of his early works, he would be free to deal forthrightly and honestly with issues far too serious to be treated cavalierly.

For his *raisonneur* Melville chose Captain "Starry" Vere, a clear-headed realist possessed of sufficient perspective as a result of broad human experience and extensive reading to enable him to weigh the most difficult alternatives and choose rationally between them. No person with lesser qualifications would serve. For the choice which Captain Vere had to make involved more than a simple distinction between blacks and whites; instead it was a choice between two standards of human behavior, to each of which man owed unquestioning loyalty. The Captain's decision, moreover, was to be Melville's as well; and Melville felt no disposition in the waning years of his life to trifle with reality and call the process truth-seeking.

Melville sympathized with Billy Budd as completely as did Captain Vere. He appreciated with the Captain the stark injustice of a situation which finds the individual condemned for adherence to a standard of behavior most men would consider noble and right. But he agreed with the Captain that justice to the individual is not the ultimate loyalty in a complex culture; the stability of the culture has the higher claim, and when the two conflict, justice to the individual must be abrogated to keep the order of society intact. Turning their backs upon one of the most cherished systems of ideas in the American tradition, a system typified by such individualists as Thoreau and Emerson, Melville and Captain Vere brought in the verdict that the claims of civilized society may upon occasion constitute a higher ethic than the claims of "natural law" and personal justice (p. [50] 245). The ultimate allegiance of the individual, in other words, is not to an absolute moral code, interpreted by his conscience and enlivened by his human sympathies, but to the utilitarian principle of social expediency.

To isolate his problem, to strip it of all irrelevant issues preparatory to making a critical examination of it, Melville chose as his setting a British vessel at sea. The ship-of-the-line *Indomitable,* a smooth-functioning[104] microcosm of society as a whole, was threatened with mutiny. Though the threat was remote, whatever would contribute to the end of knitting together the diverse individuals who made up the crew into a homogeneous unit which would act efficiently in an emergency was fully justified; conversely, that which jeopardized even slightly the clock-like functioning of the crew it was necessary to stamp out ruthlessly. His highest obligation, as Captain Vere conceived of it, was the preservation of the tight little society into which the crew had been welded, and the prevention of anything resembling anarchy. The transcendent responsibility of the leaders of the English nation, moreover, was the same as his own, writ large. An intensive study of history had confirmed his "settled convictions" against "novel opinion, social, political, and otherwise, which carried away as in a torrent no few minds in those days"; and he was "incensed at the innovators," not because their theories were inimical to the private interests of the privileged classes of which he was a member, but because such theories "seemed to him incapable of embodiment in lasting institutions," and "at war with the peace of the world and the good of mankind" (pp. [17] 163–164). The world as he viewed it was ruled by "forms"; "with mankind," Melville quotes him as saying, "forms, measured forms, are everything"; that was the import which he saw "in the story of Orpheus, with his lyre, spellbinding the wild denizens of the woods" (p. [63] 272). To preserve the ordered functioning of his crew Captain Vere was willing to sacrifice even the ideal of justice when the absolute necessity arose. What he objected to in Claggart was not that Claggart was remiss in his "duty of preserving order" but that the Master at Arms abridged the ideal of justice unnecessarily, even when the autonomy and general good of the crew were not at stake. Still, the maintenance of order came first, and it was rigorously safeguarded on the *Indomitable* "almost to a degree inconsistent with entire moral volition" (pp. [20] 172–173).

To the idea that order in society should be maintained at all cost Captain Vere adhered "disinterestedly," not because he desired such a regimented society, but because he believed it to be a practical necessity of this world. Like Plotinus Plinlimmon of *Pierre,* he preferred Christian ("Chronometrical") standards of absolute morality to the more mundane, utilitarian standard of expediency; but like Plinlimmon, he had concluded that Christian ideals were unworkable in everyday situations. He was fully aware that a regimented society abridged many private rights, but he realized also that in the absence of such a society a state of anarchy and chaos inevitably arose in which every human right was sacrificed. An ordered society at least guaranteed the preservation of *some* rights; and though this fell far short of the ideal of the preservation[105] of *all*, it was far better than the sort of "society" which, in the idealistic attempt to guarantee all rights, degenerated into chaos and so permitted their complete and total destruction. It was not a question of insuring all individual rights or a part of them; the choice was between insuring a part of them or none. The ideal society which abridged no prerogatives and guaranteed all private liberties was, in the considered opinion of Captain Vere, a figment of the imagination.

Recent events, Melville makes abundantly plain, had been responsible for the Captain's position. The Nore Mutiny, though it had been precipitated by the failure of the authorities to redress the legitimate grievances of the seamen, had threatened the military usefulness of the "indispensable fleet" upon which the stability of the entire English nation depended, and consequently had been ruthlessly suppressed (pp. [11–13] 150–153). The cataclysmic French Revolution had taught its bitter lesson, both to Captain Vere and to his creator. To the Captain the principle involved in the two events was the same: the English sailors at Nore, in running up "the British colors with the union and cross wiped out," had transmuted "the flag of founded law and freedom defined" into "the red meteor of unbridled and unbounded revolt" of the French. "Reasonable discontent," Melville pointed out, "growing out of practical grievances in the fleet had been ignited into irrational combustion as by live cinders blown across the Channel from France in flames" (p. [11–12] 151). No price was too great to pay to keep such unhinging forces of anarchy in check; in giving his life to destroy the *Athéiste,* Captain Vere sacrificed himself in defense of the *sine qua non* of civilized existence and in opposition to the false, unworkable doctrines of the French Revolution. The triumph of the *Indomitable* over the *Athéiste* was the triumph of order over chaos.

Yet how staggering was the cost of a stable society! Having decided upon the absolute necessity for maintaining unweakened the strength of the social fabric, Melville shuddered when he contemplated the price exacted in terms of human values; and *Billy Budd* became the balance-sheet upon which he reckoned the price men have to pay for the ordered society which they have to have. The most obvious price was the destruction of "Nature's Nobleman," the superlatively innocent person: every Billy Budd impressed by an *Indomitable* is forced to leave his *Rights-of-Man* behind. To the destruction of innocent persons, moreover, it was necessary to add the mental suffering of the individual forced to make moral judgments. But the total cost is not met even by the sacrifice of Billy Budds and the suffering of Captain Veres; social stability based upon expediency is paid for also with a general, blighting, human mediocrity. The standards of any civilized society are the standards of[106] the great mass of men who make up its bulk; and when maintenance of the stability of society becomes the supreme obligation of every person, the result is a levelling of the superior persons down to the level of the mass. The chief personal virtue becomes "prudence"; the end most worth seeking for becomes "that manufacturable thing known as respectability," so often allied with "moral obliquities" (p. [10] 147), and occasionally, as in the case of Claggart, indistinguishable even from "natural depravity." "Civilization," Melville remarks categorically, "especially of the austerer sort, is auspicious" to natural depravity because natural depravity "folds itself in the mantle of respectability" by avoiding "vices or small sins" and by refraining from all excesses; in short, by exhibiting the prudence which is the only virtue society demands. The natural depravity of Claggart was so insidious because it lacked the trappings in which society expects to see evil garbed, and instead, prudently enfolded itself in "the mantle of respectability" (pp. [26] 185–186). Prudence, while being the mark of the socially adjusted man who rigidly adheres to the utilitarian principle of expediency, may also be the last refuge of scoundrels.

But even when prudence did not take the extreme form of moral obliquity, even when it was not "habitual with the subtler depravity" (p. [29] 195), as it proved to be in the case of Claggart, it left its mark upon the people in the world of Billy Budd. The most "prudent" characters discharged faithfully their "duty" to their king even when to do so clashed with moral scruple, but they fell far short of the personal heroism which inspires others and vitalizes them into acts. Captain Graveling of the *Rights-of-Man* was "the sort of person whom everybody agrees in calling 'a respectable man' "; he was a lover of "peace and quiet" and the possessor of "much prudence" which caused "overmuch disquietude in him," but he was by and large a pedestrian individual who could hardly be depended upon to make any signal contribution to human progress (p. [5] 137). The old ascetic Dansker had learned from experience a "bitter prudence" which had taught him never to interfere, never to give advice, in other words, to solve the problem of his social responsibility by escaping into a shell of cynicism, and by so doing had disqualified himself for service to society (p. [34] 205). The *Indomitable*'s "prudent surgeon" was singularly unequipped to pass moral judgments and would have "solved" the problem of Billy's murder of Claggart by dropping the whole affair into the lap of the Admiral (pp. [44, 45] 229, 231). Even Captain Vere, who possessed in eminent measure the "two qualities not readily interfusable" demanded of every English sea-commander at the time "prudence and rigor" (p. [45] 234), did not earn Melville's highest accolade as a member of "great Nature's nobler order" until he let himself[107] "melt back into what remains primeval in our formalized humanity"; in short, until he forgot temporarily his "military duty," his prudence, and acted in a manner difficult to reconcile with strict social expediency (p. [54] 252).[4]

To what do these examples of prudence, the highest ethic of utilitarian philosophers, add up? Simply this: in making social expediency an ethic superior to absolute morality, Melville found himself pushed perilously close to a *Weltanschauung* which would admit slight, if any, possibility of personal greatness. Could prudence ever be truly heroic? A society which elevated prudence above all other virtues seemed to be anathema to the sort of moral adventuresomeness which Melville loved, and which for him set the great man off from the mediocre one. Yet such a society seemed to be the only sort which could safeguard men from the perils of "irrational combustion" which followed hard upon an idealism permitted to run its free course unrestrained. Here lay a crucial dilemma: was the race doomed to accept mediocrity as the price of its self-preservation, or was it still possible in a complex society for great private virtues to generate and grow?

Emotionally unequipped to reconcile himself to the bleaker alternative toward which both his experience and his reason had led him, Melville turned to history in the hope of discovering a figure of heroic dimensions whose life would free him from his impasse. Having played the role of champion of man's dignity and greatness for a lifetime, he did not feel that he could relinquish it now; and in the person of Nelson, "the greatest sailor since the world began," he found his answer.[5] Though he recognized that many changes had taken place since Trafalgar, that the "symmetry and grand lines" of Nelson's *Victory* seemed obsolete in a world of "*Monitors* and yet mightier hulls of the European ironsides," he nonetheless insisted that "to anybody who can hold the Present at its worth without being inappreciative of the Past," the "solitary old hulk at Portsmouth" spoke eloquent truth. If he could no longer embrace the simple faith of his youth when he had believed in a law "coeval with mankind, dictated by God himself, superior in obligation to any other," when he had advocated the abolition of flogging on the grounds that "it is not a dollar-and-cent question of expediency; it is a matter of *right and wrong*";[6] if the corrosive years had eaten away for him such immutable standards, he could at least salvage somehow a foundation for personal greatness and heroism. Nelson was the man he needed.[108]

---

4 Melville conjectures that this is what transpired while the Captain spoke with Billy privately in the cabin.

5 The scattered references to *Billy Budd* which follow are to Ch. iv, pp. [13–14] 154–157, passim.

6 *White Jacket* (Boston, 1892), pp. 138, 139.

He admitted that strict "martial utilitarians," believers in the rigorous application of an inexorable social expediency to every particular situation, would be inclined to take issue with his estimate of Nelson's greatness, even perhaps "to the extent of iconoclasm." For Nelson's exposure of his own person in battle at Trafalgar appeared on the surface to have been militarily inexpedient, even vain and foolhardy; his value to the cause for which he fought was so great that he should have sacrificed his natural desire for personal heroism to the higher principle of preserving a life which was indispensable to the general good. Had his life been preserved and his command of the fleet therefore been retained, the mistakes made by his successor in command might have been avoided; and his sagacity might well have averted the shipwreck with its horrible loss of life which followed the battle. So the "Benthamites of war" argued, and, Melville admitted, with some plausibility; using only the immediate circumstances of the engagement as their criteria they could convict Nelson of behavior out of harmony with the general good, and on these grounds strip him of the glory with which Englishmen had invested him.

But to this sort of iconoclasm Melville would not accede for a moment. "Personal prudence," he countered, "even when dictated by quite other than selfish considerations, is surely no special virtue in a military man; while an excessive love of glory, exercising to the uttermost heartfelt sense of duty, is the first." The Benthamites were wrong; in applying their principle of social expediency to Nelson's deed "of foolhardiness and vanity" they failed to calculate the strength of purpose which such a "challenge to death" injects into the arteries of a nation. Nelson's deed was "expedient" to a degree they lacked the vision to perceive; his name had become a "trumpet to the blood" more stimulating even to the hearts of Englishmen than the name of Wellington; the act which on the surface seemed sheer "bravado" still inspired posterity to deeds of greatness.

Unless, Melville argued, Nelson's "challenge to death" could be considered an act of supreme heroism, conformable to the highest ideals governing human behavior, no deed could be truly heroic; and this possibility he refused to entertain. The vitality of Nelson's example was immortal. In 1891, shortly after he had made his own will, Melville composed this enthusiastic tribute to another great man who had also glimpsed a premonition that death was near:

At Trafalgar, Nelson, on the brink of opening the fight, sat down and wrote his last brief will and testament. If under the presentiment of the most magnificent of all victories, to be crowned by his own glorious death, a sort of priestly motive led him to dress his person in the jewelled vouchers of his own shining deeds; if[109] thus to have adorned himself for the altar and the sacrifice were indeed vainglory, then affectation and fustian is each truly heroic line in the great epics and dramas, since in such lines the poet but embodies in verse those exaltations of sentiment that a nature like Nelson, the opportunity being given, vitalizes into acts. (p. [14] 157)

The question naturally arises whether Melville intended the digression on Nelson to illuminate the final scene of the novel. Might the answer be that the hanging of Billy Budd is Melville's final commentary upon the theme of the impracticability of absolute standards in a world necessarily ruled by expediency? Billy's noble devotion to absolute justice and right throughout the novel made him a sort of personification of the moral law; his death must have meant for Melville, consequently, that the standard of behavior to which Billy gave his allegiance, though a noble one, is simply unworkable when applied to complex social relationships. There was something unearthly about the death of Billy Budd: he was "an angel of God" (p. [44] 229), returning without fear to his Maker; his pinioned figure at the yard-end behaved like that of no mortal man; to the sailors aboard the *Indomitable* the spar from which Billy's body had hung was thought of for some years as a piece of the Cross. The luminous night of the morning when Billy was to be hanged passed away like the prophet Elijah disappearing into heaven in his chariot and dropping his mantle to Elisha. Billy was too good for this world; he properly belonged to another, not to this; and the moral principles from which he acted were appropriate enough for the world to which he belonged. But in a society composed of men, not angels—in a society in which even Claggarts are to be found—an inferior standard, that of expediency, is the only workable one.[7][110]

---

[7] This article is peripheral to a study of the concept of "expediency" in American thought, undertaken with the aid of a grant from the American Council of Learned Societies.

Billy Budd as Myth

THE RITE OF SACRAMENT*

Richard Chase

. . . .

At the deep levels of *Billy Budd* there is a massive and terrible image, which, it seems to me, moved the aged Melville so overpoweringly that he was unable to give it direct expression. As Melville says at one point in *Billy Budd*, "every ... form of life has its secret mines and dubious sides; the side popularly disclaimed." On the night before Billy Budd's execution, the ship, with its decks, is like the story itself. "The night was luminous on the spar-deck, but otherwise in the cavernous ones below—levels so very like the tiered galleries in a coal-mine."

The real theme of *Billy Budd* is castration and cannibalism, the ritual murder and eating of the Host. During his trial Billy proclaims his faithfulness to the king and to Captain Vere by saying, "I have eaten the King's bread, and I am true to the King." When, "without remorse," the dying Captain Vere murmurs, "Billy Budd, Billy Budd," he expresses faithfulness, dependence, and longing. He had eaten of the Host, and he was true to the Host. After forty years Melville had returned to the theme of *Typee*. In that book the young hero had extricated himself from the valley by a sudden exchange of passivity for action. Billy Budd is fatally passive, his acts of violence being unconsciously calculated to ensure his final submission. All of Billy's conscious acts are toward passivity, the first one being his quick acquiescence in his impressment, an act which causes the hero-worshiping sailors to regard him with "surprise" and "silent reproach." In symbolic language, Billy Budd is seeking his own castration—seeking to yield up his vitality to an authoritative but kindly father, whom he finds in Captain Vere. When anyone else stirs the depths of Billy's longing, threatening to bring his unconscious thoughts to consciousness, he flies into a sudden rage. When Red-Whiskers, a

* From Richard Chase, *Herman Melville: A Critical Study*, 269–277. Copyright 1949 by Richard Chase and used with permission of The Macmillan Company and the author. [My title. Ed.]

sailor who had once been a butcher, maliciously digs Billy in the ribs to show him "just whence a sirloin steak was cut," Billy gives him a "terrible drubbing." And when the minion of Claggart approaches Billy on the moonlit deck and, holding out two shining guineas, says, "See, they are yours, Bill," Billy Budd stammeringly threatens to toss him over the rail. The persistent feminine imagery Melville associates with Billy and his statement that "above all" there was "something in the mobile[269] expression, and every chance attitude and movement suggestive of a mother eminently favored by Love and the Graces," indicate that Billy has identified himself with the mother at a pre-Oedipean level and has adopted the attitude of harmlessness and placation toward the father in order to avoid the hard struggle of the Oedipus conflict. The Oedipus conflict entails, of course, the idea of one's incestuous guilt and one's desire to kill one's father. The psychoanalyst might say that Billy Budd has avoided the Oedipus struggle by forming an attachment to the mother at the pre-phallic level of "oral eroticism" and has allayed his fears of castration by symbolically castrating himself (by being consciously submissive) and by repressing his rage and hostility against the father in order to placate him. That all Billy's rage and hostility against the father are unconscious is symbolized by the fact that whenever it is aroused it cannot find expression in spoken language. Billy can only stutter and use his fists. This is a mechanism for keeping himself from admitting his own guilt and his own destructiveness. For indeed Billy destroys not only Claggart but himself—and even Captain Vere. For a cloud seems to pass over Vere in his last days, and he dies without achieving the rewards his character had seemed to predestine him to achieve; he dies longing for a "child-man" he had once known.

The food symbolism need not be labored. It recurs frequently, and it is the symbolism which takes us down most swiftly into the coherent lower strata of the story, where there is "a subterranean fire ... eating its way deeper and deeper." Melville even symbolizes moral qualities by their taste, the innocent character having an "untampered-with flavor like that of berries" as against the guilty character, which has the "questionable smack of a compounded wine." Frequently Billy Budd is compared with animals—a heifer, a horse, a dog, a nightingale, a goldfinch. When he is hanged, he ascends to the yard-arm like a "singing-bird," watched from below by a "wedged mass of upturned faces"—as if the sailors were birds expecting to be fed. It is said of Billy Budd (the Lamb of God) that the serpent has never bitten him, but after the accusation Claggart is described as a snake.

The idea of Billy as Host is established early in the story. When the lieutenant of the *Indomitable* goes aboard the *Rights-of-Man* in[270] search of new hands and immediately selects Billy Budd, he drinks some of the captain's grog almost as if conscious of performing a ritual. "Lieutenant," says the captain, "you are going to take my best man from me, the jewel of 'em." " 'Yes, I know,' rejoined the other, immediately drawing back the tumbler preliminary to a replenishing; 'yes, I know. Sorry.' " The captain, referring to the pacifying effect Billy has had on his troublesome sailors, then says, "A virtue went out of him, sugaring the sour ones. They took to him like hornets to treacle." Metaphors such as these evoke the primitive rite of slaughtering the young hero in order to eat his flesh and thus obtain his "virtue," his strength, or his heroic quality.

Later in the story Billy Budd spills his soup at mess, and Claggart, happening to pass by at the moment, is inwardly enraged, though outwardly he is only suavely and ambiguously satirical. Melville seems to feel that the enormous eruption of hostile emotion in Claggart may strike the reader as excessive and hence unbelievable. He therefore prefaces one of his comments on the spilled soup with a paragraph which says in effect that the most ordinary event may be a symbolic act which can arouse momentous passions:

> Passion, and passion in its profoundest, is not a thing demanding a palatial stage whereupon to play its part. Down among the groundlings, among the beggars and rakers of the garbage, profound passion is enacted. And the circumstances that provoke it, however trivial or mean, are no measure of its power.

The palatial stage is surely the conscious mind or the realm of conscious art, and the abode of beggars and rakers of the garbage is the unconscious mind. There are "beggars" in the unconscious mind, calling the ego back among the rakers of garbage, as Billy Budd calls his own ego back. And is not this whole passage intended as a statement that *Billy Budd* does not present the reader with a "palatial stage" where profoundest passions are enacted but that, instead, these passions are being enacted "down among the groundlings"? This comes close to telling us not only what is wrong with the story—simply that its profound passions do not find adequate objective representation—but also what is wrong with Billy Budd as tragic hero —that there is no "palatial stage" in his[271] personality, no conscious structure, no mind whose disintegration we should watch with pity and terror rather than merely with bewilderment and an obscure sense of loss.

When Claggart spies the spilled soup, it seemed to him "the sly escape of a spontaneous feeling on Billy's part more or less answering to the antipathy on his own." He feels that Billy has insulted him. But what is the nature of the insult? Presumably that, in spilling the soup, Billy has symbolically exposed himself to Claggart as the Host, the vessel from which issues "virtue." ("Handsomely done, my lad!" cries Claggart. "And handsome is as handsome did it, too!") The spilled soup has also exposed Claggart's guilt as an eater of the Host and, furthermore, Claggart's fear of his own unconscious desire to be like Billy; for the psychological content of Claggart's desire to share Billy's innocence is his desire to be the passive Host.

Melville tells us that Claggart's jaw is heavy out of proportion with his otherwise delicately shaped face—Claggart's unconscious motives center upon orality. This occurs to us when, for example, he smiles at Billy Budd with an ambiguously "glittering dental satire." One of Claggart's "cunning corporals" is called Squeak, "so nick-named by the sailors on account of his squeaky voice and sharp visage ferreting about the dark corners of the lower decks after interlopers, satirically suggesting to them the idea of a rat in a cellar." Squeak spies on Billy Budd and in this capacity is described as the "purveyor" who "feeds Claggart's passions."

I am sure that much of the sacramental symbolism in *Billy Budd* is conscious and intended. But some of it may be less conscious. One cannot be sure how much Melville means by pointing out that two other partisans of Claggart in compromising Billy Budd (two of Claggart's "messmates," they are called) are the Armourer and the Captain of the Hold; but it is a haunting idea that the Armourer represents Teeth and the Captain of the Hold represents Belly. Nor can one say what Thyestean implications there may be in the use of parts of the body in referring to Claggart, whose nickname is Jimmy Legs and whose official title is Master-at-Arms.

As the story concludes, the grim symbolism occurs more frequently and with more intensity. In the captain's cabin Claggart's "mesmeric glance," which Melville compares with "the hungry[272] lurch of the torpedo fish," quickly determines Billy's fate. It is the overt threat of castration which always sets off the explosion of Billy's unconscious fears and resentments. There is a terrible upwelling of his passive emotions, as if in a last attempt to control their aggressive counterparts. Briefly Billy has the expression of "a condemned vestal priestess at the moment of her being buried alive, and in the first struggle against suffocation"—images which convey both the desire for, and the fear of, castration.* But such emotions as these Billy cannot express consciously. He stutters, and strikes Claggart.

Describing the scene in which Vere informs Billy Budd of the sentence, Melville says, "there is no telling the sacrament." There is no telling; but the sacrament can be symbolized. Lying manacled

---

* The psychoanalysts tell us that suffocation is sometimes identified in the unconscious with castration. In connection with the cabin scene, the following passage is significant: "Quite often a patient begins to stutter when he is particularly eager to prove a point. Behind his apparent zeal he has concealed a hostile or sadistic tendency to destroy his opponent by means of words, and the stuttering is both a blocking of and a punishment for this tendency. Still more often stuttering is exacerbated by the presence of prominent or authoritative persons, that is, of paternal figures against whom the unconscious hostility is most intense." O. Fenichel, *The Psychoanalytic Theory of Neuroses*, pp. 312–313.

on the deck during the night, Billy is like "a patch of discolored snow ... lingering at some upland cave's black mouth." His terrible experiences are of the order that "devour our human tissues." The skeleton begins to show under Billy's cheek for the first time; he lies between two cannon as if "nipped in the vise of fate." After the hanging of this Lamb of God, after the chaplain has knelt down "on his marrow bones" to pray (as the ballad of "Billy in the Darbies" says), after the night has passed and it is full day, "the fleece of low-hanging vapor had vanished, licked up by the sun that late had so glorified it." The very patriarch of the universe feeds on Billy Budd.

The passage Melville calls "Digression" is difficult and obscure; but I venture the following account. The purser and the surgeon discuss the absence of spasm in Billy's body. (They are at mess during this discussion: we are continually reminded in *Billy Budd* of the verbal kinship of "mess" with the ritual word "mass.") The purser is "a rather ruddy, rotund person, more accurate as an accountant than profound as a philosopher." The surgeon is "spare[273] and tall" (the same words used to describe Claggart): he is caustic, austere, and something of an intellectual. The two men are opposite types. The purser is the unthinking human animal who kills, vicariously, in order to eat. He is the simple cannibal, as is indicated by his placid rotundity (his being like a purse) and by his crude belief that Billy controlled his spasm by "will power." The surgeon is, like Claggart, a lean, emotionally complex and ambivalent sadist: he is more interested in murder than in food, as may be symbolized by his hastily leaving the mess table to get back to a patient in the sick bay. Thus, this very horrifying passage is not really a digression: it is a brief scene which universalizes the theme of the story by presenting two opposite mythical types of man lingering, as it were, over the body.

As the body of Billy Budd, wrapped in canvas and weighted with cannon balls, slides over the rail, the sailors "who had just beheld the prodigy of repose in the form suspended in air" think of the same form "foundering in the deeps"—an image of the act of eating. Over the spot where Billy has sunk, gaunt sea birds wheel and scream; and though the birds are predictably moved by "mere animal greed for prey," the sight has a surprising effect on the sailors. "An uncertain movement began among them, in which some encroachment was made." It is a brief moment of potentially mutinous commotion, which we can understand by noticing that the captain and his officers are symbolically connected with the birds, a connection the sailors unconsciously make. Immediately after the hanging, there had been a similar murmurous impulse to mutiny among the sailors. But the ship's officers had acted quickly. Their authoritative voice was heard in the whistle of the boatswain and his mates, which was "shrill as the shriek of the sea-hawk," which "pierced the low ominous sound" and "dissipated" it, so that in a moment or two "the throng was thinned by one half."

In a man-of-war world, Melville is saying, law feeds on man, being only a translation into social forms of that "horrible vulturism of earth" of which he had spoken in *Moby-Dick*. And with a complex human vulturism Captain Vere feeds on Billy Budd. Notice the sexual-sacramental character of Vere's reaction to Billy's spontaneous "God bless Captain Vere." At these words, "Captain Vere, either through stoic self-control or a sort of momentary[274] paralysis induced by emotional shock, stood erectly rigid as a musket in the ship-armor's rack." The sexual spasm does not occur in Billy Budd because Billy's vitality or "virtue" has been symbolically transferred to Vere. And yet the transference is ambiguous; paralysis and rigidity suggest death just as surely as erection and the potentiality of the musket suggest life. New vitality has been given to Vere as captain and exponent of martial law (Vere as "musket"), but as man and father he has been stricken.

The intimation of Melville's passages about Lord Nelson is that had Nelson been aboard the *Indomitable* instead of Vere (the two are inferentially compared on several occasions), all this might not have happened, or—and perhaps this is the central point—if it had happened, no subsequent cloud would have passed over Nelson, as it does over Vere. Nelson is the invulnerable and fully mature father, a mythical hero standing behind Captain Vere, a less majestic figure. Nelson already has the qualities of Billy Budd, so that the ritual transference of vitality need not ruin him with its cruel ambiguities. Nelson has the heroic vitality of Billy Budd and the brilliance and audacity of the "jewel" among sailors; it is Nelson's fatherhood which allows him to make "ornate publication" of the very qualities, in sublimated form, which Billy Budd, in the form of infantile rage and hostility, represses. As Melville presents him, Nelson, the "Great Sailor," is the ultimate heroic possibility of the man-of-war world. But he is not of that order of hero represented by Jack Chase; Jack Chase symbolizes a culture beyond the boundaries of Nelson's world. Nelson would never leave his ship to take part in a republican revolution, as Jack Chase did. He is the mythical father whose very presence on board ship, as Melville says, is enough to forestall an incipient mutiny—the uprising, that is, of the sons against the father.

The imposing structure of personality Melville attributes to Nelson is beyond the reach of Captain Vere because Vere's moral stability is not proof against the uprising of the sons. In Claggart he sees his own hostility toward Billy Budd. (The relation of Vere to Claggart and Billy is the relation of a father to his sons, one of whom assumes the aggressive and hostile role of the father and the other of whom assumes the passive role of the mother.) In Billy Budd, Captain Vere sees his own imperfectly redeemed childhood.[275] Vere, imposing and even heroic as he is, must repeatedly return to his own childhood to feed on it and to murder it. For him there is no other way of supporting, of nourishing, the structure of consciousness, order, authority, and legality which constitutes the man-of-war world. The man-of-war world destroys itself by feeding on its own vitality, as the vulture feeds upon Prometheus.

This is in itself a moving idea; and so is the implied identification of Billy Budd with Christ. But is there not still another source of the massive emotion which rests uneasily beneath the imperfect surface of *Billy Budd?* Consider the connections Melville makes between the captains and literature. Nelson's ship is "poetic"; it has "symmetry" and "grand lines." Of Nelson at Trafalgar, Melville writes:

> If under the presentiment of the most magnificent of all victories, to be crowned by his own glorious death, a sort of priestly motive led him to dress his person in the jewelled vouchers of his own shining deeds; if thus to have adorned himself for the altar and the sacrifice were indeed vainglory, then affectation and fustian is each truly heroic line in the great epics and dramas, since in such lines the poet embodies in verse those exaltations of sentiment that a nature like Nelson, the opportunity being given, vitalizes into acts.

Homer is a kind of Nelson. They are the same mythical hero—great captains of the mind, the sea, and the man-of-war world. The author of *Moby-Dick* was such a captain.

Captain Vere "loved books." His name, "Vere," signifies (besides "man") "truth"; he is a speaker of the truth. Both his mien and his interests connect him with different kinds of literature than that associated with Nelson. He likes books "treating of actual men and events, no matter of what era." Such a man of truth is Herman Melville, who writes concerning *Billy Budd:* "The symmetry of form attainable in pure fiction cannot so readily be achieved in a narration essentially having less to do with fable than with fact. Truth uncompromisingly told will always have its ragged edges."

In *Typee,* Melville had already pictured himself as Billy Budd, the youth with the nameless malady who shrank with such inexplicable fear from the tattooing instrument, tipped with a shark's tooth, and who discovered that his elders—the fathers and the warriors of the tribe—were cannibals.[276]

Lord Nelson is not on "the main road"; he is on "a bypath." The central autobiographical figure in *Billy Budd* is Captain Vere. The dark and moving image of the book is Melville as the devourer of his own childhood. An old man with sons of his own, Melville is overwhelmingly moved with pity for the passive, hermaphrodite youth, an image of himself, who must continuously be killed in the rite of the sacrament if books are to be written or the man-of-war world sustained—or indeed if life is to go on at all.

Surely, then . . . I contradict myself. Billy Budd *is* a deep one and a man-trap (but if he is, he cannot be "innocent"!). His personality has extensive moral significance and psychological reality. He is highly effective, since he kills Claggart and even Captain Vere. And Captain Vere, not Billy Budd, is the tragic hero of the story.

It seems to me, however, that how one judges *Billy Budd* depends on what level of the story one is talking about. Potentially the story is one of the greatest tragedies of Western literature. But the upper level, the conscious structure, the "palatial stage" is far too uncreated, self-contradictory, and noncommittal to articulate the underlying images. At the explicit symbolic and dramatic levels of the story Melville draws back in awe from Billy Budd and can speak of him only by painful acts of will which in the very process of becoming articulate cut themselves off from the deepest sources of emotion and thus remain inexpressive. Billy Budd's stammering is Melville's own. When Billy Budd speaks articulately, he misrepresents his own deepest emotions. So does Melville.[277]

Billy Budd as Art

THE UNITY OF *BILLY BUDD**

Ray B. West, Jr.

. . . .

. . . The subject of . . . [*Billy Budd*] is adequately suggested in Melville's brief preface, the opening sentence of which reads as follows:

The year 1797, the year of this narrative, belongs to a period which as every thinker now feels, involved a crisis for Christendom not exceeded in its undetermined momentousness at the time by any other era whereof there is record.

This crisis, of course, represents the events surrounding the revolution in France, and it is significant that Melville apparently saw the events of the mutinies at Spithead and at the Nore as symbolic of the threat to world order posed by the revolution. Any reader of Melville knows

---

* From *Hudson Review*, V (Spring, 1952), pp. 120–127, reprinted by permission of the author.

that he was greatly concerned with the historic development of mankind and that he saw Christianity as the center of an order which seemed gradually but inevitably to be passing away. It was probably because of his view that he could think of himself only as a nominal, not an orthodox, Christian. Any reader of *Clarel* understands the approximate terms upon which this state of mind was based[121] during the later years of Melville's life. Both *Clarel* and *Billy Budd* might have been titled, less imaginatively, "The Crisis of Christendom", with Christendom standing not only for the formal aspects of religion, but for all of the philosophical, political, and moral concerns of Man.

In these terms Billy Budd is Man—Christian man as well as historic man. Though he is presented with obvious simplicity, he contains the ambiguities of all of Melville's heroes from Ahab to The Confidence Man. In Christian terms he is Christ, but with typical Christian ambiguity, he is both the Son of Man and the Son of God. Whence came he? In philosophical and political terms, he sailed first as a common sailor on the *Rights of Man*, but was later impressed aboard his Majesty's warship the *Indomitable*. It is remarkable how little attention critics have paid to the names of these two vessels, as well as to the ship which appears at the end of the story: the French warship *Athéiste*, formerly the *St. Louis*. The contrast between life aboard the *Rights of Man* and that aboard the *Indomitable* is the contrast between the Lockean and the Hobbesian points of view. The order of the first is that imposed by Billy's primitive innocence: the common-sense example of good backed up by physical force when necessary. The *Indomitable* is ruled by a concept of absolute order imposed by authority and depending upon fealty to the source of legislated power. Historically, however, it is the distinction between primitive society (which, of course, Melville knew well and at first hand) and the era of what he called "citified man". Theologically, it is the contrast of pagan and Christian order.

Freeman presents evidence to show that at one point Melville considered naming the *Indomitable*, the *Bellipotente*. Such a title must have seemed to him finally too inclusive, too pointedly aimed at the religious level of his tale. Nevertheless, the religious level is primary during the period of Billy's difficulties aboard the second ship, and the parallel of Billy's execution for technical mutiny and the crucifixion have been clearly and commonly seen. Christ's godlike innocence is mirrored in Billy's natural innocence; Christ's humanity in Billy's natural (physical) defect of speech; Christ's agony in submitting to the Will of Heaven in Billy's submission to the authority of Captain Vere. Captain Vere's exclamation following the death of Claggart (the naturally depraved) by the hand of Billy—"Struck dead by an angel of God. Yet the Angel must hang!"—reflects the paradox of atonement by which Christ suffered the agony of death in order to release mankind from the bondage of evil.

It is clear that Melville saw the idea of the Fall and the Atonement as an accurate image of man's predicament . . . ; this level of *Billy Budd* is the one [with] which critics have primarily concerned themselves. What is important is that Melville held it *as image*, not as orthodox religion. As such it was nearer an aesthetic than a theological concept. This is important, because it follows that the crucifixion[122] becomes tragedy, mirroring man's incompleteness; the victory over evil is transient and incomplete. . . .*

In *Billy Budd* Melville is merely consulting "historic memory", and what he discovers is that man and God are always the same. Billy is budding man, yet he is also the budding God. As primitive man Billy lives at comparative ease with his shipmates aboard the *Rights of Man*—a society similar to that pictured in *Typee*. Transferred, however, to the *Indomitable*—emerging into the era of citified man, he has left nature behind him, except as he himself represents it aboard the second vessel. As a representative of nature, he does the *natural* thing, strikes out at the evil with which he is confronted. It is Claggart's eloquence (the ability to make a fair case for an evil cause) which is the mark of his duplicity. The mark of primitive man is his completeness, his oneness with nature; but he lacks eloquence, he depends upon intuition and action. Citified man faces nature, as John Crowe Ransom has stated handsomely in a recent article, "in guilt and fear toward that Nature who no longer contained him but indifferently confronted him." Melville has Captain Vere say, after acknowledging that Billy's action was no more than "natural": "But do these buttons that we wear attest that our allegiance is to Nature? No, to the King."

The question I take it Melville is raising here is this: If the King's authority is gone, and Nature's, what then supports us? Billy dies for his impulsive act with a prayer for Captain Vere (*vir*—man) upon his lips. A little later the *Indomitable* meets up with the French warship *Athéiste* (formerly the King's ship, the *St. Louis*) and engages her. The *Indomitable* survives the engagement, sinking the *Athéiste*, but Captain Vere, who is also the old god, perhaps even the father of Billy, dies with Billy's name upon his lips, not, as Melville says, "in accents of remorse", but as though transferring his authority to his son: Billy the Son of God and the Son of Man; God become Man and Man become God.

It seems clear that this is Melville's view of the crucifixion—the old God superseded by the new; God as myth. The story of Billy Budd

---

* Deleted passages are quotations from *Clarel* and other late poems of Melville that clarify the direction of his thinking at the time he composed *Billy Budd*. Pertinent quotations from these verses are utilized later in the essay, but quoted without reference to their source. [Ed.]

then represents the origin of myth, myth which mirrors man's tragic situation; but is not an attempt at tragedy itself. It is set in a period which represents, in Melville's words, "a crisis for Christendom", a period in which atheism is averted but[123] which has only (possibly) in the story of Billy Budd brought forth a new myth to replace it. *Billy Budd* is to be seen, then, somewhat as prophecy, or as an expression of faith. . . .

[Melville's tale] is [thus] an example of how the new birth will come, winning for mankind a unity such as they knew under Christianity, under the gods of antiquity, or in their primitive innocence. . . .

If the subject of *Billy Budd* is, as we suggest, the renewal of myth, is it Melville's intention to imply that we are simply awaiting the arrival of a new Messiah? In one sense, yes. We must not assume, as did Tully, that since the old gods are gone no new ones will arise to perform the unification performed by the old. On the other hand, Melville is quite specific about a certain danger—the danger of following false gods; and he is equally specific about the method whereby he believes the new will be enabled to arise. It is this which the critics of *Billy Budd* have heretofore failed to see in those passages which they have labeled extraneous.

Let us begin first with the danger. I have said that the victim of Billy's natural wrath, Claggart, clothed his duplicity by a fairness of appearance which included his ability to speak falsehood under the appearance of truth. Undisguised truth (which is what Billy's innocence represents) is hateful because antipodal to evil. Billy is budding man—primitive man: John Locke's *tabula rasa*. Claggart is the Hobbesian man in whom cunning and intelligence have been substituted for brute force. Mythical man (or Captain Vere) stands squarely between these two opposing concepts. He is intelligent but dreamy—sometimes known as "Starry" Vere. He wears the authority of his office openly[124] and plainly, as did Lord Nelson, who insisted upon wearing the scarlet and gold-braid even in the midst of battle. The life of Vere (and Nelson) is open to scrutiny, and upon a certain level it is reflected in the beauty of their vessels, the ornaments of their office, the attractions of ceremony, and the eloquence of their commands. Upon another level, however, such ornaments only served to mask the ugly injustices afflicting the common sailors under their command. Here is Melville's dilemma, and the dilemma which supplies the dramatic framework for his tale. If we correct the injustices in the name of humanity, do we not almost commit ourselves to the giving up of all of those beauties which the old order had cherished? Yes, Melville finally concedes, we do. We exchange Nelson's ornate dress for drab, because in calling attention to himself, Nelson endangered the lives of those under him. We relinquish the ceremony of authority, because to delay weighing anchor as Nelson did was dangerous and impractical in a world where ceremony is no longer observed. We surrender the grand lines of Nelson's flagship *Victory* to the more functional and less beautiful design of the *Monitor*. Yet we do not accede to the demands of revolution—atheism. We have come full circle, but only in the sense that pagan civilization had come full circle at the time of Tully. . . .

We then are faced by the same danger which Captain Vere faced in his engagement with the *Athéiste:* civil barbarism. The *Athéiste* is, significantly, not a vessel in its own right, but one merely captured and renamed. The question of identity here is related to Melville's concept of truth and reality. Atheism, which was the product of popular science, was doomed simply because it did not express truth and reality. Captain Vere was doomed, but for an entirely different reason ("The gods are gone"); the *Indomitable* survived both the *St. Louis* and the *Athéiste,* but the implication is clear that the crisis is one merely of discovering a new captain. Melville's attitude toward popular science is further clarified in an ironic passage labeled "A Digression", which occurs in the narrative just after Billy's death. The Purser and the ship's Surgeon are discussing what everyone had considered the remarkable nature of Billy's dying. The Purser suggested that will-power might have been responsible for the absence of the usual physical manifestations, but the Surgeon ridicules such an idea, saying it is not more attributable to will-power than to horsepower. He admits that the event was phenomenal only "in the sense that it was an appearance the cause of which is not immediately to be assigned." The Purser then suggests euthanasia. *"Euthanasia",* the Surgeon replies, "is something like your *will-power;* I doubt its authenticity as a scientific term.... It is at once imaginative and metaphysical,—in short, Greek."

It seems clear that if Melville was optimistic it was not with the arrogant optimism of Nineteenth Century science. This is further indicated in the report of Billy's death supplied by a writer of popular prose, the reporter of[125] *News from the Mediterranean;* here (as with the Surgeon) the truth is hidden beneath a false appearance of truth. If Claggart represents malicious evil (natural depravity), the Surgeon represents the evil of ignorance, while the popular reporter, pretending to serve constituted authority, tells the grossest falsehood of all. All are forms of dissimulation—the dangers confronting modern man in his search for truth. Where then does truth lie?

The answer, of course, is inherent in the novel itself. . . . Christianity and all it implies has fallen into decay. The spirit exhales, but only momentarily, awaiting the propitious moment again to belly philosophy's sails. Billy's act of innocent heroism supplies the opportunity—creates the situation. Authoritarianism and a changing concept of man's individual worth had conspired to bring about the destruction of the old gods. Billy's act (and by extension, Christ's) is seen more as tragic circumstance than as actual atonement. From

Billy's act then springs the new myth, sung to the tune of a simple sailor's ballad. It is "verse, popular verse" which bellies the sails, which supplies the common man with a means of confronting the facts, not only of Billy's death, but of his own. It is not orthodox Christianity. It is not popular science. It is the simple creative act which pierces the mask of falsehood and error, which sees man's existence as an heroic submission to fate, but which is in constant rebellion against those forms which result in man's injustice to man.

If it seems odd that so apparent and so integrated a theme should have been missed by so many readers, the fact of its having been missed is only additional evidence of the difficulty which the modern reader has with the ironic style in which Billy is composed. The difficulty is multiplied in this case, because Melville did not employ (indeed, could not have employed) the lyric-ironic style of *Moby Dick*, to which we have, after a lapse of many years, become accustomed. Accompanying the positive theme of man's rejuvenation through myth, there is also, as we have indicated, the negative one of modern man's situation in an over-materialistic society: "atheized into a smatterer". In a satiric-ironic manner, Melville pretends to adopt the very style of the popular-prose writer against whom his book is at least partially directed. Despite the fact that his central theme betrays his principal intention—he had elsewhere[126] written, "It is not the purpose of literature to purvey news",—he pretended to have written a story which, as he says, "has less to do with fable than with fact". He speaks of digressions and ragged edges, as though the very essence of truth lay in its absence of form. He pretends, in other words, to have written the very book which claims arrest of the advance of truth, or fable, or of instituted creeds; but the theme itself, the form which he has created in *Billy Budd*, tinctures the very book which he pretends to have written—the book of factual information concerning a mutiny at sea.

Contrary to current critical opinion, then, *Billy Budd* as a unified work not only is not marred by digressions and irrelevancies, it is a triumph of architectonic structure. When Melville protests that as a writer of "facts" he is prevented from achieving "an architectural finial", he is merely calling attention (in a method not uncommon in literature) to his central theme, which is in fact presented as an architectural finial, since it lies imbedded in the popular ballad "Billy in the Darbies", which ends the book. . . . This is not great poetry, but it was not intended to be. Neither is it, as one critic calls it, doggerel. It is intended merely to represent the primitive, but universal, ability of man to temper the harsh facts of death, to come to terms with nature, through art. It represents Melville's final expression of faith in mankind—faith in the ability of the common man to see beyond the misrepresentations of evil, however disguised; faith that the essential beauty and heroism of man will always be recognized and celebrated in artistic form, however crude.

Billy Budd is not in itself a tragedy, although it is an expression of belief in the tragic predicament of man. If we need distinguish it by supplying a name, I would suggest that it be called satiric-allegory. It does not pretend to the organ voice of *Moby Dick*. It combines the biting irony of Swiftian satire with the lyric hopefulness of John Bunyan. That it has been so little understood need not finally surprise us when we consider the history of Melville's literary career from *Mardi* onward. Among other things, *Billy Budd* suggests the possibility that Melville believed the rich tongue of Shakespeare (the use of which he borrowed in *Moby Dick* and *Pierre*) to be as obsolete as the scarlet and gold of Lord Nelson's office. Perhaps this is why he chose to write otherwise in his final work.[127]

THE FORM OF *BILLY BUDD**

William York Tindall

Billy Budd seems to make something almost too tidy out of what remains uncertain in *Moby Dick*. Melville's story of the captain, the villain, and the tar, apparently less a story than a commentary on one, may strike the hasty reader as a product of reason rather than imagination, as something reduced to discourse for ready apprehension by basic Englishmen. What had to be said has been said by Captain Vere or Melville himself. As critics, therefore, we may feel frustrated, as Romantics we may prefer a little teasing mystery around, and as esthetes, confronted with discourse, we are sure that talking about a thing is less admirable than embodying it in image or action. Of Kierkegaard's three categories, the esthetic, the moral, and the divine, Melville seems to have chosen the second—to the applause of some and the departure of others, for *Don Giovanni* maybe.

That the matter of *Billy Budd* gratifies what Melville calls "the moral palate" is plain from the plainest rehearsal. The scene is a British frigate during the Napoleonic wars. Two mutinies have justified fears of more. Against this ominous background, Billy, an innocent aboard, is accused for no good reason by Claggart, a petty officer, of plotting mutiny. The captain, a reasonable man, doubts Claggart's

* From "The Ceremony of Innocence," R. M. McIver, ed., *Great Moral Dilemmas in Literature, Past and Present,* (New York: Harper & Brothers, 1956), 73–81, by permission of publisher and author. [My title. Ed.]

story and brings Billy in to confront his lying accuser. Overcome by a stutterer's indignation, the innocent foretopman, unable to speak a word, strikes Claggart dead with a fist like a ham. Captain Vere is faced with a dilemma. Though he believes in Billy's innocence, naval law and prudence alike demand punishment for the[73] impetuous seaman while pity and reason counsel mercy. Internal debate inclines the captain toward conviction, and Billy, condemned despite the "troubled conscience" of his judges, is hanged.

The subject is a quandary or what Melville calls "the intricacies involved in the question of moral responsibility." As the captain ponders "the moral phenomenon presented in Billy Budd" and the "elemental evil" of Claggart, he fathoms the "mystery of iniquity." The case of Billy seems, as the captain says, a matter for "psychologic theologians."

Although, as T. S. Eliot observes in *After Strange Gods*, "It is ... during moments of moral and spiritual struggle ... that men (in fiction) ... come nearest being real," Billy and Claggart, who represent almost pure good and pure evil, are too simple and too extreme to satisfy the demands of realism; for character demands admixture. Their all but allegorical blackness and whiteness, however, are functional in the service of Vere's problem, and Vere, goodness knows, is real enough. Claggart is black because, as Philipp G. Frank once observed, a sinner is necessary for the realization of a moral code; and an innocent is almost equally instructive. These abstractions, a sacrifice of verisimilitude to tactical necessity, reveal the "moral quality" of the captain's mind, which becomes a theater for contending opposites and eventual choice. Such dramatic crises are not only the favorite stuff of novelists but of philosophers and poets as well: Kierkegaard wrote *Either/Or* and Yeats "The Choice."

Not only rational, Vere's choice involves his whole sensitive, adult being. Agony shows on his face as he emerges from his interview with Billy, and a final exclamation shows how deeply he is stirred. Involving more than black and white, the captain's choice is between two moral codes, military and natural. The first is evident; the second is either that of the noble savage, in whom Melville was interested, or what Western culture takes for granted. In other words, the captain's conflict is between the balanced claims of justice and equity, order and confusion, law and grace, reason and feeling, or, as Melville puts it, "military duty" and "moral scruple." Vere's eloquent and moving speech to the drumhead court, the climax of such drama as there is, leaves little to add about these issues and his dilemma.[74]

The conflict of military with natural may occupy the stage, but Melville recognizes other codes, that of custom or respectability, for example. Claggart's "natural depravity" appears in respectable guise. Melville also recognizes the cultural, psychological, and absolute bases for morality, and hints in a very modern way at their operation.

"Moral," Melville's favorite word—in this book at least—is one which, though commonly taken for granted, is slippery. I have read a thing in which "moral" means something else on every page. What Yvor Winters means by it escapes me. Vague and general like F. R. Leavis's "awareness of life" or narrow and definite like the *quid agas* of Scholastic philosophers, the word needs fixing before use. As I shall use it and as I think Melville did, morality implies not only action but motive, attitude, and being. It involves a sense of obligation to self, community, and the absolute, which provide a frame by conscience, law, tradition, or revelation. If we demand a single equivalent, Melville's "responsibility" will do.

Vere's action, however sudden and whether we approve of it or not, is plainly responsible. Billy and Claggart act, to be sure: one bears false witness and the other delivers a blow, but neither actor follows reason and each is more important for what he is than what he does. If being as well as action can be moral, however, they are moral figures, too, existing like cherubs or fiends in a moral atmosphere. Good and bad, they occupy the region of good and evil.

It is agreed by most that moral substance is necessary for the novel. Not the pure form of Flaubert's desire, and falling far short of the condition of music, the novel is an arrangement of references to vital issues, without which it is empty. A value of Joyce's *Ulysses*, for example, is the feeling and idea of charity. That moral substance fails to insure greatness, however, is proved by the works of Horatio Alger; and that it fails to guarantee moral effect is proved by those of Mickey Spillane. The errors of censors and formalists show the folly of judging by morality alone or arrangement alone. Not moral idea but its embodiment in what Eliot called objective correlatives, suitably arranged, determines value. Far from inciting action as moralizing does, embodied morality invites contemplation, and to become an object of contemplation, substance must be distanced by form. The[75] question is not how much morality is there but how much is under control, how fully insight and moral intelligence have submitted to esthetic discipline. Our problem, then, is not morality itself but moral art or morally significant form.

Captain Vere's speech to the court adequately embodies the idea of "moral responsibility" in dramatic form; but we must find if Billy's history has found fitting embodiment. At first reading, that history seems a curious and eccentric structure of essays on ethics, digressions or "bypaths," character sketches, and chronicles of the navy, an arrangement that after uncertain progress tails inconclusively off. Such image and action as we find, failing to halt the lamentable decline, seem occasions for analysis or digression, like biblical texts in a pulpit. Since the crucial interview between Vere and Billy is disappointingly offstage, Melville seems to have avoided the dramatic possibilities of his theme. That the book calls for the dramatization he failed to give it, is proved by attempts at play and opera, which, while affirming excellence of theme, imply that action or image are better ways of presenting it. But something that continues to fascinate us in its present form and calls forth responses beyond the capacity of discourse, suggests art of another kind. Maybe Melville avoided drama in the interests of a less obvious medium.

Moby Dick assures us that Melville was an artist, not a lecturer on ethics. He not only worked three years on *Billy Budd*, but he seems to have regarded the result with far from senile favor. The first version, recently detected in manuscript by F. Barron Freeman, reveals more action and less discourse; yet this version, which corresponds more happily to what we think fiction should be, is not so effective as the one before us with all its weight of digression and analysis.

That Melville was aware of form is clear from passages in *Billy Budd*. When Captain Vere says, "With mankind forms, measured forms, are everything," he probably means usage and custom; but Melville himself, applying Vere's remark to esthetics, says that the symmetry of form desirable in pure fiction cannot be achieved in factual narrative like this. The story is not factual in fact. But Melville, wanting it to seem so, excuses apparent formlessness as a form for[76] giving the illusion of a bare report; for truth, he continues, will always have its ragged edges and matters of fact must lack the finish of an "architectural finial." Aware of loose structure and inconclusive ending, he justifies them for what seem wrong reasons. Not reasons, however, but what he made must detain us while we scout further possibilities. The curious form he made may be functional and, for all our hasty impression and his explanation, effective. Is the book as shapeless as he implies? Or, if shapeless, is shapelessness a kind of shape? Is the book as pedestrian, discursive, and factual as he claims and as we had supposed on first looking into it?

What seems at first to be factual is presented, we find, in part by images and allusions that are incompatible with pretense of factuality. Though unapparent, those images are livelier than we thought. Consider the coloring of the scene between decks before the execution as Billy lies in white amid profound blackness. Catching up the abstract whiteness and blackness of Billy and Claggart, this image of black and white embodies them. At the execution the rosy dawn that seems "the fleece of the Lamb of God seen in mystical vision" promises a kind of renewal while implying much else. Circling birds after the burial at sea offer by the aid of tradition some spiritual import. And that spilt soup, perhaps more action than image, carries suggestions beyond the demands of plot, suggestions so indefinite, what is more, that they confound its rational progress. Even the names of ships, though serving a more comprehensible purpose, are as significant as those in *Moby Dick*. Billy is removed from the *Rights of Man,* for instance, and Vere is mortally wounded by a shot from the *Athéiste.*

The words of *Billy Budd* carry more than denotation. "Sinister dexterity," at once witty and desolating, sounds like something from *Finnegans Wake*, where, indeed, it reappears. Vere's last words, "Billy Budd," are equivocal. Do they imply feeling, regret, self-realization, understanding? Are they a form for something incompletely realized? However "factual" the words of this pseudoreport, they function like the words of poetry.

Not only last words and indeterminate images but a number of hints about Billy's "all but feminine" nature plague our assumptions.[77] Roses and lilies dye his cheeks. He comports himself like a "rustic beauty" at times and like a vestal virgin at others. These qualities and appearances, astonishing in an able seaman, calling forth an "ambiguous smile" from one or another of his shipmates, suggest psychological depths and motives below the level of the plain report. By virtue of such intimations Billy seems at once more and less bottomless than we had supposed, and so do the motives of Claggart, if not those of the captain himself. Among such suggestions, avoidance of the obviously dramatic becomes implicit embodiment that escapes the limits of drama.

What pleases me most, however, is the accompaniment of biblical allusions which, however unobtrusive and irregular, recurs like Wagnerian *leitmotiv*. Time and again Billy is compared to Adam and Jesus. Billy's innocence is as much that of Adam before the Fall as that of the more secular noble savage. As a "peacemaker," a term implying beatitude, Billy seems destined for "crucifixion"; and his hanging, condensing events, becomes an ascension. Vere is compared to Abraham about to sacrifice Isaac, obeying God's will with fear and trembling. Becoming a shadow of God, Vere weighs the claims of Adam and Satan. Claggart, whose denunciation is reported in Mosaic terms as "false witness," is compared not only to the Serpent of Eden but to Ananias and to one struck dead by an angel of God, "yet," as the captain says, "the angel must hang!" Man's fall and redemption and all troubles between seem suggested by this large though not fully elaborated analogy, which, bringing to mind the mythical parallels in *Ulysses* and *The Waste Land*, removes Billy a little farther from the abstraction to which, for all his stutter and those rosy cheeks, he seems committed. However incapable of supporting this mythical burden, he becomes by its aid almost as portentous as choosing Vere. The sailors, whose testimony cannot be ignored, are more impressed by Billy than by Vere, reason and all. Not only being and secular victim, Billy becomes saint and martyr and his hanging an omen. Pieces of the spar to which he quietly ascends are venerated like pieces of the true cross, suitable for reliquaries or the holiest of duffle bags. By the aid of myth and military ritual the[78] story of Billy, transformed from an essay on good, evil, and choice, approaches what Yeats called "the ceremony of innocence."

We must conclude that Melville avoided the attractions of the obvious in the interests of indefinite suggestiveness and myth. His work, whatever its air of the factual and the discursive, is symbolist and richer for scarcity of drama and image. Such drama and images as are there function more intensely in their abstract context than profusion could. That the structure as a whole also serves esthetic purpose is likely. As we have seen, the book is a queer arrangement of discourse, action, image, and allusion, with discourse predominating. We have seen how image and action work in this mixture; but we must examine the function of discourse. In such context, discourse, increasing tension, makes allusion and image dramatic or enlarges them, and, working with allusion, image, and action may produce a third something by juxtaposition as in Eliot's *Four Quartets* or Wallace Stevens' *Notes Toward a Supreme Fiction*. Seeming now a structure of conflicts, not only of men and codes but of methods, which become a technical echo of the theme, the book emerges as a structural drama or a drama of structure. An ending that seemed weak afterthought (and was not there in the first version) now unifies all. Vere's exclamation, the saint's legend, and inconclusiveness, working together, comprise a form, which may tail off but tails suggestively off, leaving endless reverberations in our minds. There is more mystery around than we had thought, and we may agree with dying Gertrude Stein that answers are less important than questions. What at a superficial reading had the appearance of exhaustive discourse becomes inexhaustible. The shapeless thing becomes suggestive shape. Neither as loose nor as tight as it once seemed, the strange sequence of precise discourse and indefinite suggestiveness corresponds to our experience of life itself. That the form Melville made fascinates while it eludes and teases is shown no less by popular favor than by the abundance of critical comment.

However different it looks, *Billy Budd* is not altogether different in kind from *Moby Dick,* another structure of digression, discourse, action, and image. The proportions and impact may be different, the[79] images of *Moby Dick* may be more compelling, but both serve symbolic suggestion and both are forms for offering a vision of reality. Not the tidy discourse of our first impression, the work is almost as inexplicable as *Moby Dick*.

What exactly does this form present? It is impossible to answer this question for any symbolist work; for works of this kind escape discursive accounting. We may say that *Billy Budd* is a vision of man in society, a vision of man's moral quandary or his responsibility; but its meaning is more general than these, and that is why it haunts us. So haunted, I find the work not an essay on a moral issue but a form for embodying the feeling and idea of thinking about a moral issue, the experience of facing, of choosing, of being uneasy about one's choice, of trying to know. Not a conclusion like a sermon, *Billy Budd* is a vision of confronting what confronts us, of man thinking things out with all the attendant confusions and uncertainties. Disorder is a form for this and the apparently formless book a formal triumph. To do what it does it has to be a fusion of tight-loose, shapeless-shaped, irrelevant-precise, suggestive-discursive—a mixture of myth, fact, and allusion that has values beyond reference. The discursive parts represent our attempts at thinking, while the action, images, and allusions represent what we cannot think but must approximate. Arrangement of these discordant elements forms a picture of a process.

From my guess at meaning it follows that the center of this form is neither Vere nor Billy but rather the teller of the story or Melville himself. Though ghostlier, he is not unlike the Marlow of Conrad's *Lord Jim* and *Heart of Darkness* or the Quentin of Faulkner's *Absalom, Absalom!* Using Vere and Billy as materials, Melville's thought-process, like those of Marlow and Quentin, is the heart of this darkness and its shape the objective correlative, a form for something at once imperfectly understood and demanding understanding. Morality, the substance of this form, becomes an element that limits and directs the feelings and ideas created by the whole. Moral substance, what is more, may be what engages our minds while the form does its work. Value, not from morality alone, issues from the form that includes it and in which it serves. If the form[80] concerned less, I repeat, it would be trivial, but without its formal presentation the morality would remain in Sunday school.

United now, the beautiful and the good create a vision larger than either, a vision transcending the case of Billy Budd or the quandary of Captain Vere. The teller, now any man, presents man's feeling in the face of any great dilemma. Thought and feeling, outdistancing themselves, become objects of contemplation, remote yet immediate. The effect of this form is moral in the sense of enlarging our awareness of human conditions or relationships and of improving our sensitivity. In such a form Kierkegaard's esthetic, moral, and divine become a single thing.[81]

MELVILLE'S USE OF THE BIBLE*

Nathalia Wright

. . . .

When the theme of the Crucifixion is taken up finally in *Billy Budd*, the New Testament story is clearly visible. Fundamentally, of course, the two main characters in the novel are embodiments of two abstractions. In one sense Budd is simple nature, a barbarian, "Adam ... ere the urban Serpent wriggled himself into his company." Yet his innocence is more than that of a natural man, completely unarmed in the world. It is a divine innocence, incorruptible by society or the forces of darkness. It is a communicable quality, too, to such an extent that Billy's captain on[128] the *Rights of Man* says of him, as Jesus said of himself: " 'Not that he preached to them or said or did anything in particular; but a virtue went out of him, sugaring the sour ones.' "

The spiritual antithesis of Billy is Claggart, the master-at-arms, who represents "depravity according to nature." It is a quality not consisting of petty vices nor engendered by experience, but innately residing in his inmost being. He is not so much an evil man as an evil principle, described by such words as those in Proverbs 21:10, which Melville marked: "The soul of the wicked desireth evil...." Admittedly Melville had some Biblical parallel in mind, for when he came to analyze Claggart he indulged in an illuminating digression. Recording a youthful conversation with a friend on the subject of penetrating character, he quoted the friend as saying:

"Coke and Blackstone hardly shed so much light into obscure spiritual places as the Hebrew prophets. And who were they? Mostly recluses."

At the time my inexperience was such that I did not quite see the drift

---

* From *Melville's Use of the Bible* (Durham: Duke University Press, 1949), 126–136, by permission of the publisher.

of all this. It may be that I see it now. And, indeed, if that lexicon which is based on Holy Writ were any longer popular, one might with less difficulty define and denominate certain phenomenal men. As it is, one must turn to some authority not liable to the charge of being tinctured with the Biblical element.[129]

Yet while Billy and Claggart are essentially abstractions, arrayed against each other by their very natures, for the purposes of the plot they play the roles of Jesus and Judas. Though he is not a creature of the secondary or auxiliary nature of Judas, Claggart is as effective a betrayer of an innocent man to authority. His first attempt is by bribery: he has a seaman offer Billy two guineas to join a proposed mutiny group. When that temptation is withstood, Claggart falsely charges that Billy is disloyal to the king. Only in this way, by treachery, can evil reach good. So Jesus was betrayed by Judas after he had resisted the temptations of Satan in the wilderness, and above him on the cross was hung the same charge: treason.

Both these indictments, moreover, go unanswered. When Budd is brought into the cabin and hears Claggart's accusation he does not utter a word in self-defense, just as Jesus remained silent before the priests and elders. The experience has brought out his defect of speech and he is momentarily paralyzed, though making agonized efforts to speak and defend himself. Perceiving the situation, Vere offers him more time in which to reply, but he is not successful in soothing the sailor:

Contrary to the effect intended, these words, so fatherly in tone, doubtless touching Billy's heart to the quick, prompted yet more violent efforts at utterance—efforts soon ending for the time in confirming the paralysis, and bringing to the face an expression which was as a crucifixion to behold.

Then comes Budd's response to Claggart's accusation, not consciously but instinctively. There can be no compromise between the two forces which they represent, and Claggart falls fatally under Budd's blow. Nor can there be compromise between what remains: between Budd and the king's statute, under which he is now subject to trial. It does not matter that in nature he is free; it does not matter[130] that in breaking an immediate law he thereby kept one higher. Nor does his intent enter into the case; he is judged solely by his deed. The purity of his conscience is reserved for consideration until the Last Assizes, where, as Vere remarks, it will surely acquit him. Here he is the double victim of malignity and of custom.

Thus poignantly and dramatically did Melville distinguish between the false and the true charge against Budd. The distinction is the same in the trial of Jesus. The charge of treason which the members of the Sanhedrin proffered, though necessary for his official execution, was not only false, it was superficial in their own minds. Their true grievance against him was the fact that in obeying the spirit of the law, even more faithfully than they, Jesus violated its letter. Under a similar primitive code both he and the Handsome Sailor are condemned: the Mosaic law and the Mutiny Act. The similarity between the two codes is not insignificant. For the Mutiny Act, demanding a life for a life, is in effect the same penalizing legalism as the Old Testament ethic. . . .

Throughout these scenes Captain Vere stands in two relationships to Budd. Primarily he is the military superior and disciplinarian. He sacrifices everything to the end of having Billy convicted, calling a drumhead court together lest in the delay he be swayed by the essential right and wrong of the case from the execution of his duty as administrator of the drastic law. Like Pilate, he condemns to death a man whom he knows to be innocent, though unlike Pilate he accepts the full responsibility of his act. Melville may have known, too, that apocryphal story that Pilate was haunted by the memory of Jesus during his last years as praetor of Hispania Tarraconensis. Not far from this locality Vere murmurs Budd's name as he lies dying on Gibraltar.[131]

Yet Vere also appears in the role of Billy's father; as Abraham to Isaac, as God to Jesus—or rather, not as Abraham to Isaac. Among numerous figures of speech emphasizing the general father-son relationship of the two men this one, brief as it is, provides a revealing contrast with the particular relationship which Melville was also at pains to establish between them. In the private interview between the foretopman and his captain before the execution Melville imagines:

The austere devotee of military duty, letting himself melt back into what remains primeval in our formalised humanity, may in the end have caught Billy to his heart, even as Abraham may have caught young Isaac on the brink of resolutely offering him up in obedience to the exacting behest.

The figure is moving, but the parallel can be carried no further. For Isaac did not die. Even waiving the fact that his near sacrifice is a deliberate scheme of the Old Testament Jehovah, the obedience of Isaac and of Billy Budd are two different things. Isaac was not taken into Abraham's confidence any more than Abraham was taken into Jehovah's. All is blind obedience, dependent on a jealous and capricious deity.

Not so is the sympathy between Budd and Vere. The sailor and the officer meet as equals; neither conceals anything from the other. When confused at the trial Budd turns to Vere, his accuser, for counsel. His only concern is to have himself cleared in the mind of his captain, to be understood if not to understand; when that is accomplished he has no fear of the future. Their interview alone in Vere's cabin is not unlike the episode in Gethsemane. Afterward the foretopman possesses a peace marvelous and ineffable, which even the chaplain cannot fathom. As he goes to his death his last words are, " 'God bless Captain Vere!' "[132]

. . . .

But Melville read something . . . [else] into the Crucifixion story. There he found one more illustration for his notion that beyond the farthest known truth there is yet an untrodden realm, an undisclosed mystery. Unlike Jehovah in the Old Testament, God the Father seems to practice as well as to command obedience;[133] hence his enigmatical willingness for Jesus to die. And so in *Billy Budd* even he who administers the law is bound by it. It is the fact that Vere did not formulate the Mutiny Act which makes possible the community of spirit between him and Billy Budd. Both are subject to a power beyond themselves.

What this power is, what this realm is in which, as in Hebrew wisdom, God himself does not reign, Melville never concluded. But it is clearly not simply evil. It is beyond good or evil; it is beyond conflict. The realm in which Budd meets Vere is not the same as that in which he meets Claggart, and beyond them all is an utterly amoral, mysteriously influential *terra incognita*. The last of all Melville's symbols, the death of Captain Vere in the encounter with the *Athéiste*, is a fitting one. Religion, even in its noblest aspect, remained for him penultimate.

The mystery in *Billy Budd* is thus not altogether one of iniquity. It is the mystery of a boundless creation, an infinite number of superficially exclusive, deeply related spheres. Symbolic of their existence and of their interdependence is the fact that all nature is affected at Budd's death, as it was at the death of Jesus. . . . The moral conflict is not confined to its own world but reaches beyond it, even to the unyielding elements. When Budd's body is hoisted aloft the violent motion usually noticeable at hangings is absent; it is suspended quietly above the heads of his comrades. At the same moment the appearance of the sea and sky becomes phenomenal:

... the vapoury fleece hanging low in the east, was shot through with a soft glory as of the fleece of the Lamb of God seen in mystical vision, and simultaneously therewith, watched by the wedged mass of upturned faces, Billy ascended; and ascending, took the full rose of the dawn.[134]

It is not accidental that the description contains a suggestion of the Ascension and of the doctrine of the Atonement. For in the manuscript of *Billy Budd* the word "shekinah" is crossed out in favor of "rose," and at the beginning of the next chapter Melville first referred to Billy's "ascension" but changed it to his "execution."

Finally, when Billy's remains are lowered into the sea, throngs of birds fly screaming to the spot and circle it as the ship passes out of sight. And at last it is related that for several years the sailors of the *Indomitable* knew the whereabouts of the spar from which Billy was suspended, following it from ship to dockyard to ship again. "To them a chip of it was as a piece of the Cross."

. . . .[135]

MELVILLE'S *NUNC DIMITTIS**

Newton Arvin

. . . .

. . . The real feeling of *Billy Budd* . . . is very deep and very affecting; it triumphs even over the stiff-jointed prose, the torpidity of the movement, the excess of commentary, and Melville's failure to quicken any of the scenes with a full dramatic life. In spite of these blemishes of form and manner, the persons in *Billy Budd* and the moral drama they enact have too much largeness, as well as too much subtlety, in their poetic representativeness, not to leave a permanent stamp on the imagination.

For the tale of the Handsome Sailor and his unhappy end has an archetypal depth and scope that no reader can quite mistake; it is Melville's version of a primordial fable, the fable of the Fall of Man, the loss of Paradise. There are vibrations in it of the Book of Genesis, of the *Works and Days,* of Milton; there are other vibrations that are pure Melville. Billy himself, at any rate, is on one level Primal Man; he is Adam; indeed, it is said of him that, in the nude, he "might have posed for a statue of young Adam before the fall." His physical beauty, certainly, is such as the First Man's would necessarily be; but so, too, and of course more vitally, is the purity of his innocence, his incapacity so much as to imagine evil, his utter freedom from all malice and envy, and his helplessness in the presence of the wrong. His goodness, moreover, is not mere blank innocence; it is an active and disarming *good nature* also, and it draws upon him the spontaneous affection of his mates. But there is a complete absence from it of any intellectual element whatever; the illiterate and mindless Billy

---

* From *Herman Melville: A Critical Biography,* by Newton Arvin, copyright 1950 by William Sloane Associates, Inc., by permission of William Sloane Associates, Inc. [My title. Ed.]

is "radically" a barbarian. And perfect as Billy is in the innocence of his heart, he is touched nevertheless by the primordial imperfection of humanity. His stutter[294] is a symbol of this, and there is a mysterious justice in the fact that this stutter is his undoing.

If Billy is the Adam of this naval Eden, Claggart is of course its Satan. Malign as he is, Claggart, like the great Enemy in *Paradise Lost*, has a certain nobility of form and type. In physical presence, with his tall figure, his shapely forehead, and his curling black hair, he is quite without meanness, and it is only his strangely protuberant chin and his unwholesome pallor of complexion that hint at the depravity of his being. That depravity is inherent and terrible, but it does not express itself in what are called vices or small sins. As a naval officer, Claggart is a model of dutifulness and patriotism, and intellectually he is a man of marked superiority. He is dominated, indeed, by his intellectuality; dominated by it, at any rate, in his *means,* for his aims are mad; with all his "rationality," he is completely exempt, at heart, from the law of reason. Instinctively he hates the good; hates Billy precisely because he is innocent and guileless. In the deepest sense Claggart is a rebel and a traitor, like his great exemplar; a rebel against the law of reason and a traitor to the image of man. There is a Guy Fawkes, as Melville says, prowling in the hid chambers of his nature, and it is wholly suitable that the charge he brings against an innocent man should be the charge of mutiny. It is true that Billy has been guiltless of what he is accused of; guiltless of rebellion and disobedience; but was not that the sin to which Satan tempted the first of men? and is it not fitting that Claggart should now impute it to Billy? There is a strong suggestion of the old serpent in the master-at-arms, and when, after his death, Billy and Captain Vere attempt to raise his body to a sitting posture, "it was like handling a dead snake."

Now that he has struck dead an officer of the Navy, Billy is indeed objectively guilty, under the Mutiny Act, of a crime of exactly the same heinousness as that with which he was falsely charged. It may be that, as the officer of marines protests, Budd *intended* neither mutiny nor homicide; Adam did[295] not *intend* disobedience either, and, as Captain Vere observes, "Budd's intent or non-intent is nothing to the purpose." The Mutiny Act, like war, of which it is the offspring, "looks but to the frontage," and Captain Vere, as the embodiment of naval authority, the Jehovah of the drama, has no choice but to administer, dutifully and grimly, the harsh terms of that Act. In order to do so, he must suppress not only the heart within him but his private conscience: it is the "imperial" conscience, formulated in the Naval Code, under which he officially proceeds. This means adjudging to death a youth toward whom he is drawn emotionally as a father to a son. Imaginably, Billy might *be* his son, for Billy is a foundling and one in whom noble descent is as evident as in a blood horse; and the aristocratic Captain Vere, a bachelor, "was old enough to have been Billy's father." The sacrifice of Billy by Captain Vere is a re-enactment of the sacrifice of Isaac by Abraham, though it is a completed one; and Vere does not turn aside from his duty, anguishing though it is. Billy is hanged at the yard-arm, and Vere, a few months later, mortally wounded by a shot from the *Athéiste,* dies with Billy's name on his lips.

Such is this rewriting of the first three chapters of Genesis, this late-nineteenth-century *Paradise Lost.* Budd owes much of its subliminal effect on the imagination to the fact that it repeats, with variations, that primordial pattern. Yet quite as real as the repetition, and at least as vital, are the variations. There is no Eve in this Eden, for one thing, but far more importantly, the tale does not have, after all, the unequivocal spiritual and moral simplicity of the Christian legend or of any of its theological formulations. It abounds in what Melville himself calls ambiguities; it suggests no unambiguous dogma. There is a strain of irony in it that has no parallel in Genesis or in Milton. . . .[296] Unlike the world of theology, Melville's world is insuperably incomprehensible, and he makes no claim to comprehending it.

The drama of the Fall of Man is a drama in which divine and absolute justice is countered by infernal evil in a contest for the immortal soul of God's creature, Man, and in which Man, yielding to the temptation of the evil spirit, turns rebel against God's will, disobeys it, and involves himself and all his posterity in the guilt of Original Sin. Billy, on the contrary, is no rebel against divine justice, and he is not guilty, even symbolically, of disobeying some transcendent will. He is an unwitting, impulsive offender against the Mutiny Act, the child of war, itself an evil and infecting with evil everything that relates to it. Captain Vere makes no mistake about that. To the protest of the officer of marines that Billy intended no mutiny, he replies: "Surely not, my good man. And before a court less arbitrary and more merciful than a martial one that plea would largely extenuate. At the Last Assizes it shall acquit." If there is a divine justice, Billy is innocent in its eyes; he goes to his death as a penalty for breaking a law that has no absolute sanction whatever. His impediment in speech is a symbol of his irreducible imperfection as a man; it is not a symbol of total depravity, and Vere's real feeling about Billy breaks out when, gazing at Claggart's dead body, he cries: "Struck dead by an angel of God."

There is a far more enigmatic intertangling of good and evil in this universe of Melville's final vision than in the universe of theology or of dogmatic ethics: evil and good, as Rolfe had said, do indeed play, braided, into one cord. Billy may be as blameless as Oedipus of any conscious evil intention, yet a malign fate, working upon his inevitable limitations as a human being, brings it about that he commits in fact a capital crime. Meanwhile, Claggart's iniquity, terrible though it is, is not the absolute and transcendent wickedness of the principle of Evil itself, the Evil of the Father of Lies. It is, as Melville insists, "a depravity according to nature,"[297] born with him and innate, not the product of training; but it embodies some mysterious principle in human experience that "by no means involves Calvin's dogma as to total mankind." It takes chiefly the form of an instinctive hatred of the innocent and the good, but a hatred so spontaneous and so insane that it suggests a dreadful perversion of love. Claggart's glance, indeed, sometimes follows "belted Billy," moving about the deck, "with a settled meditative and melancholy expression," his eyes strangely suffused with tears. At such moments the diabolic master-at-arms looks like the man of sorrows. "Yes, and sometimes the melancholy expression would have in it a touch of soft yearning, as if Claggart could even have loved Billy but for fate and ban."

It is his miserable destiny, however, to be incapable of loving the good, indeed to be incapable of love itself, and there is no greater misery. For there is a solid reality in this incomprehensible universe, this universe of equivocations and contrarieties; it is the reality of "the heart within you." To mind "the issues there" is to know that, even in the dark midst of evil and hate, goodness exists, and that its essential reality is that of love. Neither goodness nor love can flourish in a nature "dominated by intellectuality," as Claggart's is, and certainly not in a nature like that of the ship's surgeon, with his materialistic, scientific rationalism. They attain their fairest form, perhaps, in a nature as pristine and even primitive as Billy's is, but they are not irrevocably at war with the life of the mind, and indeed they attain their highest form in association with it. Captain Vere is a man with "a marked leaning towards everything intellectual," a passion for books and learning, and a habit of abstracted meditation. Yet he is an image of the high virtue in which the sternest sense of severe and painful duty is united to a capacity for the purest and tenderest love, the love of father for son. And it was in the full imaginative realization of that love, given and received, that Melville brought his work as a writer to its serene conclusion.[298]

After the drumhead court has pronounced its just and inexorable sentence, Captain Vere and Billy have a final interview alone together in the stateroom where Billy is confined. What occurred there was never known, says Melville, . . . [but] whatever took place in the stateroom between the ideal father and the ideal son, its effect was indeed sacramental, an effect of the purest unction and the most complete reconcilement. When, during the night that follows, the chaplain of the vessel comes upon Billy lying asleep on the upper gundeck, he gazes down on the sleeping countenance and feels that even he, "the minister of Christ," has "no consolation to proffer which could result in a peace transcending that which he beheld." Ishmael, in the end, after so long a banishment, had been taken back to his father's heart. Billy's final words, as he stands the next morning with the noose about his neck, are an expression of rapturous surrender: "God bless Captain Vere!"[299]

THE USES OF MILTON*

Lawrance Thompson

. . . .

I have said that Melville's ulterior concept, in *Billy Budd*, inverts Milton's ulterior concept, in *Paradise Lost*. Man's fault, says Melville, is God's fault. The many cross-references between *Billy Budd* and *Paradise Lost* are sometimes obvious and sometimes subtle; but one of the most obvious is the direct quotation which Melville uses as his title or motto for Chapter Thirteen: "Pale ire, envy and despair." Milton uses those words to describe Satan's mixed feelings when first he looks on Adam in the Garden of Eden; Melville uses those words to describe Claggart's mixed feelings when he looks on Billy. Envying Billy his innocence, Claggart yet views that innocence with disdain: "... to be nothing more than innocent! Yet in an aesthetic way he saw the charm of it, the courageous[379] free-and-easy temper of it, and fain would have shared it, but he despaired of it." Thus the reader's attention is made to concentrate on the relationship between innocence and ignorance, with many possible extensions of that relationship. Melville's handling of it recalls the remarks of Milton's Satan as he enviously soliloquizes, while watching Adam and Eve:

> Yet let me not forget what I have gain'd
> From thir own mouths; all is not theirs it seems:
> One fatal Tree there stands of Knowledge call'd,
> Forbidden them to taste: Knowledge forbidd'n?
> Suspicious, reasonless. Why should thir Lord
> Envy them that? can it be sin to know,
> Can it be death? and do they only stand
> By Ignorance, is that thir happy state,
> The proof of thir obedience and thir faith?
> O fair foundation laid whereon to build
> Thir ruin!
>
> (*Paradise Lost,* IV, 512–522)

---

* From *Melville's Quarrel with God* (Princeton: Princeton University Press, 1952), 379–381, by permission of the publisher. [My title. Ed.]

After Melville has suggested a correlation between Milton's Satan and Claggart, he lets the narrator tuck in a more darkly significant kind of correlation:

With no power to annul the elemental evil in himself, though he could hide it readily enough; apprehending the good, but powerless to be it; what recourse is left to a nature like Claggart's surcharged with energy as such natures almost invariably are, but to recoil upon itself, and, like the scorpion for which the Creator alone is responsible, act out to the end the part allotted it.

Once again the narrator has established an analogy merely for purposes of describing Claggart's specific iniquity. Melville uses this seemingly innocent remark for sinister purposes, and thus shifts the weight of meaning from Claggart to the dark allegorical concept: the fault is not Claggart's any more than the fault which ruined Satan was Satan's. Each commits actions "for which the Creator alone is responsible." In *Paradise Lost,* Satan works out ironic variations on that same theme. When God's agent Ithuriel asks who he is, Satan answers, "Not to know mee argues yourselves unknown." Later, as we have noticed, when Satan plots the corruption of Adam he speaks with unheard bitterness: "Accept your[380] Maker's work; he gave it me, Which I as freely give." So Claggart implies, allegorically.
 . . . .[381]

MILTON AND MELVILLE*

Henry F. Pommer

 . . . .
The automatism of Claggart's evil, the serpent imagery of . . . the book, the allusions to Satan and the quotation from Milton, the envy aroused by Billy's beauty of body and of character, the incipient love and actual suffering in Claggart's soul, and his misleading appearance determine his position as the ultimate of Satanic villainy in Melville. . . .
With no more than the usual accuracy of epigram, one might

* From *Milton and Melville* (Pittsburgh: University of Pittsburgh Press, 1950), 89–90, by permission of the publisher.

say[89] that in Claggart Melville reacted classically to Satan, whereas in Ahab he reacted romantically. In the former case he condemns a man who does wrong in the eyes of the world; in the latter he sympathizes with such a man, justifies his means by referring to his ends, and makes a hero of a devil. In *Billy Budd* his attitude towards Claggart is roughly analogous to that of Christ when he told God,

> Whom thou hat'st, I hate, and can put on
> Thy terrours, as I put thy mildness on,
> Image of thee in all things; and shall soon,
> Arm'd with thy might, rid Heaven of these rebell'd;
> To their prepar'd ill mansion driven down,
> To chains of darkness, and the undying worm;
> That from thy just obedience could revolt,
> Whom to obey is happiness entire.

. . . .[90]

A CAUTION ABOUT SOURCES*

Norman Holmes Pearson

. . . .

Thus when we read in *Billy Budd* of the relationship between Billy, Claggart, and Vere, we are given a situation analogous to, and dependent upon, Milton's poetry and the Bible which stood behind it. This is Melville's use of the earth as the shadow of Heaven. What must be remembered is that there is only a shadow, and that Melville establishes momentary resemblances rather than complete identities. Thus Billy may without conflict be like pre-lapsarian Adam; like Christ who took the fallen Adam's place to carry out the obedience Adam denied; and like Isaac in relation to Abraham. But Billy never loses his identity as a sailor. Claggart may be like Satan, the Arch-Enemy who would attempt to rule the earth after his own fall and man's, and[107] yet retain his character as master-at-arms of the *Indomitable*. Vere, too, may bear the same relationship of ultimate command to an Adam-Christ and to a Satan, who was his renegade cheva-

---

* From "Billy Budd: 'The King's Yarn,'" *American Quarterly*, III (Summer, 1951), 107–108, by permission of publisher and author. [My title. Ed.]

lier, that a captain of a man-of-war does to his men, in an analogy of captaincy to the authority of God which is without the blasphemous assumption of Godhead. These are simply shifting similitudes, which reënforce but do not tie down.

. . . .[108]

BILLY BUDD, ANTIGONE, AND THE WINTER'S TALE*

Richard Chase

. . . .

It is high praise indeed to speak of a story as just missing equality with the small body of great tragic literature. And that is how we nowadays think of *Billy Budd,* which Melville wrote in the years between 1888 and 1891, the year of his death. A comparison of *Billy Budd* with the *Antigone* of Sophocles can, I think, be taken just literally enough to point to the decisive difference of achievement.

Both works are concerned with the defeat by abstract legality of an individual who possesses in more than usual measure certain timelessly precious human attributes. If we mean by a tragic hero a man of high estate who falls from prosperity by a flaw in his character or because he is guided by a power beyond his control or because of a mistake he makes, we may say of both *Billy Budd* and *Antigone* that the tragic hero himself is of only secondary interest. In the formal structure of these works Captain Vere and Creon are tragic heroes; yet in each instance the author's main interest, his most abundant flow of emotion, is directed toward someone else; in Sophocles, it is Antigone; in Melville, Billy Budd.

In both works, the tragic hero is personally superior to the legal ideology he believes he must enforce. The two characters are adequately conceived by their authors. But we must admit that Sophocles is more successful with his Antigone than is Melville with his Billy Budd. In Antigone's insistence on the proper burial of her dead brother we see the full lineaments of a marvelously rich and mature

* From "Introduction," copyright 1950 by Richard Chase, in *Selected Tales and Poems* of Herman Melville. Reprinted by permission of Holt, Rinehart and Winston, Inc., and the author. [My title. Ed.]

character and a profound commitment to certain sources of moral and spiritual health. In comparison with Antigone, we must see that Billy Budd is not quite adequately conceived for the part he is supposed to play, the part, that is, of innocence and generosity in tragic[xiii] collision with the rigid proscriptions of society. In some ways at least, Billy Budd strikes us as not quite believable. There are contradictory elements in his character; he is, for example, "innocent," yet he has had "experience." We ought to desire the tragic writer to show us innocence as it has survived or been produced by experience, by knowledge of life. The mindless innocence of Billy Budd, like that of a child, is wonderfully touching and valuable. Yet it is not quite the stuff of tragedy. Melville, as we see, was not free of the vast commitment of the American Man to the American Boy.

Captain Vere is finely portrayed. Somewhat in the manner of Captain Delano, he is an admirable if (in relation to the ultimate possibility of human character) fundamentally second-rate man. Claggart is also perfectly imagined—a man depraved by nature and by "Cain's City."

I would suggest that the relative failure of Billy Budd as a fictional character can be accounted for in a very simple manner. Melville was too personally involved with Billy Budd. Whether he was picturing his own son Malcolm (who shot and killed himself at the age of twenty) or speaking of his own youth or of Christ or making a general statement of the perpetual sacrifice of boyish innocence to law and society, the idea of Billy Budd appeared so overwhelmingly moving to the aged Melville that he was not able to express it in artistically cogent language. If the reader wishes to look into the subterranean depths of the story, its "secret mines and dubious sides," he might well begin with the large number of figures of speech having to do with the act of eating; for example, the "mesmeric glance" of Claggart at Billy Budd, which Melville compares with "the hungry lurch of the torpedo fish." These metaphors show what Melville, in his darkest vision of life, is really saying. He is saying that the "horrible vulturism" of the world, of which he had written in *Moby Dick*, is a basic principle of things. Society, law, adulthood, worldly accomplishment can sustain themselves only by feeding on youthful innocence and generosity. In this sense, the theme of *Billy Budd*,[xiv] as of Melville's *Typee*, and, indeed, as of the sacrament of communion, is the ritualistic sacrifice of the hero.

But even as Melville shows us these dark and terrible ideas, we are aware that he is counterposing another range of meaning. Neither nature nor society is totally destructive of what is admirable in human life. By some genial, liberating grace, innocence and beauty are empowered to renew themselves in the very teeth of destruction. And so we are enabled to feel that *Billy Budd,* though not quite successful as tragic drama, remains immensely moving as a drama of pathos and myth. In this respect, its kinship is with the late plays of Shakespeare and with the New Testament, in its affirmation that out of the death inflicted by nature and society there issues new life.

. . . .

Melville is the most Shakespearean of American writers, a fact that will be brought home afresh to anyone who compares *Billy Budd* with such a play as *The Winter's Tale.** Like *Antigone* and *Billy Budd, The Winter's Tale* is concerned with the destruction of innocence and beauty by an inhumanly enforced legality. It is jealousy and suspicion which immediately cause Leontes, King of Sicilia, to bring about the death of his queen, Hermione, and his son, Mamillius. But mirrored in the jealous king we see the proscriptions of society conspiring with the destructive powers of nature—though, like Creon and Captain Vere, Leontes is personally superior to the law he lives by. In the "welkin eye" of Mamillius and of Billy Budd (Melville borrowed the phrase from Shakespeare) we see the idyllic world of eternal boyhood—described as follows by Polixenes as he recalls his boyhood friendship with Leontes:

> We were as twinn'd lambs that did frisk i' the sun
> And bleat the one at th' other. What we chang'd [p. xv]
> Was innocence for innocence; we knew not
> The doctrine of ill-doing, nor dream'd
> That any did.

The hanging of Billy Budd, at once a death and a resurrection, has the same force in Melville's story as the resurrection of Hermione at the end of Shakespeare's play, for both writers affirm that in some magical way innocence and beauty still exist in the world, that however evil nature and man may be they are still graced with a kind of minimal creative principle. Claggart's death is sudden and final. Captain Vere dies without having achieved the fame that might otherwise have come to him. But "the fresh young image of the Handsome Sailor" lives on in the heart of men. Of Melville, of Shakespeare, and of Sophocles (in *Oedipus at Colonus*) it may be said that in the works of their advanced age they took up the themes of the pathos of death, the crimes of society, the magically creative and restorative powers of nature, the myth of rebirth. . . .[xvi]

---

* A comparison brought in detail to my attention by Professor Andrew Chiappe.

MELVILLE'S VERSION OF TRAGEDY*

Richard Harter Fogle

. . . .

Billy Budd is, it seems to me, entirely comprehensible as Melville's version of tragedy. But to affirm this it is necessary to provide some definition both of tragedy and of irony as the terms are used here, though no more is attempted than an informal description sufficient for the immediate purpose. Tragedy, then, is a heightened and dignified action, intentionally so complicated as to involve its personae in the greatest conceivable difficulties, in order to elicit from them in their struggle the fullest potentialities of which they are capable. As to irony, we know that there are many notions of it, and perhaps no certain center can be found. We shall need to distinguish between different usages in order to specify the respects in which *Billy Budd* is or is not ironic. It is not ironic in the sense of irony ordinarily used by those who claim that it is; that is, a more or less complete reversal of the ostensible meaning, with, to add the words of A. R. Thompson in *The Dry Mock,* an effect of painful mockery. It is not painful, it is not sharp-edged, except by distortion of a part to misrepresent the total effect. It is ironic in that it frequently means more —not other—than it seems to say. Correspondingly *Billy Budd* is ironic in the modern sense of irony somewhat overworked by T. S. Eliot[109] —who called it wit—, I. A. Richards, and the New Critics: that is, a consciousness of the difficulties which any belief or attitude must face, an awareness of complexity. Indeed, one might concede to *Billy Budd* any ironies, of character, word, situation, or general attitude, which do not impeach its essential good faith and render verbalization itself a worthless currency. But precisely this destructive irony is what the ironist critics have fixed upon.

Billy Budd can like *Moby Dick* be justly described as Melville's nineteenth century version of classical tragedy, with old form revivified by new issues. According to Aristotelian prescription it portrays men as better than they are. The principals are exceptional: Billy, Captain Vere, and Claggart stand high in the hierarchy of natural man, above

---

* From *"Billy Budd*—Acceptance or Irony," *Tulane Studies in English,* VIII (1958), 109–113, by permission of Tulane University, *Tulane Studies in English,* and the author. [My title. Ed.]

the limited comprehension of the mere worldly-wise. The last meeting of Vere and Budd is too sacred for the common view. "But there is no telling the sacrament, seldom if in any case revealed to the gadding world wherever under circumstances at all akin to those here attempted to be set forth two of great Nature's nobler order embrace." As to Claggart, his evil is an object of moral and aesthetic appreciation, a quality to be savored by connoisseurs.

To heighten and dignify the tragic action Melville, as in *Moby Dick* with Ahab, magnifies his characters by investing them in heroic myth, legend, and history. The background is "a crisis for Christendom not exceeded in its undetermined momentousness at the time by any other era of which there is a record." The Handsome Sailor has mythical proportions. He is Aldebaran, a pagod, a grand Assyrian bull; at the yard-arm he is "young Alexander curbing the fiery Bucephalus. A superb figure, tossed up as by the horns of Taurus against the thunderous sky." He is Hercules refined by the influence of Venus, in him "something suggestive of a mother eminently favored by Love and the Graces." Melville thus states the problem of his modern tragedy: "Passion, and passion in its profoundest, is not a thing demanding a palatial stage whereon to play its part. Down among the groundlings, among the beggars and rakers of the garbage, profound passion is enacted. And the circumstances that provoke it, however trivial or mean, are no measure of its power. In the present instance the stage is a scrubbed gun-deck, and one of the external provocations a man-of-war's man's spilled soup." But his stage is so framed and so lighted as to display the tragic patterns to the best dramatic advantage. Antique myth,[110] Christian allusion at its most spacious, and finally the aesthetic distance of a more poetic age of sail are all utilized to magnify and embellish. (One may remark here in passing that it is a waste of ingenuity to prove that Billy is not the Handsome Sailor. Insofar as the Sailor is mythic hero he cannot be, for this is not a man but an archetype. Billy is as close to being the Handsome Sailor as any human, closely scanned, is likely to get. How much use was Melville able to get out of Bulkington in *Moby Dick?*) One final comment upon magnification: there is a commemorative quality about *Billy Budd* which very interestingly fuses the tragedy of hero and common man, which blends the diverse tones of *Moby Dick* and *John Marr and Other Sailors*. It is a tale at once of Lord Nelson and Greenwich pensioners, of mutiny, age-old oppression and pain, of military splendor. "To the mutineers those battles and especially Trafalgar were a plenary absolution; and a grand one; for all that goes to make up scenic naval display and heroic magnificence in arms. Those battles especially Trafalgar stand unmatched in human annals."

Like classical tragedy, *Billy Budd* makes a clear distinction between the sphere of the actual and the sphere of the ideal. True judgment of Billy lies with natural law, here also divine, the realm of absolute justice—chronometrical, as Plotinus Plinlimmon would have it in *Pierre*. " 'At the Last Assizes it shall acquit,' " says Vere. But Vere is equally clear on the distinction between a natural and a man-of-war world. The killing of Claggart is divine justice, but on the *Indomitable* it is the murder of a superior officer under wartime conditions. " 'Struck dead by an angel of God. Yet the angel must hang!' " " 'We proceed under the law of the Mutiny Act.' " In *Billy Budd* this tragic discrepancy is born of the dogma of the Fall of Man, which inevitably brings it into being. The law of the mutiny act is the law of a fallen world, in which an unfallen man like Billy cannot long exist. The immediate tragedy originates in a second Fall, the mutiny at the Nore, which has made any union of these worlds impossible. Age-old abuses of government, first rationally and properly protested at Spithead, have finally roused the "red meteor" of the Nore. "Reasonable discontent growing out of practical grievances in the fleet had been ignited into irrational combustion as by live cinders blown across the Channel from France in flames." The Revolution, one sees, is also a Fall. Many parallels with Melville's early writing have been suggested by critics of[111] *Billy Budd*. At this point one might add to the list *The Encantadas*, and most particularly Sketch Seventh, "Charles's Isle and the Dog-King." The Encantadas are a fallen world in which no rational government can flourish, in which oppression on the one hand is countered on the other by unbridled license.

In still another respect *Billy Budd* follows the classic formula of tragedy. The mainspring of the plot is a reversal, the *peripateia* defined by Aristotle as a hallmark of the complex tragic action, in which carefully laid plans produce results directly opposite to expectation, with, if well-managed, an artistic effect of combined surprise and inevitability. Thus Vere's well-planned arrangements lead to the killing of Claggart and the execution of Billy. He is not, we recall, deceived by Claggart's accusation. He brings the two men privately to his cabin, in order to confront the liar with truth in a manner as little harmful as possible to the general welfare. He fully understands Billy's inability to speak, but by his very kindness he brings on the fatal blow. "Contrary to the effect intended, these words so fatherly in tone, doubtless touching Billy's heart to the quick, prompted yet more violent efforts at utterance—efforts soon ending for the time in confirming the paralysis, and bringing to the face an expression which was as a crucifixion to behold. The next instant, quick as the flame from a discharged cannon at night, his right arm shot out, and Claggart dropped to the deck." Inevitability accompanies surprise, as Aristotle has laid down, for Melville has carefully paved the way by his references to Billy's stutter—his one connection with a fallen world—and his sudden violence once before aboard the merchantman *Rights of Man*. " 'Quick as lightning Billy let fly his arm. I dare say he never meant to do quite as much as he did, but anyhow he gave the burly fool a terrible drubbing.' "

With so many of the traits and qualities of tragedy, *Billy Budd* can claim also the final attribute of tragic reconciliation. In his defeat and passion the tragic hero yet brings about a partial redemption, he keeps alive some hope for the future, some confidence that goodness survives. So the story of Billy does not die, but is preserved and transmitted among seamen, and bits of the boom from which he was hanged are kept like pieces of the true Cross. This effect and survival of his memory might be contrasted with the effect of the announcement by Vere of Billy's impending execution, which "was listened to by the throng of standing sailors in a dumbness[112] like that of a seated congregation of believers in hell listening to the clergyman's announcement of his Calvinistic text."

This reconciliation is not precisely Greek, nor yet the Hebraic catharsis of *Samson Agonistes*—"nothing is here to wail, nothing for tears." There is no firm base of belief on which to ground it. The system with which we are to be reconciled is too vast and ambiguous. In one dimension of meaning Captain Vere is certainly God the Father, as Billy is God the Son; but as Nathalia Wright has well remarked Vere is not omnipotent. He acts in accordance with a law that is not of his own framing. There is something beyond him. . . .

As tragedy *Billy Budd* undoubtedly possesses tragic irony, the irony of fate. Its ironies would seem bitter to those who are inclined to view them bitterly. One might well think that Melville is presenting in *Billy Budd* a second crucifixion, which in this man-of-war world will inevitably be re-enacted whenever Christ should reassume the estate of man. His irony, however, is the natural attitude of a capacious, energetic, and subtle mind in pursuit of as much meaning as it can grasp, and its honest admission of the presence in reality of a something finally ungraspable. It magnifies and intensifies, it deepens and enriches, rather than diminishing by a mere irony of wailing mockery. Viewed in the full context of the tragedy of *Billy Budd*, this irony is neither a scream nor a sneer.[113]

BILLY AND OEDIPUS*

Herbert Weisinger and Adrian J. Jaffe

. . . .

Thus Melville has succeeded in writing what is in essence a perfect tragedy. Budd is the tragic hero who falls afoul of a set of circumstances which he did not cause, but which he cannot by the same token battle. Like Oedipus, Budd must suffer for the commission of a crime he did not intend to commit and which was, moreover, forced upon him. And like Oedipus, Billy Budd recognizes at the end the justice of Vere's decision and calls out before his death, "God bless you, Captain Vere," for without this understanding on Budd's part the tragedy would have no more meaning than if Othello had died without discovering that Desdemona was in fact innocent of adultery with Cassio. Thus the moral order, as in Greek tragedy, is questioned as the human being is pulled toward acquitting Billy Budd, and then in Vere's decision it is again reaffirmed and strengthened as we know that divine law still prevails on earth and that everything is in its proper place. It is a harsh and difficult acceptance that we must make, one that goes against every fiber of our human feeling, but it is of the very nature of the problem that this should be the way it is.

. . . .[143]

* From "Billy Budd, Foretopman," *The Laureate Fraternity: An Introduction to Literature* (Evanston: Row, Peterson and Co., 1960), 143, by permission of the publisher.

5. SPECIAL PROBLEMS

The Characters

THE CASE FOR CAPTAIN VERE*

Milton R. Stern

. . . .

. . . With Pierre's death, the story of the quester is complete. What remained now for Melville was to create a hero.

What would happen if there were a man who did manage to understand the proper relationship between heart and mind, a man who was not blind to history, a man who had a political or social position —say a ship's captaincy—which would allow him to translate his realizations into action? What if this man were exposed to a choice between pure ideal and "fallen" human history, with its present actuality of a crime-filled man-of-war world? Wanted: a hero.

Captain Vere is the man created to fill this position.

Billy Budd, like the early Pierre, is pictured as the childlike barbarian, the pure creature whose only experience really is just the experience of his own inner purity and ideality. His spontaneous responses preclude control by mind. This Christ figure also deceives by silence, albeit unwittingly, and finally becomes a murderer and a causer of his own death. Billy himself is the lure which Vere painfully rejects with all the insight created by an understanding of human history. Vere is educated, with the reader, to see Claggart as Satan and Baby Budd as Christ. But Vere's one overriding fact is the fact of the temporal world, the reality of his human community to which he owes his primary allegiance. He cannot choose the ideal which, by itself, is beautiful. And Claggart becomes the other facet of Budd.

---

* From *The Fine Hammered Steel of Herman Melville* (Urbana: University of Illinois Press, 1957), 26–27, by permission of the publisher and the author. [My title. Ed.]

Budd is the ideal, Claggart is the consequence. He is the completely mad and satanized quester who has withdrawn from quest. He is Ahab, retired in his New Bedford home, staring silently and crazily out at the sea. He is Ahab who has given up the chase, but who still watches. ... This demonized isolato seeks out and hates and yearns to believe in ideal Billy in exactly the same monomaniacal relationship which Ahab has to the white whale. Just as the reader sees that for Ahab the whale is only what Ahab thinks he is, and the whale, in a sense, becomes Ahab, so for Melville, Christ and Satan are ultimately one entity with a dual face. Like all Melvillean dualities, absolute identities are man-made products which unite in the flow of historical consequence in the Great God Time. The bright and the dark are the *same*.[26]

Vere rejects both lure and quester. His heartbroken rejection of Budd as a beautiful impossibility in favor of an ugly reality, his decision to force his position of command to operate according to what his head dictates and his heart detests, is his acceptance of this world as the only possible one. It is not, as many critics have attempted to demonstrate, an acceptance of historical necessity in a naturalistic universe. It is a consequent call for man to control his fate by controlling his actions in the historical world—and it is also Melville's statement of inability to find the way to do so. Vere decides to remain unwithdrawn, to accept the responsibility of the human community by accepting the responsibility of command. His decision to maintain order because of man's blindness is his sacrifice of self to the necessities of moral responsibility historically defined. Moreover, it is in his sacrifice of individual self to his social self that Vere finds his greatest identity, in the book as well as in the reader's mind. Vere is the polar opposite and instinctive antagonist to the quester. He offers the alternative behavior which had to be created once the quester's behavior was anatomized and rejected.

In *Billy Budd* the cast of characters changes. The quester as such drops out and the hero takes his place. And here the limitations (or perhaps the accuracy) of Melville's nineteenth-century naturalism become most apparent. For even the hero does not create a purged world. The lesson of Vere's sacrifice is lost. The lesson of Billy Budd's final realization is lost. The world gains not social insight but myth, and the cycle continues. Various studies have tried to identify Melville with his questers. But if he is to be identified with any of his characters, it must be with Captain Vere rather than with anyone else except Ishmael. (The two combined offer a very fair approximation of Melville's political, social, and metaphysical perceptions.) He is the man who turns to history for direction, yet who, when faced with the mystery of *human* nature, calls "Billy Budd! Billy Budd!" He calls for the perfection-aspiring human heart, and not in accents of remorse. . . .[27]

THE CASE AGAINST CAPTAIN VERE*

Leonard Casper

Billy Budd has often been considered Herman Melville's "testament of acceptance" because of Billy's unrebellious nature and because of the final blessing which he bestows on the officer who has condemned him to hang. Such an argument depends on the assumption that Melville can be identified completely with Billy. Similarly, it demands the conclusion that the man who rebelled against orthodox religious and political thought all his life and who, despite his unending interest, found no resolution of the tensions between good and evil, finally succumbed and accepted moral expediency and horological law. Because such a startling conversion is unprepared for by any of Melville's writings—his novels, poetry, journals, or letters—one is inevitably led to question the validity of such an interpretation of Billy Budd and to review again the case against Captain Vere.
. . . .[145]

. . . Although . . . [Captain Vere] is treated with some sympathy and much[149] understanding by Melville, it is fair to ask if the author ever accepts his reasoning.

Discussing natural depravity, Melville says

> Civilization, especially if of the austerer sort, is auspicious to it. It folds itself in the mantle of respectability...

And he goes on to describe how irrationality often lurks behind a reasonable exterior. Although this ostensibly is an explanation of Claggart's character, is there any of it which does not apply equally to Vere? Could Melville have written this, with Vere's austere nature, doubtful sanity, and cool judgment before him, and have not intended Vere to be read into this description? Or is this indictment by indirection?

Certainly Vere's behavior demands explanation because of its unnaturalness. Although he cannot take seriously the charge that Billy is a mutineer and for a while treats the boy like a son, his attitude changes completely when Billy unwittingly kills his false accuser. The captain seems to forget the first extenuating circumstance: he himself has just warned Claggart that, in something as serious as a mutiny

---

* From *Perspective*, V (Summer, 1952), 146–152, by permission of the publisher and the author.

charge, false-witness incurs a death penalty. Not only does he forget this, but he has already reached a decision before the court-martial is summoned. Billy must hang! The trial is a pretense at deliberative justice, and is made to appear so by Melville.

Other officers are surprised at Vere's strange attitude. The surgeon is struck by Vere's implied desire for secrecy. Aware of the danger of mutiny and of all the circumstances of the event which has just occurred, still he believes that as usual the accused should be referred to the Admiral for trial. Furthermore, Melville allows the surgeon "professionally" to surmise that Vere is a victim of mental aberration—and note that just previously his "professional eyes" correctly judged that Claggart is dead. The lieutenant and captain of marines equally consider improper Vere's decision to hold a drumhead.

The court-martial itself is improperly conducted by Vere who, as a witness, should have disregarded his rank; yet he knowingly testifies from the ship's weather side. After several moments of investigation have passed, he suddenly terminates interpretation of motives and circumstances and limits the court's judgment to the death blow itself. This is tantamount to having the court-martial sit merely as a coroner's jury. They are to decide the cause and causer[150] of death. Punishment follows inevitably. Vere's reported strangeness of manner reveals that Melville is carefully indicating that all this is a mistrial, a miscarriage of justice. The officers are shocked at the prejudgment evident in Vere's utterances.

Having silenced the captain of marines and Billy with overruling glances, Vere proceeds to the summary of his case. His rationalizations result in "virtuous expediency" being inevitable. By refusing all natural considerations, Vere makes his verdict unnatural, a perversion as serious as Claggart's.

By shifting responsibility for his decision to the King, Vere denies that he is a free agent with an individual sense of discrimination and judgment. He assumes the attitude of freely-willed fatalism and self-determinism evident in such characters as Ahab in *Moby-Dick* and, shortly, Billy Budd himself in his acceptance of the death penalty. His decision is not to make a decision, but to hand down a prejudgment; by limiting his free will, he makes the whole seem fated.

The question of free will in *Billy Budd* is important because those who argue that this is a testament of acceptance seem to imply that the basis for resignation is a sense of real fatalism not only exhibited by Vere and Billy, but believed in by Melville.

Billy's resignation, his acceptance of the death penalty, rises directly from his uneducated sense of fatalism, a sense that inhuman forces make his death necessary, however unjust those forces may be; and his fatalism is calm and triumphant because to him death is endurable. However, despite his acceptance of necessity in this sense, he never explicitly accepts Vere's argument of expediency or necessity.

He never says, "It is *right* that I die." He only implies, "I seem fated to die, right or wrong, and I am ready."

If this interpretation is correct, then Billy's final unstammered "God bless Vere" does not mean that he is accepting his fate as just or Vere's verdict as proper. Instead it is a form of absolution and Christian forgiveness (or perhaps even indifference), peculiarly ironic because it is echoed by the crew, automatically, in the more conventional sense of recognition of justice performed. Whatever the interpretation of Billy's words, obviously Melville outlives him and reflects his own opinion in the immediate murmur among the crew at the unnecessary death, in their wise revulsion and doubt.

In a post-mortem scene the implication of a conversation between the purser and the surgeon is that free will probably does exist. Among the Greeks one sense of the word euthanasia was the wilful sacrifice of one's self for one's country; the fact that the death was[151] willed was supposed to induce pleasure; this is obviously the sense in which the purser uses the word when he asks if Billy's death was a case of euthanasia because his limbs did not twitch. The scientist cannot refute, but can only deny, that in death Billy exhibited any will power. If this conclusion can be accepted as Melville's tentative one (all of his conclusions were open to further demonstration), then we must see that his viewpoint is much broader than Billy's self-deluding, fatalistic one; and therefore the two figures are not congruent.

Vere himself is not allowed to die such a noble death. Instead, in the description of his demise, it is intimated that he was not always wholly unselfish, but that he may have been secretly ambitious.

His death is connected with Billy's through an interesting and subtle device, an ironic newspaper report of the latter's death. The reporter says that Claggart's splendid character refutes Dr. Johnson's statement that patriotism is the last refuge of a scoundrel. Since Claggart is, actually, a depraved person, it must be obvious that Melville's opinion coincides wholly with Dr. Johnson's. And Starry Vere, of course, is the principal patriot in the story.

The story ends, not with Captain Vere, but where its center of gravity has been all the time: with the crew (the people) and their attitude toward Billy, their instinctive refusal to believe him capable of mutiny or of wilful murder (despite all the "reasons" given them). Their expression of sympathy for him, as he has become idealized in their memories, certainly is no testament of acceptance.[152]

BILLY BUDD*

W. H. Auden

If, when we finish reading *Billy Budd,* we are left with questions which we feel have been raised but not answered, if so to speak the equation has not come out to a finite number, as in a work of art it should, this is not due to any lack of talent on Melville's part, but to the insolubility of the religious paradox in aesthetic terms.

For any writer who attempts a portrait of the Christ-like is faced with the following problems. His central figure

a) must be innocent of sin, yet a man like us in all things tempted as we are. If he is given any aesthetic advantages, he at once ceases to be the God-Man and becomes the Man-God, the Aesthetic Hero, Hercules, who must be admired, but cannot be imitated. His sinlessness must be the result of faith, not of fortune.

b) He must be shown as failing in a worldly sense, i.e., as coming into collision with the law of this world, otherwise there is no proof that his sinlessness is due, not to faith, but to mere worldly prudence.[144]

c) Failure and suffering, however, are in themselves no proof of faith, because the collision with the law may equally well be the result of pride and sin. The crucified Christ is flanked by two crucified thieves.

d) The suffering must at one and the same time be willed and not-willed. If it seems entirely against the will of the sufferer, he becomes pathetic, if it seems entirely brought about by his own actions, he becomes tragic, and it is impossible to distinguish between pride and faith as the cause of his suffering.

. . . .

Melville . . . solves this problem. This Passion of Billy Budd is convincing, but fails in respects where Cervantes succeeds, and the ways in which he fails are interesting for the light they throw on the romantic conceptions of life. Like many other romantics Melville seems to hold:

1) That innocence and sinlessness are identical, or rather perhaps

---

that only the innocent, i.e., those who have never known the law, can be sinless. Once a man becomes conscious, he becomes a sinner. As long as he is not conscious of guilt, what he does is not sin. This is to push St. Paul's remark "Except I had known the Law, I had not known sin" still further to mean that "Except I had known sin, I[145] would not have sinned." Thus when Billy Budd first appears he is the Prelapsarian Adam:

Billy Budd in many respects was little more than a sort of upright barbarian, much such perhaps as Adam presumably might have been ere the urbane Serpent wriggled himself into his company.

He may have done things which in a conscious person would be sin—there appears to have been a certain Bristol Molly—but he feels no guilt.

2) That the unconscious and innocent are marked by great physical beauty, and therefore that the beautiful are sinless. This is true for Billy Budd as it was for Bulkington and Queequeg.

If the story were to be simply the story of the Fall, i.e., the story of how the Devil (Claggart) tempted Adam (Budd) into the knowledge of good and evil, this would not matter, but Melville wants Budd also to be the Second Adam, the sinless victim who suffers voluntarily for the sins of the whole world. But in order to be that he must know what sin is, or else his suffering is not redemptive, but only one more sin on our part. Further, as long as Billy Budd is only the Prelapsarian Adam, our nostalgic image of what we would still be if we had not fallen, his beauty is a perfectly adequate[146] symbol but the moment he becomes the Second Adam, the saving example whom we all should follow, this beauty becomes an illegitimate aesthetic advantage. The flaw of the stammer will not quite do, for this is only an aesthetic weakness, not a deliberate abandonment of advantages. It succeeds in making Billy Budd the innocent who "as a sheep before the shearer is dumb so openeth he not his mouth," but it makes his dumbness against his will not with it. We can never look like that, any more than, once we have become conscious, we can go back to unconsciousness, so how can we imitate his example? He becomes an aesthetic hero to admire from a distance. Melville seems to have been aware that something must happen to Billy to change him from the unconscious Adam into the conscious Christ but, in terms of his fable, he cannot make this explicit and the decisive transition has to take place off-stage in the final interview between Billy and Captain Vere.[147]

CLAGGART—I*

W. H. Auden

Similar insoluble paradoxes are raised by the demonic, the religious passion in reverse. For the demonic must be moved solely by pride, just as the religious must be moved solely by faith and love. Absolute pride cannot be manifested aesthetically because it tolerates no weakness except itself which thinks of itself as absolute strength.[147]

Absolute pride denies that the six other deadly sins are its children and despises them as weakness, being incapable of seeing that it is the source of all weakness. The Devil, therefore, cannot himself be lustful, gluttonous, avaricious, envious, slothful, or angry, for his pride will not allow him to be anything less than proud. He can only pretend in disguise to be any of these without actually feeling them; he can only "act" them. His acts must appear to be arbitrary and quite motiveless. No accurate aesthetic portrayal, therefore, is possible; Iago has to be given some motive, yet if the motive is convincing, he ceases to be demonic.

So with Claggart. Just as the bias in Melville's treatment of Billy Budd is a tendency to identify consciousness and sin, so he makes Claggart identify innocence with love; "To be nothing more than innocent," he sneers on seeing Billy Budd. This is no doubt what the serpent says to Adam, but it is not what he says to himself, which is rather "To be nothing more than loving." For the difference between God and the Devil is not that God does not know the meaning of good and evil and that the Devil does, but that God loves and the Devil will not love. That is why the motive for Claggart's behaviour, half-stated only to be withdrawn because no motive will really do, is homosexual desire.

In *Moby Dick*, where Ahab's pride revolts against lack of absolute strength, against being finite and dependent, the sexual symbolism centres round incest and the Oedipus situation, because incest is the magic act of[148] self-derivation, self-autonomy, with the annihilation of all rival power.

* From *The Enchafèd Flood*, by W. H. Auden. Copyright 1950 by the Rector and Visitors of the University of Virginia. Reprinted by permission of Random House, Inc.

In *Billy Budd,* the opposition is not strength/weakness, but innocence/guilt-consciousness, i.e., Claggart wishes to annihilate the difference either by becoming innocent himself or by acquiring an accomplice in guilt. If this is expressed sexually, the magic act must necessarily be homosexual, for the wish is for identity in innocence or in guilt, and identity demands the same sex.

Claggart, as the Devil, cannot, of course, admit a sexual desire, for that would be an admission of loneliness which pride cannot admit. Either he must corrupt innocence through an underling or if that is not possible he must annihilate it, which he does.[149]

CLAGGART—II*

Geoffrey Stone

. . . .

For the modern reader, trained in a non-moral casuistry for which the declared motive is never the true one, the fact that Claggart looked on "belted Billy rolling along the upper gundeck ... with a settled, meditative, and melancholy expression, his eyes strangely suffused with incipient feverish tears" will at once suggest a key to the story's meaning. And when Melville says that "sometimes the melancholy expression would have in it a touch of soft yearning, as if Claggart could even have loved Billy but for fate and ban", it will be plain that the iniquity considered here is the one to which Sodom has given its name. There is no doubt that the story lends itself not at all implausibly to this interpretation: if Claggart entertains a perversion of love for Billy, it is psychologically quite credible that such a love should be further perverted into hate. Actually, this provides no explanation to the mystery of iniquity. Would evil cease to operate in the world if the "ban" were removed or would Billy never have been hanged had Claggart been questioned by a psychiatrist before being mustered into the King's navy?

Quite possibly Melville intended that Claggart's immediate motives—obscure even to Claggart—were to be understood for what is now called ambivalent, but if Melville sought to disguise this matter

---

* From *Melville* by Geoffrey Stone, copyright 1949, Sheed & Ward, Inc., New York, by permission of the publisher. [My title. Ed.]

of the sexually illicit, it was a concealment[312] prompted by politeness, not by the belief that here was a piece of esoteric doctrine, ex-
plaining the most obscure mysteries, to be revealed only to the initiate.
Each age has things it does not talk about, but they are not necessarily
mysterious. Melville constantly addresses himself to the metaphysical
implications of Claggart's depravity, and if these are not his chief
concern with the matter, we are left with the curious spectacle of a
highly intelligent old man devoting the last three years of his life to
pondering a simple case of thwarted pederasty. . . .[313]

THE DANSKER: THE ARCHETYPE
OF THE WISE MAN*

James Baird

    . . . .
    . . . If one wishes to see the archetype of the wise man in less
distinctive guise, he has in Melville's work at least one example for
study. He is the old Dansker of *Billy Budd*, known[249] to his shipmates
as "Board-her-in-the-smoke." Among the crew of the *Indomitable*, he
is the "salt seer," as Melville calls him. In the narrative he has the
function of a Teiresias of the British Navy. He is the dispassionate
observer of Billy's innocence and Claggart's evil. He it is who warns
Billy that "Jimmy Legs" (Claggart) is "down upon him." He is oracular, as Melville intends him; he is the "old sea-Chiron" who thinks that
for the nonce "he had sufficiently warned his young Achilles." In his
role as the seer, the old Dansker is the voice of fate. But this old veteran of weathered face, of a complexion like parchment, of many
scars is, more particularly, a pure distillation of the ethos of the
mariner's custom, of the culture of all men who go down to the sea in
ships.

Now the first time that his small weasel eyes happened to light on Billy
Budd, a certain grim internal merriment set all his ancient wrinkles into
antic play. Was it that his eccentric unsentimental old sapience, primitive
in its kind, saw, or thought it saw, something which in contrast with the
warship's environment looked oddly incongruous in the Handsome Sailor?

---

    * From *Ishmael* (Baltimore: Johns Hopkins Press, 1956), 249–251, by permission
of the publisher. [My title. Ed.]

The primitive wisdom of the ancient Dansker is the least symbolized wisdom appearing in Melville's art. It matches the primitive flowing sea beneath the *Indomitable;* it has no form save the shadowy outline of an old sailor who is dusk to the sharp light in which Billy, Claggart, and Captain Vere are shown. The Dansker is wise with the weary wisdom of the Furies and the Norns, heavy with the knowledge of human error and distorted purpose. I can think of no character in literature nearer this hoary old seer of *Billy Budd* than Shakespeare's Old Man who enters with Ross after the murder of Duncan in *Macbeth* (Act II, Sc. iv) or Marlowe's Old Man who comes to warn Faustus (Scene xiv). With either or both of these he is the seer of primordial wisdom. In the art of Melville he is the character who stands nearest to the pure archetype; he is the least symbolic sage, and the only one who may be[250] assigned to that area of dream content in which archetype and nothing else is seen.

. . . .[251]

The Digressions

THE DIGRESSIONS IN *BILLY BUDD**

Mary Foley

Herman Melville's *Billy Budd* represents the conflict between two kinds of form—the metaphysical form by which an individual thing is what it is, and the external form (or pattern, or law) by which individual things exist in relation to each other. In this novel the conflict first occurs between naval law and an extraordinary malefactor, Billy Budd. Naval law, absolutely necessary to the existence of naval society, is established to deal with the "Divine average," the ninety-nine cases out of one hundred in which metaphysical form produces an "ordinary" crime. (For the sake of simplicity, "ordinary" may be

---

* A student's paper, not heretofore published; printed with the author's permission.

here defined as meaning "that situation in which agent, intention and act correspond sufficiently to produce the same emotional and rational verdict.") Billy Budd is the one hundredth case. His metaphysical form is rare. He is unusual and, therefore, in conflict with form (or pattern, or law).

For Melville, a spirit in conflict with form might be—but is not necessarily—superior to that form. A violation of the ordinary course of things can be a Billy Budd or an "Athéiste." Either one endangers order (or law, or form) and thereby threatens the existence of society which, being by definition "the usual," functions well under law. This is the basic paradox of *Billy Budd*—that a spirit in conflict with form, whether better or worse than ordinary, cannot endure in society because that spirit is itself incapable of form.

The digressions which conclude the novel are Melville's illustration of another conflict between organic form and externally imposed form. Each of the five digressions is an attempt to apply some law or pattern to the novel's events. Since *Billy Budd* already has its own organic form, the efforts to give it form through a preconceived standard are doomed to, at best, the achievement of partial truth. But the partial truths they embody are a necessary part of the whole truth the complete tale embodies.

The first digression represents the formula by which science would handle the phenomenon of Billy Budd. The ship's doctor is doggedly empirical in rejecting what he cannot touch ("will power," for example), while defining his terms like a Schoolman. His science, predicated upon absolute laws of cause and effect, admits of no peculiarities which cannot be referred to those laws. Thus, he explains Billy Budd by restricting his singularity to the absence of muscular spasms—and explains this absence in relation to natural but undetermined causes. This scientific formularization must completely reject euthanasia ("an easy, happy death") which, while congruent with the moral rarity which Melville emphasizes throughout the novel, is unscientific and, therefore, in conflict with the doctor's law.

The second digression offers the reaction of superstition—a form in its way as rigid as science. Where pure "head"—the doctor—sees natural but unknown causes, pure "heart"—the sailors—see preternatural forces at work. Recognizing Billy's more-than-physical transcendence, they find "no prosaic significance" in the sudden convergence of sea fowl following Billy's funeral. Although Melville partially rejects the almost mythic construction which the crew places upon this event, his explanation that the birds' behavior was "dictated by mere animal greed for prey" does not totally invalidate the crew's view. By recognizing a more basic aspect of Billy's nature than the doctor does, the sailors know him better than the doctor can. Their superstitious assignment of cause and effect is, nevertheless, as much the application of external form as is the doctor's empiricism. The sailors too, therefore, attain only partial truth.

In this digression the crew's reconstruction of events is interrupted by Captain Vere's insisting upon the form of routine work. Just as at Billy's trial, however, the routine is slightly awry: the ship's schedule is carried on "at an hour prior to the customary one." At the trial, normal court-martial procedure prevailed, but earlier than usual, since the case should really have been reserved for the admiral. Captain Vere's devotion to form is here in conflict with the great foe of human order—Time. The captain perpetually imposes order upon events as rapidly as possible, lest the passage of time should make such ordering impossible. (One of his main arguments for condemning Billy is the possibility that any lapse of time will be taken by the sailors as a sign of weakness of discipline.)

In the course of this digression the ambivalence of Melville's view of Vere, the apostle of law and order, becomes apparent. In phrases like "an officer like Captain Vere, a martinet as some deemed him," the juxtaposition of "martinet" and "Vere" suggests the conflict between the author's recognition of the necessity of order and his aversion to the destruction of Billy, which is necessary to maintain that order.

The third digression is Melville's own repudiation of form, his rejection of traditional literary form in favor of the looser structure of truth. Warning the reader that "truth uncompromisingly told will always have its ragged edges," he goes on to provide ragged edges. The death of Vere has, superficially, little connection with the rest of the story. "Well-wrought" fiction would have assigned his death to some poetically just agent. Vere's destruction by the French ship *Athéiste* (formerly *St. Louis*) is, upon examination, precisely in keeping with the book's main theme. As Billy represents the "Revolutionary Spirit" in its amiable aspects, *Athéiste,* flying the flag of the French government which deliberately embodied that spirit, represents conflict with form in its positively destructive aspects.

The fourth digression applies the standard of bureaucratic morality to Billy's case. According to the journalistic syllogism: Bad men strike their superiors. Billy struck a superior. Thus, Billy was bad. The article's emphasis upon "the efficiency of his majesty's navy" and its final assurance that "Nothing amiss is now apprehended aboard HMS *Indomitable*" repeat Melville's thesis that authority will willingly sacrifice the unusual for the sake of order.

The final digression represents an effort to come to terms with the story of Billy Budd through art. The sailors' vision of Billy is based upon the false information that his death was "unavoidably inflicted from the naval point of view"; but this vision is modified by their instinctive perception of Billy's innocence. Theirs is the conflict between reason and instinct, the order of logic and the rebellion of emotion. The ballad of "Billy in the Darbies" attempts to reconcile the image of Billy as an ordinary sailor with that of Billy as a hero somehow worthy of poetic immortality. Although the poem itself does not even suggest that Billy was remarkable, its very existence implies just that, since very few sailors do become ballad heroes. The grotesqueness of images like "pendant pearl," and " 'tis me, not the sentence they'll suspend," suggests that even the form of poetry cannot capture the truth of Billy Budd.

The digressions in *Billy Budd* thus serve a dual function. First, they echo the novel's basic conflict between metaphysical and external form. Second, they demonstrate the impossibility of reducing truth to a single formal standard. Each digression captures some aspect of the story and distorts the rest. But distortions actually vindicate the novel's lack of conventional form, embodying as they do the apparent formlessness which is the necessary organic form of the whole.

BILLY IN THE DARBIES*

M. L. Rosenthal and A. J. M. Smith

The following dramatic monologue appears in Herman Melville's novel *Billy Budd*. It gives us the hero's thoughts on the eve of his execution aboard ship for the crime of killing one of the ship's officers. The crime had been an unintentional one, and it has done no discredit to the much-loved young sailor who committed it. The sympathetic quality of Billy's character can be seen in the humble way he has of putting things, in his[372] affectionate tone when speaking of his messmate, and in his inability to visualize his own death as being of any great importance. At the same time, there is a saintly quality to his thoughts, as though he had long ago agreed that he was dying in a good cause. . . . Notice how the slight touch of humor deepens the pathos of Melville's effect here, and how Billy's resignation to his destiny makes the pathos a minor aspect of his essentially heroic character—in which there is not a trace of whining or self-pitying bitterness. ("Darbies" are manacles. The Dansker and Taff are shipmates of Billy's: Taff is now dead.)

* From M. L. Rosenthal and A. J. M. Smith, *Exploring Poetry*. Copyright 1955 by The Macmillan Company and used with permission of the publisher and author.

. . . .[373]

This monologue, in addition to what it tells us of Billy's character, becomes, indirectly, something more—a humble, loving but fatalistic view of the world. Through the doomed sailor's thoughts, first of all, we receive a picture of the good life as one in which a few creature-comforts would be available and in which men would judge each other's motives genially and affectionately. Even if he has some "bad" thoughts, Billy's mind does not rest with them. It passes sadly over to details of his coming execution, halts momentarily with the all-too-answerable question "But aren't it all sham?"—but finally moves to calm acceptance of his lot. He knows, as a matter of fact, that it *is* "all sham," that the laws of society have arbitrarily made him the scapegoat in a ritual-travesty of justice which he does not quite understand. But although he could not at first imagine his own death, he at last comes to see himself as already, literally, dead: "I am sleepy, and the oozy weeds about me twist."

As so often happens, in the dramatic monologue and in other kinds of poetry as well, the "story" here involves a projection into the future: first a recognition that a change must come about and a parallel tension at the prospect (as in Billy's inability to get his imagination fastened on the precise fact of his own physical death), then the realization of its full meaning, and finally the crystallization of an attitude or insight (in this case, Billy's complete acceptance of his future condition).

We too must "accept." We must accept the truth of this projection of imagination. We shall do so if we feel that we know the speaker's essential character, if the progression of his thoughts and feelings is credible, and if the external objects he observes and the way they enter his consciousness are acutely enough conceived. In such case, the "meanings" the monologue carries along with it will be seen as having their own truth and life and will exercise a certain power over us whether we are prepared to believe in them generally or not. Artifice and realism move together in[374] Melville's poem to bring this conviction about in us. Every reader separately will have to come to his own conclusions, of course, about the degree of psychological realism present in Billy's thinking. But realism is not in any case the only consideration, for the phrasing and the balanced movements of the poem are not always of the kind one would expect in a simple, untutored person like Billy. There are humble picturings—"down on his marrow-bones," "a nibble-bit o' biscuit," and "a blur's in my eyes." And there are others with the poet's own trademark on them—"the moon-shine astray," "a jewel-block they'll make of me," "pendent pearl from the yard-arm-end," "his cheek ... like the budding pink." There is a rough correspondence between the alternation of the two kinds of language and the swinging, up-down movements of the physical visualization in this poem. The chaplain goes *down* on his knees; the moon comes *up* and then, in forecast, *down;* Billy imagines himself *up* in the air, then *down* to the moment before he is *raised* to be hanged; and so on until the movement is quieted in his vision of himself *sinking* and, finally, rocking slowly at the *bottom* of the sea. Through much of the monologue, the sense of emotional depression grows deeper the more clearly Billy visualizes his coming death. Yet the closing lines, with their steadily downward movement until they reach a point of final rest at the ocean-bottom, actually represent a heightening of his morale as his agitation of spirit subsides and he moves into total acceptance. The poet behind the scenes—somewhat like a theatrical director—has been experimentally manipulating basic dramatic feeling toward this final impression. To do so, he has had to distort nature and add something to it. Without such distortions and additions, however, poetry and the other arts would lose their inner truthfulness to the felt meaning of experience.[375]

The Author

HERMAN MELVILLE*

W. H. Auden

HERMAN MELVILLE
(For Lincoln Kirstein)

Towards the end he sailed into an extraordinary mildness,
And anchored in his home and reached his wife
And rode within the harbour of her hand,
And went across each morning to an office
As though his occupation were another island.

Goodness existed: that was the new knowledge
His terror had to blow itself quite out

* From *The Collected Poetry of W. H. Auden,* copyright 1940 by W. H. Auden, by permission of Random House, Inc., and Faber and Faber Ltd., Publishers.

To let him see it; but it was the gale had blown him
Past the Cape Horn of sensible success
Which cries: "This rock is Eden. Shipwreck here."

But deafened him with thunder and confused with lightning:
—The maniac hero hunting like a jewel
The rare ambiguous monster that had maimed his sex,
Hatred for hatred ending in a scream,
The unexplained survivor breaking off the nightmare—
All that was intricate and false; the truth was simple.[146]

Evil is unspectacular and always human,
And shares our bed and eats at our own table,
And we are introduced to Goodness every day,
Even in drawing-rooms among a crowd of faults;
He has a name like Billy and is almost perfect
But wears a stammer like a decoration:
And every time they meet the same thing has to happen;
It is the Evil that is helpless like a lover
And has to pick a quarrel and succeeds,
And both are openly destroyed before our eyes.

For now he was awake and knew
No one is ever spared except in dreams;
But there was something else the nightmare had distorted—
Even the punishment was human and a form of love:
The howling storm had been his father's presence
And all the time he had been carried on his father's breast.

Who now had set him gently down and left him.
He stood upon the narrow balcony and listened:
And all the stars above him sang as in his childhood
"All, all is vanity," but it was not the same;
For now the words descended like the calm of mountains—
—Nathaniel had been shy because his love was selfish—
But now he cried in exultation and surrender
"The Godhead is broken like bread. We are the pieces."

And sat down at his desk and wrote a story.[147]

QUESTIONS FOR STUDY: THEME
AND PAPER TOPICS

NOTE: The criticism collected in this book and in the references cited in the checklist gives ample testimony to the richness of *Billy Budd*. The tale, however, is by no means thereby exhausted, for it still raises a wealth of issues. The questions that follow are in no way exhaustive, nor are they intended to direct the student or the teacher toward any particular approach to the story. But it is hoped that they are suggestive and flexible enough to provide a wide variety of provocative discussion and papers. The best questions and topics will of course ideally come from the student himself.

Study Questions

1. What are the esthetic advantages, or disadvantages, of Melville's having conceived of a ship for his locale?

2. In what different way is *Claggart* as appropriate a name as the names of Billy, Vere, and the three ships: *Rights-of-Man, Indomitable,* and *Athéiste?*

3. The three major characters, Billy, Claggart, and Vere, all die. What do their deaths have in common? In what ways are they different? How are they related? In what sense are the deaths "comments" on one another? Do they collectively embody a single comment? If so, what is it?

4. Compare Braswell's reading of the story as "spiritual autobiography" with Auden's poem. In what ways are they similar? In what ways dissimilar?

5. Observe the color symbolism in the tale, the use of *rose* in connection with Billy and of *pallor* with Claggart. How closely may we associate them, respectively, with "heart" and "head"? How is the opposition between dark and light used generally? In what other ways does Melville assign symbolic values to his characters?

6. What differing esthetic premises appear to lie behind the five essays in Section III? Are the premises mutually exclusive? Which ap-

proach seems best to take into account the complete tale? What kind of comment do the authors collectively make about the nature of the tale? Much criticism of *Billy Budd* is dominated by a consideration of Melville's attitude toward Vere. How crucial is this question to these five critics? Is it a necessary critical problem of the tale?

7. How far are we to press the Christian parallels? "Are we to regard them as overtones and images," as Bruce Harkness and Royal Gettman have asked, "or are we to regard them as echoes and counterparts?" Can Billy effectively be the "upright barbarian," Adam, *and* Christ? Can Vere be God, father to Billy, *and* the ideal temporal Governor? Are Auden's objections to the characterization of Billy and Claggart valid ones?

8. Is the function of the early digressions (that is, the dedication to Jack Chase, the references to the French Revolution and the mutinies at Nore and Spithead, the Nelson digression) similar to that of the ending ones? Discuss the contribution made to the tale as a whole by each of these. Compare and contrast Nelson, Captain Graveling, and Vere as *captains*. Does Melville intend them as comments on one another?

9. How convincing is Melville's understanding and depiction of the *psychological* motivations behind the actions of Billy, Claggart, Vere, and the Dansker? Do their symbolic functions reduce or strengthen their worth as believable human characters? Discuss each character in this connection.

10. Is it a serious limitation to read the story simply as a conflict between a natural world and a civilized one? Stallman and Watters see the following additional antitheses suggested by the story: depravity versus innocence, intuition versus "knowledge of the world," the earthly versus the heavenly, head versus heart, military duty versus private conscience, war versus religion, landsmen versus seamen, society versus the individual. Does one of these more accurately reflect that conflict? Does one of your own?

11. Examine carefully the background information given about Billy, Claggart, and Vere. What considerations seem to have determined the kind and amount of information Melville provides about these three characters? Take into consideration theme, characterization, and technique.

12. Is the uncertainty about the meaning of *Billy Budd* a reflection on the esthetic achievement of the tale? What are, finally, its strengths and weaknesses as a story, as a unified work of art?

Theme Topics

1. Following is a list of authors referred to in *Billy Budd:* Sir William Blackstone, Edmund Burke, John Calvin, Camoëns, Sir Edward Coke, Charles Dibdin, Diderot, Oliver Goldsmith, Hawthorne, G. P. R. James, Samuel Johnson, Martial, Andrew Marvell, Milton, Montaigne, Thomas Paine, Plato, Ann Radcliffe, Tennyson, Voltaire.* Discover where in *Billy Budd* the reference or references are made to each. Find out what you can about each author and his works; then explain Melville's purpose in thus referring to him. What contribution is thereby made to the tale?

2. State explicitly the central theses in the two articles under the section *"Billy Budd* as Testament." Then support that thesis which most nearly parallels your own reading of the story. (The same can be done with each of the sections, or with selected essays from different ones —the case for or against Captain Vere, for example, or Auden's doubts about the characterization of Billy and Claggart.)

3. Select one of the following episodes from the tale: Billy's last words, Vere's last words, the moment of Claggart's death, "Billy in the Darbies," Vere's speech to the court-martial, the conversation between the purser and the surgeon, the dedication to Jack Chase, Billy's hanging, the spilt soup episode, the unreported conversation between Vere and Billy as Vere reports the court-martial's verdict, the newspaper account of Billy's death, the Nelson digression, the function of the Dansker or of the Chaplain, the reference to the *Somers,* and so on. Then examine and evaluate the function performed by the episode, the contribution it makes to the meaning of the whole.

4. Explicate Auden's poem, using as model the technique and method Rosenthal and Smith employ in their examination of "Billy in the Darbies." In what way is the poem an interpretation of *Billy Budd?* Is it in any sense also an evaluation of it?

5. Reread the Biblical account of Adam's expulsion from Eden and make your own analysis of Melville's intention in that regard in *Billy Budd.* Compare your results with Arvin's. Do the same with the Biblical accounts of Christ (or with Milton's *Paradise Lost*) and test

---

* Suggested to me by Gordon Roper's useful "An Index of Herman Melville's *Mardi, Moby-Dick, Pierre,* and *Billy Budd"* (Unpublished Ph.D. dissertation, University of Chicago, 1944), 255–257.

your findings against the findings of the appropriate critics. Do the allusions work, as Tindall suggests, in a fashion similar to the mythical parallels in Joyce's *Ulysses* or Eliot's *The Waste Land?*

6. Compare Billy with Othello, Vere with Hamlet, or Claggart with Iago. For more recent parallels, compare and contrast Billy with Huck Finn, or with Maisie Farange (from James's *What Maisie Knew*), Morgan Moreen (from James's "The Pupil"), Holden Caulfield (from Salinger's *Catcher in the Rye*), George Willard (from Anderson's *Winesburg, Ohio*), Ike McCaslin (from Faulkner's *The Bear*), or Tommo (from Melville's first novel, *Typee*).

7. One might also make comparative studies of the tale as a whole with the works listed above or with *Antigone, Oedipus Rex,* or *Oedipus at Colonus;* or with Hawthorne's "The Birthmark," specifically referred to in the tale.

8. Analyze, specify, and evaluate the varying critical methods employed by Braswell, Glick, Chase, West, and Tindall in order to define what literary criticism should be. Contrast these methods with those employed by the critics in Section I.

9. Take what you consider to be Melville's resolution of the central moral issue in *Billy Budd;* examine it, test it, and evaluate it in the light of your own beliefs regarding the basic nature of goodness, evil, justice, or fate.

10. Compare the tale *Billy Budd* with the play by Coxe and Chapman or the opera by Crozier and Britten. In what special ways are they both interpretations and evaluations of the tale?

Topics for Longer Essays and Term Papers

1. Trace the critical reputation of *Billy Budd* from Weaver's brief remarks in 1921 through the almost equally brief but radically different comments of Fiedler (see checklist) in 1960. Does this also become a brief history of American critical thought over the same four decades, its strengths, weaknesses, and variety? Compare and contrast the British and American reactions to the story.

2. Place *Billy Budd* in its proper perspective as the culmination of a development begun in Melville's *Mardi* and continued through *Moby-Dick* and *Pierre.* Or take another track and trace Melville's de-

velopment through his sea stories, beginning with *Typee* and *Omoo,*
through *Redburn, White-Jacket, Moby-Dick,* and his short tales of the
sea, on to *Billy Budd.* Or, more simply, take an early novel, a middle
one, and *Billy Budd.* Such studies could be focused on major themes,
major characters, major moral resolutions, and so on. The possibilities
are many. One might also trace Melville's development from *The
Confidence-Man* to *Billy Budd* by way of the considerable amount of
poetry he wrote in between.

3. Trace the history of the *Somers* affair and its relation to Melville and his family. Begin with the items by Anderson, Freeman,
Arvin, and Harrison. In what ways does knowledge of the affair affect
one's understanding and evaluation of Melville's tale.

4. Compare and contrast *Billy Budd* with late tales by other major
nineteenth-century American novelists—with Hawthorne's *The Marble
Faun,* for example, Twain's *The Mysterious Stranger,* and James's
"The Beast in the Jungle" or "The Jolly Corner." Do they throw light
on one another in any meaningful way? Do they allow you to make
any generalizations about American fiction?

5. At least one critic (Jean Jacques Mayoux) approaches the problem of Melville's treatment of innocence in *Billy Budd* by pointing
to Kafka's *The Trial* as a contrasting treatment of essentially the same
problem. In what ways are the two views alike? In what ways different? Or contrast *Billy Budd* with Camus's *The Fall.*

6. Contrast Melville's treatment of innocence in *Billy Budd* with
one of James's American innocents—with Christopher Newman, say,
or Daisy Miller. In what ways is Twain's view of innocence (in *The
Innocents Abroad,* for example) essentially different from Melville's
and James's? How about Twain's view in *Huckleberry Finn?*

7. In his *The American Novel and Its Tradition* (Garden City:
Doubleday Anchor Books, 1957), pp. 5–7, Chase says this:

. . . The American novel has usually seemed content to explore, rather than
to appropriate and civilize, the remarkable and in some ways unexampled
territories of life in the New World and to reflect its anomalies and dilemmas.
It has not wanted to build an imperium but merely to discover a new place
and a new state of mind. Explorers see more deeply, darkly, privately and
disinterestedly than imperialists, who must perforce be circumspect and pru-
dential. The American novel is more profound and clairvoyant than the
English novel, but by the same token it is narrower and more arbitrary, and
it tends to carve out of experience brilliant, highly wrought fragments rather
than massive unities.

In fact, he continues, ". . . many of the best American novels achieve
their very being, their energy and their form, from the perception and
acceptance not of unities but of radical disunities." Examine *Billy*

Budd in terms of the various ways it does or does not fit this generic definition of the American novel.

8. Tindall says that the "teller" of *Billy Budd* ". . . is not unlike the Marlow of Conrad's *Heart of Darkness,*" that Melville's thought-process, like that of Marlow, "is the heart of this darkness and its shape the objective correlative, a form for something at once imperfectly understood and demanding understanding." Reread the latter part of Tindall's essay and then Conrad's *Heart of Darkness* and compare the technique of the two tales. See also Thompson, Freeman, and Braswell on the narrative technique in *Billy Budd*. In what ways does what Conrad depicts as the center of experience parallel what Melville depicts in *Billy Budd?* Tindall also suggests that the narrative technique in Faulkner's *Absalom, Absalom!* is essentially the same. Test it in relation to *Billy Budd*.

9. In Conrad's *Lord Jim* the character Stein makes this well-known statement:

A man that is born falls into a dream like a man who falls into the sea. If he tries to climb out into the air as inexperienced people endeavour to do, he drowns. . . . No! I tell you! The way is to the destructive element submit yourself, and with the exertions of your hands and feet in the water make the deep, deep sea keep you up.

Does this passage throw any light on *Billy Budd?* Compare the two novels.

10. McElderry, the Gollins, Cameron and Sutton (see checklist) have all found what they describe as earlier treatments of the *Billy Budd* theme. Read the various works they cite and discover your own parallels. Test your readings against Withim's use of their findings.

11. Provide annotations for some or all of the allusions in *Billy Budd*. What is their collective contribution to the meaning and worth of the tale? See Pearson.

BIBLIOGRAPHY

An Annotated Checklist of Studies of *Billy Budd*

NOTE: I have provided brief descriptive annotations only for those important studies whose titles are either misleading or unspecific. The entries preceded by an asterisk (*) are printed in complete or nearly complete form in this collection; those preceded by a dagger (†) are excerpted in this collection and carry annotations only when the unexcerpted portions are of major importance.

Anderson, Charles Roberts. "The Genesis of *Billy Budd*," *American Literature*, XII (Nov., 1940), 328–346. Important first extensive treatment of sources.

Arvin, Newton. "A Note on the Background of *Billy Budd*," *American Literature*, XX (March, 1948), 51–55. Additional evidence on the *Somers* affair.

*———. *Herman Melville*. New York: William Sloane Associates, Inc., 1950. Pp. 292–299. Reprinted as a Compass Book (New York: The Viking Press, 1957).

*Auden, W. H. *The Enchafèd Flood or The Romantic Iconography of the Sea*. New York: Random House, 1950. Pp. 144–149.

*———. "Herman Melville," *Collected Poems of W. H. Auden*. New York: Random House, 1945. Pp. 146–147.

†Baird, James. *Ishmael: A Study of the Symbolic Mode in Primitivism*. Baltimore: Johns Hopkins Press, 1956. Pp. 249–251, 272–273, 426–427. Reprinted as a Harper Torchbook (New York: Harper & Brothers, 1960).

Berthoff, Warner. " 'Certain Phenomenal Men': the Example of *Billy Budd*," *ELH*, XXVII (Dec., 1960), 334–351. Billy and Vere represent complementary "motions of magnanimity under the most agonizing worldly duress . . ."

Blackmur, R. P. "Introduction," *American Short Novels*. New York: Thomas Y. Crowell Co., 1960. Pp. 5–8. Views *BB* as Melville's "continuing allegory of how it is that we seek what we must shun."

Bowen, Merlin. *The Long Encounter: Self and Experience in the Writings of Herman Melville*. Chicago: University of Chicago Press, 1960. Pp. 216–233. Views *BB* as a study of moral blindness: anti-Vere.

*Braswell, William. "Melville's *Billy Budd* as 'An Inside Narrative,' " *American Literature*, XXIX (May, 1957), 133–146.

———. *Melville's Religious Thought: An Essay in Interpretation*. Durham: Duke University Press, 1943. Pp. 122–124. Reprinted (New York: Pageant Books, Inc., 1959).

Brown, John Mason. "Hanged from the Yardarm," *As They Appear*. New York: McGraw Hill Book Co., Inc., 1952. Pp. 186–192. Compares the tale with the play.

Brumm, Ursula. "The Figure of Christ in American Literature," *Partisan Review*, XXIV (Summer, 1957), 403–412, *passim*.

Cameron, Kenneth W. *"Billy Budd* and *An Execution at Sea," Emerson Society Quarterly*, No. 2 (First Quar., 1956), 13–15. Reprints an earlier treatment of the *BB* theme.

Campbell, H. M. "The Hanging Scene in Melville's 'Billy Budd,'" *Modern Language Notes*, LXVI (June, 1951), 378–381.

———. "The Hanging Scene in Melville's 'Billy Budd': A Reply to Mr. Giovannini," *Modern Language Notes*, LXX (Nov., 1955), 497–500.

Carpenter, Frederic I. *American Literature and the Dream*. New York: Philosophical Library, Inc., 1955. Pp. 79–82, 203–205. *BB* as an expression of the problem of liberty and authority; compares *BB* with Wouk's *The Caine Mutiny*.

———. "Melville: The World in a Man of War," *University of Kansas City Review*, XIX (Summer, 1953), 257–264. Reprinted in Carpenter, above.

*Casper, Leonard. "The Case against Captain Vere," *Perspective*, V (Summer, 1952), 145–152.

Chase, Richard. "A Note on *Billy Budd," The American Novel and Its Tradition*. Garden City, N.Y.: Doubleday Anchor Books, 1957. Pp. 113–115. A reply to R. W. B. Lewis (see below) and a "political" reading of *BB*.

———. "Dissent on Billy Budd," *Partisan Review*, XV (Nov., 1948), 1212–1218. Expanded in Chase, *Herman Melville* (see below).

†———. *Herman Melville: A Critical Study*. New York: The Macmillan Co., 1949. Pp. 258–277, 298. Questions the conscious esthetic achievement of *BB*.

*———. "Introduction," *Selected Tales and Poems* of Herman Melville. New York: Rinehart Editions, 1950. Pp. xiii–xvi.

Clive, Geoffrey. *The Romantic Enlightenment*. New York: Meridian Books, 1960. Pp. 161–165. *BB*, Kierkegaard's *Fear and Trembling*, and *Crime and Punishment*.

———. "The Teleological Suspense of the Ethical in Nineteenth Century Literature," *Journal of Religion*, XXXIV (April, 1954), 75–87. Same as Clive, above.

Cowie, Alexander. "Herman Melville," *The Rise of the American Novel*. New York: American Book Co., 1948. Pp. 394–395.

Coxe, Louis O., and Robert Chapman. *Billy Budd: The Play in Three Acts*, with "Foreword" by Brooks Atkinson. Princeton: Princeton University Press, 1951. "Foreword" is Atkinson's review of the play, New York *Times*, Feb. 11, 1951.

Cramer, Maurice B. "'Billy Budd' and 'Billy Budd,'" *Journal of General Education*, X (April, 1957), 78–91. Compares play with tale.

Cunliffe, Marcus. *The Literature of the United States*. London: Pelican, 1954. Pp. 118–119.

Feidelson, Charles N. *Symbolism and American Literature.* Chicago: University of Chicago Press, 1953. Reprinted as a Phoenix Book. Chicago: University of Chicago Press, 1959. Pp. 212, 344–345. Questions the "acceptance" thesis.

Fiedler, Leslie. *Love and Death in the American Novel.* New York: Criterion Books, 1960. Pp. 359, 362, 434–435.

*Fogle, Richard Harter. "*Billy Budd*—Acceptance or Irony," *Tulane Studies in English,* VIII (1958), 107–113.

———. "*Billy Budd:* the Order of the Fall," *Nineteenth-Century Fiction,* XV (Dec., 1960), 189–205. Defends Vere.

*Foley, Mary. "The Digressions in *Billy Budd,*" in *Melville's Billy Budd and The Critics,* ed. by William T. Stafford. San Francisco: Wadsworth Publishing Company, Inc., 1961. Pp. 161–164.

Forster, E. M. *Aspects of the Novel.* New York: Harcourt, Brace and Co., 1927. Pp. 204–206.

———. "Letter," *The Griffin,* I (1951), 4–6. Explains his treatment of Vere as villain in his libretto (see below) for the Benjamin Britten opera of *BB.*

———, and Eric Crozier. "Libretto" for Benjamin Britten's *Billy Budd: Opera in Four Acts.* London: Boosey & Hawkes, Ltd., 1951.

Freeman, F. Barron. "Introduction," *Herman Melville's Billy Budd.* Cambridge: Harvard University Press, 1948. Pp. 1–126. Extended analysis of the biographical background, sources, composition, text, style, technique, and significance of *BB.*

*Freeman, John. *Herman Melville.* New York: The Macmillan Co., 1926. Pp. 131–136.

Freimarck, Vincent. "Mainmast as Crucifix in *Billy Budd,*" *Modern Language Notes,* LXXII (Nov., 1957), 496–497.

Gerould, Gordon Hall. *The Patterns of English and American Fiction: A History.* Boston: Little, Brown and Co., 1942. Pp. 354, 358. *BB* "predicts" Conrad.

Gettmann, Royal A., and Bruce Harkness. "Billy Budd, Foretopman," *Teacher's Manual for A Book of Stories.* New York: Rinehart & Co., Inc., 1955. Pp. 71–74.

Giovannini, G. "The Hanging Scene in Melville's *Billy Budd,*" *Modern Language Notes,* LXX (Nov., 1955), 491–497. Reply to H. M. Campbell (see above).

*Glick, Wendell. "Expediency and Absolute Morality in 'Billy Budd,'" *PMLA,* LXVIII (March, 1953), 103–110.

Goldsmith, Arnold L. "The 'Discovery Scene' in *Billy Budd,*" *Modern Drama,* III (Feb., 1961). Defends the discovery scene in the dramatic version of *BB.*

Gollin, Richard and Rita. "Justice in an Earlier Treatment of the *Billy Budd* Theme," *American Literature,* XXVIII (Jan., 1957), 513–515.

Hayford, Harrison, ed. *The Somers Mutiny Affair.* Englewood Cliffs: Prentice-Hall, Inc., 1959.

Heilman, Robert. *Magic in the Web; Action and Language in Othello.* Lexington: University of Kentucky Press, 1956. Pp. 37, 43, 113, 116, 247–248. Compares Iago and Claggart.

Hillway, Tyrus. "Melville's *Billy Budd,*" *Explicator,* IV (1945), Item 12. Defends Vere.

———. "*Billy Budd:* Melville's Human Sacrifice," *Pacific Spectator,* VI (Summer, 1952), 342–347. BB's death as "heroic tragedy."

Howard, Leon. *Herman Melville: A Biography.* Berkeley: University of California Press, 1951. Pp. 324–328. About sources and conditions under which BB was written and a view of its meaning as "the best thing possible 'in this incomprehensible world.'"

Kazin, Alfred. "Ishmael in His Academic Heaven," *New Yorker,* Feb. 12, 1949, pp. 88–89. Review-essay of Freeman's edition of BB.

Krieger, Murray. *The Tragic Vision.* New York: Holt, Rinehart and Winston, Inc., 1960. Pp. 256, 260, 263–264. Questions the tragic achievement of the tale.

Lesser, Simon. *Fiction and the Unconscious.* Boston: Beacon Press, 1957. Pp. 92–93. A psychological reading.

Levin, Harry. *The Power of Blackness.* New York: Alfred A. Knopf, Inc., 1958. Pp. 194–197. BB is at best "a truce."

Lewis, R. W. B. *The American Adam: Innocence, Tragedy, and Tradition in the Nineteenth Century.* Chicago: University of Chicago Press, 1955. Pp. 146–152. BB as an "American" Adam in terms of Horace Bushnell's definition of American innocence.

McElderry, B. R., Jr. "Three Earlier Treatments of the *Billy Budd* Theme," *American Literature,* XXVII (May, 1955), 251–257.

Mason, Ronald. "*Billy Budd* and the Victory of Innocence," *The Spirit Above the Dust: A Study of Herman Melville.* London: John Lehmann, Ltd., 1951. Pp. 245–260. Also on BB and *The Tempest.*

Matthiessen, F. O. "Billy Budd, Foretopman," *American Renaissance: Art and Expression in the Age of Emerson and Whitman.* New York: Oxford University Press, 1941. Pp. 500–514. As the acceptance of "necessity" and parallels with Jonathan Edwards, Shakespeare, Keats, and other Melville works.

Mayoux, Jean Jacques. *Melville,* tr. by John Ashbery. New York: Grove Press, 1960. Pp. 125–128. As "acceptance" in contrast to Kafka's *The Trial.*

Miller, James E., Jr. "*Billy Budd:* The Catastrophe of Innocence," *Modern Language Notes,* LXXIII (March, 1958), 168–176. BB as a culminating "Titanic Innocent"—following Taji, Ahab, Pierre, and Mortmain.

———. "Melville's Search for Form," *Bucknell Review,* VIII (Dec., 1959), 275–276. Melville turns to Christian myth in BB to demonstrate ". . . its weakness and final inefficacy."

Montale, Eugenio. "An Introduction to *Billy Budd* (1942)," *Sewanee Review,* LXVIII (Summer, 1960), 419–422. English translation of an introduction to an Italian edition of BB.

*Mumford, Lewis. *Herman Melville*. New York: Harcourt, Brace and Co., 1929. Pp. 353–357.

†Murry, John Middleton. "Herman Melville's Silence," *Times Literary Supplement*, No. 1173, (July 10, 1924), 433. Reprinted in *John Clare and Other Studies*. London: Peter Neville, 1950. Pp. 209–212.

Noone, John B., Jr. *"Billy Budd:* Two Concepts of Nature," *American Literature*, XXIX (Nov., 1957), 249–262. Important idealogical reading in terms of Hobbes, Locke, and Rousseau.

†Pearson, Norman Holmes. "Billy Budd: 'The King's Yarn,'" *American Quarterly*, III (Summer, 1951), 99–114. Important demonstration of how literary associations (especially Milton), sources, and parallels enrich and are necessary to a reading of *BB*.

Phelps, Leland R., "The Reaction to *Benito Cereno* and *Billy Budd* in Germany," *Symposium*, XIII (Fall, 1959), 294–299. Includes important discussion of Thomas Mann's reaction to *BB*.

Plomer, William. "Introduction," *Billy Budd, Foretopman*. London: John Lehmann, Ltd., 1947. Pp. 7–10. *BB* as "final protest against the nature of things."

†Pommer, Henry F. *Milton and Melville*. Pittsburgh: University of Pittsburgh Press, 1950. Pp. 83–85, 87–90.

Reed, Henry. "Books in General," *New Statesman and Nation* (May 31, 1947), p. 397. Melville cherished his "ambiguities" to the end.

*Rosenthal, M. L., and A. J. M. Smith. *Exploring Poetry*. New York: The Macmillan Co., 1955. Pp. 372–375.

Roudiez, Leon S., "Strangers in Melville and Camus," *French Review*, XXXI (Jan., 1958), 223–225. Compares *L'Etranger* with *BB*.

Sale, Arthur. "Captain Vere's Reasons," *Cambridge Journal*, V (Oct., 1951), 3–18. Couples Claggart and Vere and views BB's death as ironic.

Schiffman, Joseph. "Melville's Final Stage, Irony: A Re-examination of 'Billy Budd' Criticism," *American Literature*, XXII (May, 1950), 128–136.

Sedgwick, William E. *Herman Melville: The Tragedy of Mind*. Cambridge: Harvard University Press, 1944. Pp. 231–249. *BB* as acceptance in contrast to *Typee, Redburn,* and *Pierre*.

Short, Raymond W. "Introduction," *Four Great American Novels*. New York: Henry Holt and Co., 1946. Pp. xxxi–xxxii. Brief comparisons with Shakespeare.

———. "Melville as Symbolist," *University of Kansas City Review*, XV (Autumn, 1948), 38–46. On Melville generally.

Snell, G. P. *Shapers of American Fiction, 1798–1947*. New York: E. P. Dutton & Co., Inc., 1947. Pp. 77–78.

Snyder, Oliver. "A Note on 'Billy Budd,'" *Accent*, XI (Winter, 1951), 58–60. *BB* as "a great political Mystery drama."

Spiller, Robert E. *The Cycle of American Literature*. New York: New American Library, 1957. P. 83.

Stallman, R. W., and R. E. Watters. *The Creative Reader.* New York: The Ronald Press Company, 1954. Pp. 334–338. Provides notes and questions for discussion.

Stein, William Bysshe. "The Motif of the Wise Old Man in *Billy Budd*," *Western Humanities Review,* XIV (Winter, 1960), 99–101.

†Stern, Milton R. *The Fine Hammered Steel of Herman Melville.* Urbana: University of Illinois Press, 1957. Pp. 26–27, 206–239.

——. "Introduction," *Typee and Billy Budd.* New York: E. P. Dutton & Co., Inc., 1958. Pp. xx–xxv; "A Note about the Text," 269–274.

Stewart, Randall. *American Literature and Christian Doctrine.* Baton Rouge: Louisiana State University Press, 1958. Pp. 98–102. Compares *BB* with Hawthorne's "The Birthmark," Claggart with Iago. Also in "The Vision of Evil in Hawthorne and Melville," *The Tragic Vision and the Christian Faith,* ed. by Nathan A. Scott, Jr. New York: Association Press, 1957. Pp. 257–262.

†Stone, Geoffrey. *Melville.* New York: Sheed & Ward, Inc., 1949. Pp. 306–319. *BB* reveals Melville's continued ambiguity.

——. "Herman Melville: Loyalty to the Heart," *American Classics Reconsidered,* ed. by Harold C. Gardiner, S.J. New York: Charles Scribner's Sons, 1958. Pp. 227–228.

Sutton, Walter. "Melville and the Great God Budd," *Prairie Schooner,* XXXIV (Summer, 1960), 128–133. *BB* read in terms of Schopenhauer.

†Thompson, Lawrance. "Divine Depravity," *Melville's Quarrel with God.* Princeton: Princeton University Press, 1952. Pp. 331–332, 355–414. Extensive analysis viewing *BB* as irony, Claggart as agent of Vere, Vere as agent of God.

Thorp, Willard. "Herman Melville," Robert E. Spiller, ed., *Literary History of the United States.* New York: The Macmillan Co., 1948. Pp. 469–471.

——. "Introduction," *Herman Melville: Representative Selections.* Cincinnati: American Book Co., 1938. P. lxxxiv.

Thurston, Jarvis, and others. "Billy Budd, Foretopman," *Short Fiction Criticism: A Checklist of Interpretation since 1925 of Stories and Novelettes (American, British, Continental) 1800–1958.* Denver: Alan Swallow Press, 1960. Pp. 156–159.

*Tindall, William York. "The Ceremony of Innocence," R. M. McIver, ed., *Great Moral Dilemmas in Literature, Past and Present.* New York: Harper & Brothers, 1956. Pp. 73–81.

Van Doren, Carl. *The American Novel 1789–1939* (Rev. ed.). New York: The Macmillan Co., 1940. Pp. 101–102.

——. "Foreword," *Billy Budd, Benito Cereno and the Enchanted Isles.* New York: The Readers Club, Inc., 1942. Pp. viii–ix.

——. "A Note of Confession," *Nation,* CXXVII (Dec. 5, 1928), 622.

von Abele, Rudolph. "Melville and the Problem of Evil," *American Mercury,* LXV (Nov., 1947), 592–598. Surveys Melville's works generally.

Wagner, Vern. "Billy Budd as Moby Dick: An Alternate Reading," A. Dayle Wallace and Woodburn O. Ross, eds., *Studies in Honor of John Wilcox* Detroit: Wayne State University Press, 1958. Pp. 157–174. And Claggart as Ahab!

Warner, Rex. "Introduction," *Billy Budd and Other Stories*. London: John Lehmann, Ltd., 1951. Pp. vii–xi.

*Watson, E. L. Grant. "Melville's Testament of Acceptance," *New England Quarterly*, VI (June, 1933), 319–327.

Watters, R. E. "Melville's Metaphysics of Evil," *University of Toronto Quarterly*, IX (Jan., 1940), 170–182. Primarily on *Mardi, Moby-Dick,* and *Pierre.*

———. "Melville's 'Sociality,'" *American Literature*, XVII (March, 1945), 33–49. Acceptance of an "embracing sociality."

*Weaver, Raymond M. "Introduction," *The Shorter Novels of Herman Melville*. New York: Liveright Publishing Corp., 1928. Pp. xlix–li.

*———. *Herman Melville: Mariner and Mystic*. New York: George H. Doran Co., 1921. P. 381. Reprinted as a Pageant Book. New York: Pageant Books, Inc., 1960.

Weir, Charles, Jr. "Malice Reconciled: A Note on Herman Melville's 'Billy Budd,'" *University of Toronto Quarterly*, XIII (April, 1944), 276–285.

†Weisinger, Herbert, and Adrian H. Jaffe: "Herman Melville," *The Laureate Fraternity: An Introduction to Literature*. Evanston: Row, Peterson and Co., 1960. Pp. 142–143; "Study Questions," 177.

West, Ray B., Jr. "Primitivism in Melville," *Prairie Schooner*, XXX (Winter, 1956), 379–385. See West, below.

*———. "The Unity of 'Billy Budd,'" *Hudson Review*, V (Spring, 1952), 120–127.

White, Edgar Walter. "Billy Budd," *Adelphi*, XXVIII (First Quar., 1952), 492–498. Compares the tale with the Britten opera.

Winters, Yvor. *Maule's Curse: Seven Studies in the History of American Obscurantism*. Norfolk: New Directions, 1938. Pp. 86–87. Reprinted in *In Defense of Reason* (Denver: Alan Swallow, 1947), pp. 230–231.

*Withim, Phil. "*Billy Budd:* Testament of Resistance," *Modern Language Quarterly*, XX (June, 1959), 115–127.

*Wright, Nathalia. *Melville's Use of the Bible*. Durham: Duke University Press, 1949. Pp. 126–136.

Zink, Karl E. "Herman Melville and the Forms—Irony and Social Criticism in 'Billy Budd,'" *Accent*, XII (Summer, 1952), 131–139.

For continuing studies of *Billy Budd,* see the annual bibliographies (May issues) of *PMLA,* the quarterly issues of *American Literature,* and the monthly issues of *Abstracts of English Studies.*